How to Engage Policy Makers with Your Research

How to Engage Policy Makers with Your Research

The Art of Informing and Impacting Policy

Edited by

Tim Vorley

Pro Vice-Chancellor and Dean of Oxford Brookes Business School, Oxford Brookes University, UK

Syahirah Abdul Rahman

Lecturer in Business and Management, Oxford Brookes Business School, Oxford Brookes University, UK

Lauren Tuckerman

Lecturer in Business and Management, Oxford Brookes Business School, Oxford Brookes University, UK

Phil Wallace

Communications and Engagement Coordinator, Digital Futures team, University of Manchester, UK

Cheltenham, UK • Northampton, MA, USA

Published by
Edward Elgar Publishing Limited
The Lypiatts
15 Lansdown Road
Cheltenham
Glos GL50 2JA
UK

Edward Elgar Publishing, Inc.
William Pratt House
9 Dewey Court
Northampton
Massachusetts 01060
USA

Paperback edition 2023

A catalogue record for this book
is available from the British Library

Library of Congress Control Number: 2022937606

This book is available electronically in the **Elgar**online
Geography, Planning and Tourism subject collection
http://dx.doi.org/10.4337/9781800378964

ISBN 978 1 80037 895 7 (Hardback)
ISBN 978 1 80037 896 4 (eBook)
ISBN 978 1 0353 2210 7 (Paperback)

Printed and bound by CPI Group (UK) Ltd, Croydon, CR0 4YY

Contents

Contributors

Syahirah Abdul Rahman is Lecturer in Business and Management at Oxford Brookes Business School. She is the Co-Investigator of the Economic and Social Research Council (ESRC)/Innovate UK funded Innovation Caucus

Vicki Belt is Deputy Director of Impact and Engagement at the Enterprise Research Centre, based at Warwick Business School

Rowena Bermingham is working for the Government Office for Science

Annette Bramley is Director of N8 Research Partnership

Sarah Chaytor is Director of Research Strategy and Policy, UCL and Co-Investigator at CAPE (Capabilities in Academic-Policy Engagement)

Dan Chedgzoy is Sheffield City Council Embedded Researcher at SIPHER (Systems Science in Public Health and Health Economics Research) Consortium

Simon Collinson is Deputy Pro Vice-Chancellor for Regional Economic Engagement and Director of the University of Birmingham's City-Region Economic and Development Institute (City-REDI) and West Midlands Regional Economic and Development Institute (WMREDI)

Ekkehard Ernst is Chief Macroeconomist at the International Labour Organization

Sarah Foxen is Knowledge Exchange Lead at the Parliamentary Office for Science and Technology (POST) in the UK Parliament

Lucy Gavens is Consultant in Public Health with Lincolnshire County Council. Lucy was previously the Consortium Manager of SIPHER Consortium

Cristian Gherhes was Research Fellow at Oxford Brookes Business School and is now Founder and CEO at Lexyfi

Mary Gogarty is Greater Manchester Combined Authority Embedded Researcher and Lead Analyst at SIPHER Consortium

Anne Green is Professor of Regional Economic Development at the University of Birmingham's City-REDI

Lisa Hanselmann is Senior Project Manager for the UK Research and Innovation Interdisciplinary Circular Economy Centre for Mineral-based Construction Materials, Department of Civil, Environmental and Geomatic Engineering

Clementine Hill O'Connor is Research Associate in the School for Social Work and Social Policy at the University of Strathclyde and Research Associate at SIPHER Consortium

Heidi Hinder is Portfolio Manager at the ESRC, part of UK Research and Innovation

Dan Hodges is Deputy Director of Strategy at Innovate UK

Ima Jackson is Senior Lecturer at Glasgow Caledonian University's Department of Nursing and Community Health

Debbie Johnson is Lead Specialist in Research at Innovate UK

Katy Jones is Research Fellow in the Centre for Decent Work and Productivity at Manchester Metropolitan University

Melanie Knetsch is Deputy Director of Innovation and Impact at ESRC

Helen Lawton Smith is Professor of Entrepreneurship at Birbeck, University of London

Adam Luqmani is Joint Head of Business Engagement at the Engineering and Physical Sciences Research Council (EPSRC), and worked recently as a Business Engagement Portfolio Manager at ESRC. Both EPSRC and ESRC are part of UK Research and Innovation

Eoin McFadden is Head of the Innovation Strategy Unit at the Northern Ireland Department for the Economy

Anand Menon is Professor of European Politics and Foreign Affairs at King's College London and Director of UK in a Changing Europe Initiative (UKICE)

Geeta Nathan is Head of Economics and Insights at Innovate UK

Jen Nelles is Senior Research Fellow at the ESRC/Innovate UK funded Innovation Caucus, based at Oxford Brookes University

Raquel Ortega-Argilés is Professor of Regional Economic Development at the University of Birmingham's City-Region Economic and Development Institute (City-REDI)

Alice Owen is Professor of Business, Sustainability and Stakeholder

Engagement at the Sustainability Research Institute at the School of Earth and Environment, University of Leeds

Monder Ram OBE is Professor of Small Business and Director of the Centre for Research in Ethnic Minority Entrepreneurship at Aston University

Graeme Reid is Chair of Science and Research Policy at University College London

Rebecca Riley is Associate Professor of Enterprise Engagement at the University of Birmingham, and Impact and Business Development Director at the University of Birmingham's City-Region Economic and Development Institute (City-REDI)

David Christian Rose is Elizabeth Creak Associate Professor of Agricultural Innovation and Extension at the University of Reading

Jill Rutter is Senior Research Fellow at UKICE and Senior Fellow at the Institute for Government

Lauren Tuckerman is Lecturer in Business and Management at Oxford Brookes Business School. She is the Co-Investigator of the ESRC/Innovate UK funded Innovation Caucus

Chris Tyler is Director of Research and Policy at UCL in the Department of Science, Technology, Engineering and Public Policy (STEaPP)

Matjaz Vidmar is Lecturer in Engineering Management at the University of Edinburgh

Tim Vorley is Pro Vice-Chancellor at Oxford Brookes University and Dean of Oxford Brookes Business School. He is the Primary Investigator and Director of the ESRC/Innovate UK funded Innovation Caucus

Phil Wallace was Project Manager of the ESRC/Innovate UK funded Innovation Caucus, and is now Communications and Engagement Coordinator in the Digital Futures team at the University of Manchester

Judy Wasige is Community Engagement Officer in the College of Social Sciences at the University of Glasgow

Sarah Weakley is Research and Knowledge Exchange Lead at Policy Scotland with the University of Glasgow's College of Social Sciences

Abbreviations

ACH	Ashley Community Housing
ARI	Areas of Research Interest
BAME	Black, Asian, and Minority Ethnic
BMDC	Bradford Metropolitan District Council
BEIS	Department for Business, Energy and Industrial Strategy
BPFS	business, professional, and financial services
City-REDI	City-Region Economic and Development Institute
CLG	Communities and Local Government
CREME	Centre for Research in Ethnic Minority Entrepreneurship
DfE	Department for the Economy
DIF	Discretionary Investment Fund
DTP	doctoral training partnerships
DWP	Department for Work and Pensions
ECRs	early career researchers
EMBs	ethnic minority businesses
EPSRC	Engineering and Physical Sciences Research Council
ERs	embedded researchers
ERC	Enterprise Research Centre
ESRC	Economic and Social Research Council
EU	European Union
GOS	The Government Office for Science
HEIs	Higher Education Institutions
IAAs	Impact Acceleration Accounts
ICPA	International Centre for Policy Advocacy
ICT	information and communication technology

INTARAAP	Intersectional Anti-Racist Academic Activism for Policy-making
IWC	in-work conditionality
KE	knowledge exchange
KPIs	key performance indicators
LEPs	Local Enterprise Partnerships
LERU	League of European Research Universities
MPEC	Model of Employment Trends in Colombia
MPEP	Peruvian Employment Projections Model
MTPE	Ministry of Labour and Employment Promotion
NGOs	non-governmental organisations
PIN	Productivity Insights Network
PR	public relations
R&D	research and development
REF	Research Excellence Framework
ROTA	Race on the Agenda
SCQF	Scottish Credit and Qualifications Framework
SDC	The UK Sustainable Development Commission
SDGs	The UN Sustainable Development Goals
SGSSS	Scottish Graduate School of Social Science
SMEs	small and medium-sized enterprises
SNA	social-network analysis
SRS	Skills Recognition Scotland
The IWC Project	Universal Credit and In-Work Conditionality – a productive turn? project
The N8	The N8 Research Partnership
UKICE	UK in a Changing Europe Initiative
UKPRP	UK Prevention Research Partnership
UKRI	UK Research and Innovation
WMREDI	West Midlands Regional Economic Development Institute

PART I

Understanding the need and articulating the offer

1. Introduction to *How to Engage Policy Makers with Your Research*

Syahirah Abdul Rahman, Lauren Tuckerman, Tim Vorley and Phil Wallace

It is a common assumption that power for policymaking is held by politicians that the public sees in various media in their daily lives. The power-bearing image of politicians is so strong that there have been centuries of studies on the art of politics and persuasion, from Aristotle's political theory to the TED talks of political journalist Steve Richards on 'How to Train Your Prime Minister'.

In reality, however, there are many actors that facilitate change in the policies that govern our lives who often go unnoticed. These actors, such as civil servants working in public sector departments, local councils and think tanks, are the ones responsible for confronting policy problems and finding solutions for them. Utilising knowledge to influence and impact policy makers creates opportunities for learning for both policy makers and academics alike. The symbiotic relationship also facilitates evidence for how new ideas can be best implemented to create positive change. There are therefore countless opportunities to be reaped by the academic community when engaging with policy makers.

In recent years, the potential of academia in creating impact and resolving policy challenges has been increasingly recognised. The Government Office for Science's (GOS) report entitled *Engaging with Academics: How to Further Strengthen Open Policy Making* mentioned that policymaking is about bringing together evidence to create real-world outcomes. The report explained that academics could be essential in investigating, assessing and advising government policy through their expertise on a given subject. The report also takes note that there are academic areas that are more approached than others, for example, in natural sciences or in areas that are more likely to provide technical evidence. Nonetheless, the report advises policy makers to consider all disciplines, including that of social sciences and humanities (GOS, 2013).

The consideration of all academic disciplines as having potential to create policy impacts has had increasing attention over the past decade. In 2012, for example, the League of European Research Universities (LERU) published a report which begins with the claim that like other disciplines, social sciences' and humanities' research can generate new knowledge that has deep, nuanced and intrinsic value (LERU, 2020). The report goes on to say that the understanding gathered from social sciences and humanities 'is as important as contributions from natural-scientific and technological disciplines to the creation, implementation and evaluation of effective public policies and innovative structures underpinning corporate performance' (LERU, 2020, p. 3). The COVID-19 pandemic further brought forward the value that academics can bring in understanding social and cultural influences on behaviours, communications and decision-making in policy spaces (Van Bavel et al., 2020).

When we think of academic engagement with policy, the most basic assumption made is that the result of such collaborations should be tangible. This is true for most cases, where, for example, survey data, statistical analysis or even qualitative case studies have been used in policy decision-making. However, in other cases, the influence of academics on policy is much more indirect, 'one small piece in a larger mosaic of politics, bargaining, and compromise' (Jennings and Callahan, 1983, p. 3). In reality, indirect academic influence is much more robustly present in policy than realised. For example, intangible knowledge in the form of academic ideas and insights frame the way policies are formed, at the very least contributing to the way policy makers conceptualise issues and frame their solution options. Historically, academics have influenced the development of politics and policies through the intellectual exploration of ideas and philosophies that influence social challenges. The works of philosophers such as Durkheim, Weber and Marx are so prominent to governance that, a century later, we can still find traces of their theories in policies worldwide.

Since the late 1990s, evidence-based policymaking has had broad support from organisations such as the Economic and Social Research Council (ESRC) (Marston and Watts, 2003) and the interest in including academic evidence in policymaking has only increased since then. In 2013, the UK government launched the What Works Network as an initiative to embed robust evidence-based policymaking at the heart of local and national government. As part of the project, the government has identified evidence gaps that are a priority for government departments, specifically to assist academics in identifying where their research may have direct impact on policy. Similarly, the UK government's Areas of Research Interest (ARI) can be used to explore opportunities for research impact. The support for academic evidence in policymaking can also be seen in a study by Dr Beswick and Dr Geddes, who evaluated academic engagement with UK legislatures and found that major legislatures in the UK are eager to increase and improve collaborations with universities and academics (Beswick and Geddes, 2020). The UK Parliament, for example, recognises the potential benefits of academic research to policymaking activities, although more engagements have been conducted with think tanks and civil society. Regardless, there is real value in bridging the gap between academia and policy. Engaging with policy makers can be both fruitful in undertaking research, as well as being an effective pathway to impact. In working with policy makers across different portfolios from the economy, to health, to transport and beyond, and at different scales from the local to the international, academics have much to contribute.

Despite an abundance of opportunities that academics can reap from policy engagement, research has shown that in some areas of academia, especially non-technical ones, there is still a lack of policy–academic engagement. Taking the above example of social sciences, a study in 2016 has shown that only 29 per cent of all social scientists have said that they are motivated to carry out user-inspired research (Bullock and Hughes, 2016). This shows a discrepancy in the engagement that academics in the areas of social sciences do with users of their research, given that nearly three-quarters of social scientists have also reported that their research is most relevant to non-commercial sectors such as in policy.

Nonetheless, there is still an ongoing assumption that academia and policy simply do not see eye to eye. Both communities belong in two separate worlds, each with their own logics. They speak different profession-based languages (see Chapter 4), they belong to institutions that have different aims and goals, and traditionally they sought out different types of purposes in conducting research. While academics have considerable insight, arguably the biggest challenges are in engaging and communicating with policymaking communities. Regardless, successful collaborations have been on the rise in recent years, with governments, local and national, putting financial and non-financial efforts to facilitate academics' involvement in policy spaces (which is typified by funders' approaches to encouraging policy impact for academics, discussed in Chapter 9). This book aims to assist academics in reaching successful collaborations with policy makers. In doing so, it also aims to help academics overcome the challenges of collaborating with policy makers using real-life examples of successful academic engagements.

This book in itself is unique in its approach, being a collaboration between 37 contributors from policymaking and academia. Authors include policymaking insiders from government departments such as the ESRC, UK Parliament, Policy Scotland and Innovate UK, and academics who have had experiences working with policy makers. The range of contributions shows that our perspective on policy and policymaking is broad, considering policy from local, regional, national and international levels and reflecting the range of actors involved in policymaking. The book is divided into three main sections. Part I focuses on how academics articulate the value and relevance of their research in relation to what policy makers are looking for. Part II considers the different ways in which academics can engage with policy makers in undertaking research and having an impact. Lastly, Part III explores the ways academic research is informing, influencing and impacting policy. While the book is structured in terms of how academics articulate the value of their research, engage with policy makers and influence policy, as the book highlights, this is often far from a linear process.

Part I starts with Chapter 2 by Graeme Reid and Sarah Chaytor who discuss methods in developing a better understanding of the complex landscape of policymaking so that academics can better engage with policy makers. In doing so, the chapter explores the distinctive functions, needs and approaches to engagement within the policy domain, including responses to analysis, advice on policy development, campaigning, scrutiny and evaluation. Following this, David Christian Rose and Chris Tyler discuss in Chapter 3 the value of research evidence to policy makers and make a number of suggestions to researchers about how to engage productively with them. The authors draw on a study of research use in the UK Parliament to bring research and policy together.

A common theme that arises from Chapters 2 and 3 is the importance of ensuring that, when working collaboratively, both academics and policy makers must ensure that they are speaking the same language. Sarah Foxen and Rowena Bermingham examine this topic in Chapter 4 by exploring the barriers to finding a common language for both policy makers and academics. The authors draw from their linguistic backgrounds to bring in theories of communication to understand why academics and policy makers talk differently, how this creates a barrier to working together and what is needed to enable mutual understanding. Knowing the right way to communicate with policy makers can be an invaluable skill for academics, as creating a successful research impact involves engaging with a wide range of stakeholders. Anand Menon and Jill Rutter discuss in Chapter 5 the experiences they have with working with media to leverage a relationship with policy makers. Using their experiences with the UK in a Changing Europe Initiative, the authors suggest that achieving policy impact can be facilitated via a broader strategy of informing public opinion more generally. The book then turns to Chapter 6 by Matjaz Vidmar, who proposes a distinctive approach to generating insight for policymaking which involves the researcher situating themselves in the multiple stakeholder contexts to understand the phenomena studied.

Part I closes with the pragmatic considerations of co-producing research with policy makers. Chapter 7 by Clementine Hill O'Connor, Lucy Gavens, Dan Chedgzoy and Mary Gogarty discusses the co-production of policy-relevant research using the example of embedding researchers within a large, multi-disciplinary programme. The chapter offers insights into how the use of embedded researchers within a large, multi-disciplinary research programme can help to understand the motivations and expectations of policy and academic partners' involvement. They describe some of the practicalities of establishing and managing embedded researcher roles. Following this, Chapter 8 by Annette Bramley discusses strategic research alliance using the case study of The N8 Research Partnership. The chapter highlights the usefulness of strategic research alliances in policy–academia collaborations, especially in the sharing of resources and risks. Ending Part I is Chapter 9 by Melanie Knetsch and Lauren Tuckerman, taking into consideration the views of the funder on the value of research impact and collaborations with academics.

Having outlined the value of academic research to policymaking, Part II focuses on the different modes of collaboration that can be undertaken between policy makers and academics. It starts with the mode of engagement known as critical friends in Chapter 10 by Debbie Johnson, Geeta Nathan and Syahirah Abdul Rahman. The chapter focuses on the facilitation role of the Innovation Caucus, an innovation-focused research centre that acts as a critical friend to provide expert academic critique which informs Innovate UK's strategy for UK business innovation. Chapter 11 by Sarah Weakley looks into the use of targeted policy engagement events as opportunities for researchers and policy actors to come together in both in-person and virtual spaces to influence the design, implementation and evaluation of policy. This chapter details some of the common features of targeted policy engagement events from the perspective of an academic knowledge broker in a university using two case studies: one detailing an in-person, day-long seminar and the other describing a virtual policy discussion series.

While many might assume that engagement with policy makers usually happens in the later years of an academic's career, Chapters 12 and 13 demonstrate that this is not always the case. There are opportunities to be had among early career researchers (ECRs) too in influencing and shaping policy discussions. Chapter 12 by Tim Vorley and Cristian Gherhes explores this notion by looking into the usage of collaborative doctoral research for ECRs who are interested in shaping their research agenda early on in their careers to fit with policymaking discussions. Similarly, in Chapter 13, Lauren Tuckerman discusses the usefulness of doctoral internships for this endeavour. Using her own experiences conducting a doctoral internship in the Scottish government, the author reflects on how doctoral internships can be a means for ECRs to build their network and research portfolios that can have long-lasting research impact. Besides academics and policy makers, there are other stakeholders who are integral to the facilitation of a successful policy–academia collaboration. In Chapter 14, Phil Wallace, Heidi Hinder, Adam Luqmani and Lisa Hanselmann discuss the importance of knowledge exchange, project management and communication activities in building long-term capacity in a policy–academia collaboration.

Part II closes by exploring the notion that the potential of making impact does not have to be limited to local and domestic organisations only. This book shows the variety of opportunities that researchers can have if only they know where to look and how best to situate their research profile to the needs of policymaking engagement. Chapter 15 by Helen Lawton Smith reflects on the author's experiences in using mission research to situate themself as an expert in several Organisation for Economic Co-operation and Development (OECD) regional entrepreneurship policy research projects. Chapter 16 by Ima Jackson and Judy Wasige explores the important topic of underrepresented and racialised communities in the process of policy research and impact. They discuss finding opportunities in collaborations during their experiences of using community engagement to make a long-lasting impact on policy-making. The authors use an Intersectional Anti-Racist Academic Activism for Policy-making (INTARAAP approach), and in their case study describe the creation of a national process to provide an interface between the skills shortages in the public and private sectors and professional and vocational qualifications acquired by those from beyond the UK. Chapter 17 by Dan Hodges and Syahirah Abdul Rahman further expands on the importance of locating opportunities using creative means by discussing the mode of com-missioned research. In describing real-life examples, the authors demonstrate how positive results can be borne out of short- to medium-term commissioned research projects and, more importantly, how academics and policy makers can ensure that repeated collaborations can be gained through commissioned research projects.

Part III unpacks the different types of ways that academics can inform, influence and impact policy using real-life examples. The section begins with examples of international and regional impacts that academics have had in collaborating with policy makers. Ekkehard Ernst starts the conversation in Chapter 18 of engaging with policy makers in the challenging environments of middle income countries, providing unique insight into how to work towards policy impact in uncertain contexts. Rebecca Riley, Simon Collinson, Anne Green and Raquel Ortega-Argilés discuss their experiences with the City-Region Economic and Development Institute (City-REDI) in Chapter 19. The chapter advises those who are interested in developing a policy-focused research institute in looking at aspects of establishing the purpose, audience and client base; understanding the mechanisms of influence; key challenges and how to overcome them; and the importance of co-creation and collabora-tive approaches and the relationship with policy research experts.

While impact can be found more obviously in policymaking spaces when collaborating with policy makers, in fact, research engagement can also be influential to smaller communities that are often taken for granted. In Chapter 20, Vicki Belt talks about the Enterprise Research Centre (ERC), the UK's leading independent academic research centre focusing on growth, productivity and innovation in small and medium-sized enterprises (SMEs). The chapter extracts some generalisable, practical tips for researchers seeking to achieve policy influence and impact, with special relevance to those based in smaller research centres and institutes. Collaborations with policy makers can also be extremely rewarding for academics who will find opportunities to tap into the networks and activities in policymaking and use the space to experiment with their conceptual framework. Chapter 21 by Jen Nelles, Tim Vorley and Eoin McFadden delves into the Productivity Insights Network (PIN) and Ireland's Department for the Economy (DfE), focusing on its experimental methods to combine theory-led research in the infusion of new ideas and perspectives on DfE's productivity puzzle.

Engaging with policy makers is one of the key methods for academics to make 'real-life impact' on important social issues. Providing research expertise to policy discussions can have invaluable effects in the shaping of social policies. Chapter 22 by Monder Ram looks into how research that begins with addressing racial inequalities in the UK has led to the development of the Centre for Research in Ethnic Minority Entrepreneurship (CREME), who work closely with practitioners to encourage entrepreneurship among ethnic minority communities as a part of the solution to resolve racial inequalities. The next chapter is written by Alice Owen, who discusses engagement with policymaking for sustainability in Chapter 23. The author uses a range of UK policy development experiences at national, regional and local levels, working in executive and non-executive roles, to offer routes for influencing effectively. Lastly, the book closes with Katy Jones in Chapter 24 discussing her real-life insights into how to begin influencing policy as an ECR. Drawing on an example of a small-scale, ECR-led project funded by the ESRC's PIN, this chapter shows how policy engagement is possible regardless of the scale of a research project, and how continued engagement has the potential to lead to bigger and better things.

Taken together, the chapters in this book provide a wide-ranging, comprehensive and detailed set of perspectives on collaborations between academics and policy makers. The different insights offered by these various perspectives will provide useful lessons for academics, policy makers, knowledge exchange officers and researchers who are interested in the practical ways associated with beginning, developing and successfully carrying out collaborations between academia and policy. These insights, lessons and perspectives are much needed, given that in the UK, and increasingly worldwide, there is a growing need for academics to gain research impact and for policy makers to have more evidence-based policy activities.

REFERENCES

Beswick, D. and Geddes, M. (2020). 'Evaluating academic engagement with UK legislatures exchanging knowledge on knowledge exchange'. https://www.sps.ed.ac.uk/sites/default/files/assets/pdf/evaluating-academic-engagement-with-uk-legislatures-web.pdf (accessed 25 August 2021).

Bullock, A. and Hughes, R. (2016). 'Knowledge exchange and the social sciences: A report to ESRC from the Centre for Business Research'. https://esrc.ukri.org/files/collaboration/knowledge-exchange-and-the-social-sciences/ (accessed 25 July 2020).

Government Office for Science (GOS) (2013). *Engaging with Academics: How to Further Strengthen Open Policy Making.* https://assets.publishing.service.gov.uk/government/uploads/system/uploads/attachment_data/file/283129/13-581-engaging-with-academics-open-policy-making.pdf (accessed 1 September 2021).

Jennings, B. and Callahan, D. (1983). 'Social science and the policy-making process'. *The Hastings Center Report*, 13(1), 3–8.

League of European Research Universities (LERU) (2020). *Social Sciences and Humanities: Essential Fields for European Research and in Horizon 2020.* https://www.leru.org/files/Social-Sciences-and-Humanities-Essential-Fields-for-European-Research-and-Horizon-2020-Full-paper.pdf (accessed 1 September 2021).

Marston, G. and Watts, R. (2003). 'Tampering with the evidence: A critical appraisal of evidence-based policy-making'. *The Drawing Board: An Australian Review of Public Affairs*, 3(3), 143–63.

Van Bavel, J.J., Baicker, K., Boggio, P.S., Capraro, V., Cichocka, A., Cikara, M., Crockett, M.J., Crum, A.J., Douglas, K.M., Druckman, J.N. and Drury, J. (2020). 'Using social and behavioural science to support COVID-19 pandemic response'. *Nature Human Behaviour*, 4(5), 460–71.

2. What do policymakers want from researchers? Developing better understanding of a complex landscape

Graeme Reid and Sarah Chaytor

2.1   SCIENCE ADVICE IN CRISIS

The coronavirus pandemic has seen science advice go from nerdy obscurity to headline news. From the government's claims to be 'following the science' to public debate about the use of scientific knowledge in combating the virus, the role of evidence and expertise in informing public policy are centre stage like never before.

Science advice has featured prominently in the handling of crises under previous governments. During the Second World War, both the Prime Minister and the Minister of Defence appointed scientific advisers, paving the way for the appointment of the first cross-government Chief Scientific Adviser (CSA) in 1966[1] (Institute for Government, 2012). More recently, outbreaks of disease in farm animals, the Fukushima earthquake in Japan and the eruption of the Eyjafjallajökull volcano in Iceland have thrust scientific advice temporarily into the spotlight.

This time, however, the prominence and persistence of science in the media coverage stands out. Prime-time media coverage of uncertainty in scientific data, professional disagreements between eminent scientists and the lively political debate about what 'the science' tells us and how far it should affect policy decisions have given the wider public a crash course in the use of evidence in public policy. Time will tell whether the Covid experience has raised the profile of research evidence in policymaking more generally and whether it has a lasting effect on the expectations of ministers when they commission policy advice.

The demand for high-quality evidence to tackle the virus means that researchers' understanding of public policy has also taken a higher profile. A growing appetite amongst policy professionals for academic expertise has been apparent in recent years. Some of this trend might be explained by, until very recently, the significant decline in departmental research and development (R&D) budgets at the same time as the public policy environment has been growing increasingly complex (Campaign for Science and Engineering, 2017). There has also been a growing awareness amongst research funders, universities and individual researchers of the potential benefits of engaging with public policy. Awareness was boosted by the introduction of Research Excellence Framework (REF) impact case studies, which can bring in significant amounts of Quality-Related (QR) funding from Research England. More recent debate over how to reflect policy engagement in Research England's new Knowledge Exchange Framework added yet more emphasis.

Recent UK Research and Innovation (UKRI) investments in initiatives such as the Economics Observatory, the International Public Policy Observatory and the Capabilities in Academic-Policy Engagement project[2] (see Box 2.1) provide important signals to universities and researchers of the significance of academic–policy engagement. Universities increasingly recognise that engaging with public policy demonstrates the societal value of academic research and expertise[3] (King's College London and Digital Science, 2015). Individual researchers can also derive benefits, ranging from personal satisfaction from making 'public good' contributions (the ability to influence the direction of policy or form powerful networks) to the professional (gaining insights and knowledge to help shape future research proposals and secure funding) to reputational advantage (developing a good REF impact case study).

Many parts of the academic community are still developing their understanding of the reality and practicalities of the public policy sphere. Only a minority of university researchers have experience of responding to the needs of policymakers. The variety of public policy functions and the distinctive responsibilities and ambitions of different parts of the policy world make it difficult to identify the particular role universities can play to systematise and share insights. Limited understanding within the government of how to work most effectively with universities and rapid turnover of policy officials exacerbates the problem (Sasse and Norris, 2019). Significant and long-standing cultural and practical barriers persist, with academics and policy professionals working on different timescales, responding to different incentives, to address different priorities[4] (Institute for Government, 2018 and Institute for Government, 2019). This is further compounded by specific barriers for under-represented groups, early-career researchers and, in the context of engagement with Whitehall and Westminster, those who live outside London[5] (Geddes, 2018; House of Commons Liaison Committee, 2019).

BOX 2.1 UNDERSTANDING STRUCTURAL BARRIERS: EMERGING INSIGHTS FROM CAPE

The Capabilities in Academic-Policy Engagement (CAPE) project is a partnership between UCL and the Universities of Cambridge, Manchester, Northumbria and Nottingham to improve the use of evidence in public policy by understanding the efficacy of different engagement mechanisms and exploring what works in different institutional, geographical and policy contexts. Working with policy partners including the Government Office for Science, the Parliamentary Office for Science and Technology, the Alliance for Useful Evidence and the Transforming Evidence Hub, CAPE aims to develop activities, improve the diversity of engagements and participants and build greater collaboration between universities.

The structural barriers to academic–policy engagement have been repeatedly emphasised in conversations with over 40 different policy stakeholders from local, regional and national government during the first phase of the CAPE project. Frequent reference has been made to the sense of a gulf between academic and policy communities: a willingness to engage in and of itself is not sufficient to overcome the significant impediments that still exist. In particular, policy stakeholders have expressed a need for much greater, more rapid research synthesis and evidence reviews – something undervalued by academics (and research funders) compared to original research and challenging to deliver on the timescales needed by policy communities.

CAPE has heard clear expressions from policy stakeholders of their appetite for developing genuine collaboration and co-creation with researchers, combined with a frustration that this can be very difficult to do. Navigating evidence used in public policy as part of a complex political process is rarely straightforward and there is considerable uncertainty on both sides. CAPE discussions have focused on how to build the social infrastructures that can enable ongoing, active knowledge exchange and dialogue between researchers and policy professionals, rather than just one-off interactions, in order to co-create both policy questions and potential solutions.

Working with stakeholders from local, regional and national levels of government, CAPE is starting to tease out some of the differences in academic–policy engagement at these different policy levels. These include varying capacity and resources for accessing academic expertise; different policy priorities or different approaches; and different rates of policy development and implementation.

2.2   BRIDGING THE DIVIDE

This leaves researchers navigating a complex and rapidly evolving landscape without clear routes for engagement and without a clear understanding of the most effective approaches to policy engagement. Difficulties in understanding what policymakers want impede effective responses and can perpetuate barriers to engagement. Furthermore, the distinctive roles and needs of civil service analysts, policy officials, government lawyers and special advisers is not always clear to academics who seek to contribute to policy development. That is before we open up the distinctive roles of central, devolved and regional governments or the different roles of government and parliament.

On the policy side, there are clear and persistent attempts to reach further into the academic world. Parliamentary Select Committees frequently appoint academic advisers and invite evidence from academic experts; a 2019 report explored how Select Committees could make better use of research evidence (House of Commons Liaison Committee, 2019). The Parliamentary Office for Science and Technology assimilates academic research findings in briefings for parliamentarians. The Parliamentary and Scientific Committee hold regular meetings that bring together parliamentarians and academics to discuss topical issues.

Strategic initiatives such as the publication of government Areas of Research Interest (ARI) and of parliamentary ARI around Covid-19 reflect some significant attempts to bridge the divide. These documents set out topics where there are knowledge or evidence gaps with the intention of prompting the research community to respond. The significance of the introduction of such publications is the provision of a clear signal to the academic community of policy needs and interests. ARIs were at the heart of a recent Government Office for Science project that brought together academic responses to inform the development of policy to support recovery from the pandemic (see Box 2.2). The quotes below also show the attitudes towards absorbing research from policymakers' perspectives.

POLICY PERSPECTIVE

Policy can be very hard to define. You know what it is when you see it but it's difficult to actually describe. It is also very different in different places, for different people, for different problems ... Government policymaking is driven by ministers' priorities. It is important that academics provide evidence to the right people on the right things at the right times – and this requires a good understanding of the policy landscape.

Professor Alan Penn, Chief Scientific Adviser, Ministry of Housing, Communities and Local Government

The 'Areas of Research Interest' published by Government Departments provide a really useful framework to help stimulate and source advice from [researchers, academics, trade bodies and others]. We now need to ensure that Government is ready to absorb more external advice and make good use of it – the last year showed how well the research sector can respond to challenges when it needs to.

Chris Pook, Deputy Director, Science and Innovation, Systems and Capability, Government Office for Science

BOX 2.2   AREAS OF RESEARCH INTEREST (ARIS): REBUILDING A RESILIENT BRITAIN

The Rebuilding a Resilient Britain programme was launched during the Covid-19 pandemic to address aspects of Britain's recovery from the pandemic over the medium to long term.

Professor Annette Boaz and Dr Kathryn Oliver, funded by the Economic and Social Research Council and working with the Government Office for Science with government departmental CSAs, identified a set of topics and themes based on existing departmental ARIs that should be addressed as a priority. These ARIs were divided into nine themes, which were addressed by nine working groups consisting of researchers, funding bodies and policymakers.

Each working group produced a report identifying existing evidence, gaps in the evidence base and key messages around the ARIs (note that the reports are the views of the working group members and are not indicative of government policy). These are linked below.

The reports have been made available online as a resource for academics, policymakers and funders interested in what the groups collated on what is already known; and where the current research gaps seem to be on nine topics of cross-cutting interesting to government departments.

However, as acknowledged in a recent Universities Policy Engagement Network (UPEN) report, the ARI are most helpfully understood as starting points for further engagement and iteration between the policy and academic communities, rather than fixed research questions (Heckels et al., 2020). This highlights the importance of further work to increase engagement between academic and policy communities in order to address identified policy needs, recognised in both the Government Office for Science's ARI Fellowships programme and the creation of parliament's Knowledge Exchange Unit. Knowledge brokers are key to building connection between academic and policy communities (see Box 2.3).

BOX 2.3   THE RISE OF THE KNOWLEDGE BROKERS

The growing emergence of an academic–policy engagement sphere within the university sector – encompassing researchers, university staff, policy professionals and others – seeks to strengthen engagement between the academic and public policy communities and increase the use of evidence in policy. Over the past decade, a number of universities – our own included – have responded to policy needs for evidence by establishing strategic initiatives to increase researchers' engagement with public policy. The rapid growth of the UPEN, from around eight institutions at inception in 2017 to more than 70 as of May 2021, indicates the increasing recognition of the need for dedicated knowledge mobilisation resources within universities.

2.3   WHAT DO POLICYMAKERS WANT?

The public policy sphere encompasses government, parliament, local and regional authorities, public bodies and intermediary organisations such as think tanks and non-governmental organisations (NGOs). Within the civil service there are analysts, policy officials, strategy teams and professionals from law, medicine, economics, statistics and, of course, the natural and social sciences. Furthermore, some policy actors are both suppliers and users of evidence, as in the case of think tanks, NGOs and some charities. The term 'policymakers' therefore denotes a heterogeneous collection of individuals, roles and functions each with distinct requirements and no unambiguous definition.

Effective engagement requires understanding different policy audiences at the different levels and points of the policy process. Policy functions also vary significantly, including evidence analysis, policy development, scrutiny of policy, implementation of policy and policy evaluation, as shown in Table 2.1. Furthermore, a single policy stakeholder may occupy more than one function – for example, backbench MPs or peers may have interests related both to campaigning on particular interests, and to scrutinising policy through membership of a select committee.

These different audiences, roles and functions will have different needs and may require different modes of engagement – for example, whereas ministers are largely concerned with advancing the political agenda of the government, backbench members of a parliamentary select committee are responsible for scrutinising government policy. What policymakers want can range from formal submission of evidence to inquiries, written briefings on particular topics, evidence reviews across a topic, undertaking formal advisory roles to

Table 2.1　　Examples of key policy stakeholders and functions

Policy Stakeholder	Function					
	Evidence analysis	Policy development	Scrutiny	Implementation	Evaluation (assessing impact of policy)	Campaigning
MPs	X		**X**		X	X
Parliamentary staff			**X**		X	
Ministers		**X**		X	X	X
Civil servants	**X**	X		X	X	
Local councillors/authority members		**X**	X	X	X	X
Local/regional authority staff	X	X		**X**	X	
Non Departmental Public Bodies (NPDBs)	X			**X**	X	
NGOs/intermediaries	X		X		X	**X**

Note: Predominant function indicated in bold.

informal advice through a short phone call. The quote below also emphasises the need to pay attention to the dynamics within policymaking realms.

POLICY PERSPECTIVE

Peers have busy schedules and usually pursue several Parliamentary agenda in parallel. I pay most attention to topics in which I take a special interest and to matters of urgency. The timeliness, relevance and clarity of evidence are particularly important to me.

Lord Sharkey, Liberal Democrat peer

The coronavirus pandemic shone a useful spotlight on the uncertainties inherent in scientific evidence, as well as the need to situate it within a broader evidential, societal and policy context. The concerns and ambitions of media commentators and the wider public add further dimensions. For example, the attitudes of 'anti-vaxxers' might appear irrational, irritating or even dangerous to many, but they are nevertheless part of the context in which ministers make policy decisions on the vaccine roll-out. This reflects the complexity of the public policy sphere. Policy development is an inherently political exercise. Academic evidence is one part of a broader public policy picture, which includes public attitudes, affordability, feasibility, timeliness and other practicalities, along with the values and disposition of the elected government (Bothwell, 2015). There will always be tensions between academic priorities and policy priorities, and between evidence and other considerations in policy development. Whilst not necessarily problematic in themselves, such tensions can prompt confusion and impede engagement when not acknowledged. So recognising that what policymakers want from researchers is evidence, analysis and expertise to sit alongside other inputs to the policy process is vital for constructive engagement. The quotes below describe policymakers' feelings about different sources of evidence including academic evidence.

POLICY PERSPECTIVE

Academic evidence is one of several sources of high quality information. Academic advice is important but not definitive. It is valued by Select Committees and individual peers as a contribution to recommendations and policy debates. Other important factors include political feasibility, affordability and the compromises needed to get a policy adopted.

Lord Sharkey, Liberal Democrat peer

Academic research is one of several sources of advice to Government. Input from academics can feel quite unstructured compared to input from business, where there are often dedicated representative bodies for specific sectors.

Chris Pook, Deputy Director, Science and Innovation, Systems and Capability, Government Office for Science

Integrating different perspectives is critical: if you go and see an economist they will come up with economic policy; if you go and see an engineer they will show you an engineering solution. We need to get better at integrating advice and evidence across a range of disciplines.

Professor Alan Penn, Chief Scientific Adviser, Ministry of Housing, Communities and Local Government

2.4 THERE ARE MANY WAYS IN WHICH RESEARCH CAN IMPACT ON POLICY

The complex, multifaceted nature of the public policy landscape means that there are many ways in which research can impact on policy, both directly and indirectly. In the broadest sense, policy stakeholders need robust, reliable evidence, knowledge and expertise about the issues that matter to them at a given moment. Their demands are likely to change with the nature of the work and according to their role and could include a need for broader expertise and advice on how to interpret evidence – including evidence gaps – as well as specific demands on the current state of knowledge on a particular issue. Interactions will be used in different ways, from informing debate or consideration of policy, to helping to shape policy development and new policies, to supporting policy implementation. The quotes below indicate different ways in which impact can be achieved with policymakers.

POLICY PERSPECTIVE

Systematic reviews are highly valued by public policy professionals, as a way of rapidly understanding what is already known about an issue ... Policy professionals don't always have time to develop future scenarios, rather than just immediate analysis of the issue of the day. Research on future scenarios can often really add value.

Professor Alan Penn, Chief Scientific Adviser, Ministry of Housing, Communities and Local Government

Having an independent expert panel in developing our Local Industrial Strategy was really useful. The expert panel understood the constraints and politics behind the process and were focused on how to apply research knowledge to real world policy development.

Policy Officer from a Mayoral Combined Authority

> *Like most peers, I have a reasonably wide network of people who are well informed in my fields of interest. These networks allow me to have informal, exploratory discussions of complicated or contested policy areas where I can try out new ideas and emerging thoughts. These discussions often allow me to better evaluate formal evidence.*

Lord Sharkey, Liberal Democrat peer

Valuable impacts can include creating awareness of particular evidence; providing a new perspective on an established problem; highlighting a new concern about existing policy; or preventing a course of action. This impact may not always be straightforward or easy to measure. Some impacts might manifest in tangible contributions to or references in parliamentary inquiries and government consultations; the initiation of a new select committee inquiry or informing legislative scrutiny. However, others may simply take the form of illuminating the thinking of various actors concerned – something which can be highly impactful although not always easy to measure. Indeed, some intangible impacts arise directly but invisibly – such as shaping the thinking of a policy analyst who is working on a particular piece of legislation, leading someone to not do something, strengthening relationships and building trust.

Researchers can undertake a variety of actions which can lead to a variety of impacts (some of these are illustrated in Table 2.2), but it is almost impossible to plan or predict these from first interaction to eventual outcome. It is not always clear when academic–policy work will make a difference; it may well be some time after specific actions are undertaken.

A direct and explicit pathway between a single piece of evidence and a change in policy is rare. Setting policy change as an objective for academic researchers will almost always lead to disappointment. That is not a weakness in academic research but a reflection on the many factors that combine to develop and implement policy.

Whilst clarity of outcome is not always possible, clarity of purpose is important. Engaging with public policy is highly complex, profoundly uncertain and often rather obscure; a clear understanding of purpose can help to mitigate this. What is the aim of engagement? What part of the policy process and which policy stakeholders are involved? What is the desired outcome? Considering purpose helps researchers to identify where effort can best be spent and what constitutes success – which of course may be very different for different researchers and different policy stakeholders.

Table 2.2   Examples of engagement routes and impacts

Engagement route	Informing development of policy documents (eg white papers)	Inform development of legislation	Inform scrutiny of legislation	Inform scrutiny of policy	Informing specific policy decisions	Inform policy thinking and ongoing policy development	Inform public debate on policy issues
				Impact on policy			
Membership of ministerial advisory group					X	X	
Submission of written evidence to a consultation by government or parliament	X	X	X	X			
Undertaking research commissioned by government					X	X	
Participating in a policy review commissioned by government	X	X	X	X	X	X	X
Participating in stakeholder meetings organised by government or parliament	X		X	X	X	X	

Impact on policy

Engagement route	Informing development of policy documents (eg white papers)	Inform development of legislation	Inform scrutiny of legislation	Inform scrutiny of policy	Informing specific policy decisions	Inform policy thinking and ongoing policy development	Inform public debate on policy issues
Speaking at conferences attended by significant numbers of government officials or other policy stakeholders	X	X	X		X		X
Blog or media article; social media	X		X			X	X
Undertaking a policy fellowship or secondment to a policy organisation	X	X		X		X	
Drawing attention to an overlooked policy issue						X	X
Lobbying government or parliament by submitting unsolicited evidence or analysis						X	

2.5   NO IMPACT WITHOUT ENGAGEMENT

Understanding of the nature and impact of academic–policy engagement is still at an early stage of maturity. We would caution against a focus on 'impact' at the expense of engagement, particularly whilst concepts of what constitutes impact on public policy are still evolving. Engagement between researchers and policy stakeholders is a prerequisite to impact. Engagement is the process by which researchers can start to understand what policymakers want and helps to develop trusted relationships. It helps to create the 'right person, right time' circumstances from which impact on policy derives as well as supporting the emergence of shared insights and impacts over time.

However, universities currently have only a limited suite of tools and frameworks with which to incentivise such academic–policy engagement. Whilst they can be useful, vigilance is needed against narrowing the concept of the practice and impact of engagement with public policy to only that which corresponds to those specific frameworks. (For example, there is a risk that research outputs which do not fit neatly into a REF impact case study are not highly valued by universities whilst such material might be of significant value to policymakers.) Researchers, universities and public policy organisations need to continue to work together to understand the rich, varied and nuanced nature of public policy engagement and impact.

As the Chief Executive of UKRI, Professor Dame Ottoline Leyser has noted, there is insufficient investment in both connecting people to maximise the benefits of research – such as academic–policy engagement – or of capturing the benefits of connectivity in a way that makes a straightforward case for further investment in it (for example, understanding the impacts of researchers engaging with public policy) (Leyser, 2020). Without increased efforts to develop such 'connectivity', researchers are likely to continue to encounter difficulties in understanding and responding to policymakers' needs.

Box 2.4 builds on our experience and understanding of engaging with policymakers to provide some top tips for academics.

BOX 2.4   TOP TIPS FOR ENGAGING WITH POLICYMAKERS

MAKE TIME: IT IS A LONG GAME: Successful engagement with and impact upon public policy is unlikely to happen overnight. More often it is the result of building networks and visibility, and refining contributions until an appropriate opportunity arises.

KNOW YOUR AUDIENCE – AND RESPECT THEIR MOTIVES: 'Policymakers' are a varied collection of individuals, professionals, officials and elected representatives. Be clear about who you wish to engage with and what you can offer them.

BE FOCUSED, BE CONSISE: Policymakers are generally short of time and work to deadlines of days or even hours. Get your points across in the shortest time possible.

GET TO THE POINT QUICKLY: Policymakers usually want to know what your research means for them, not how you conducted the research or how the field has been developed. Start your message with the key points of the evidence or conclusions from your research.

GOOD ENOUGH IS GOOD ENOUGH: Policymakers are often under time pressure; be prepared to offer conclusions based on the best available knowledge (even if certainty is not possible).

2.6   THE FUTURE OF ACADEMIC–POLICY ENGAGEMENT

Universities have shown unprecedented agility in repurposing research and applying their expertise to the range of urgent challenges posed by Covid-19. So we know it can be done. But we also know that the coronavirus response demanded a massive amount of effort and disruption amongst both academic researchers and policy professionals, working at a pace which is not sustainable. It relied heavily on existing networks and knowledge of expertise. Embedding academic–policy engagement more broadly and sustainably would help to build more sophisticated networks, diversify relationships, provide a wider pool of academic expertise which could be accessed by policymakers, and enable researchers to better understand how to respond to policy need.

At present, there is no shared expectation of funding for academic–policy engagement. Whilst universities and businesses are developing a progressively stronger understanding of their relationships, universities and policy organisations are at an earlier stage of understanding the costs and benefits of interactions. The cost of academic–policy engagement is probably covered by the block grant Quality Related (QR) funding received from Research England in many institutions, but that is often not made explicit.

The ultimate purpose of academic–policy engagement is to support better policymaking. As the Government Office for Science has noted:

> Better leadership and delivery of science, and a greater use of science in departments and across government would create a stronger evidence base for decision making, enhance government performance and contribute to government social goals and economic growth. (Government Office for Science, 2019)

This will require concerted efforts from all actors. The clearer articulation of needs and interests seen in the publication of ARI from national government and parliament is a good start. But this should be embedded at every level of government (not just central government). The move towards greater devolution of policymaking, particularly to mayoral authorities, does not appear to be being matched by adequate devolution of science advice. Government at all levels needs to set clear expectations that engaging with academic evidence is an expected part of working – and to build the capabilities and resources to do so.

POLICY PERSPECTIVE

It can sometimes be hard to be confident that you have a comprehensive, objective picture of relevant expertise and evidence, rather than one from the individuals you happen to have come across. The role of networks such as UPEN and CAPE in bringing more structure to this is very helpful.

Chris Pook, Deputy Director, Science and Innovation, Systems and Capability, Government Office for Science

There is a contrast between the siloed approach often found in national government and the integration of policy responsibilities often found in local government.

Professor Alan Penn, Chief Scientific Adviser, Ministry of Housing, Communities and Local Government

The role of CSAs is very important. They often retain a foothold in academia and therefore are well placed to create a trusted interface and help navigate it on behalf of Government.

Chris Pook, Deputy Director, Science and Innovation, Systems and Capability, Government Office for Science

Likewise, universities as institutions have a role in understanding both what policymakers want and how to support researchers to respond. This requires acknowledging that dedicated effort and sustained resources are needed for academic–policy engagement. This can be, for example, through dedicated knowledge mobilisers, the provision of additional funding to support engagement, training and development for researchers, or investment in supporting networks with policy stakeholders in which researchers can participate. University 'policy units' or other centrally funded structures can play an important role here, but incentives (such as funding or career recognition) are also likely to be required to support widespread engagement from individual researchers. Approaches will vary amongst institutions, but a commitment to valuing academic engagement with public policy in terms of institutional support, provision of resources, allowance of time, career recognition and facilitation will all be important.

POLICY PERSPECTIVE

There is lots of goodwill on both the academic and policy sides but having the capacity to actually do something is critical. Policy impact is now valued by academics, but it would be useful for us to get a bit more understanding of what the drivers are for academics and the different constraints they face.

Policy Officer from a Mayoral Combined Authority

At the same time, individual researchers may need to maintain a greater awareness of the policy environment and ensure willingness to understand what policy stakeholders need and how to meet these needs. This is likely to require investing some time over the long term – for example, through attending events and meetings, networking, being active on social media and in writing blogs. Being alert to opportunities for increased engagement – such as calls for evidence or advisory roles – will enable researchers to apply their expertise in policy settings. Additionally, researchers can ensure active consideration of how policy questions and needs can be factored into research activity and funding proposals. Submitting written evidence to government consultations or parliamentary inquiries can often provide a first step to engagement but is unlikely to lead to instant recognition or the formation of immediate networks.

2.7   BUILDING SHARED PURPOSE

Academic engagement with and impact upon public policy can be a long, uncertain and complex process with no immediate pay-off. The process itself (relationships built, thinking altered) can be as valuable as the tangible outcome (production of a briefing). Ultimately, we suggest, establishing successful academic–policy engagement as an ongoing and embedded activity for both communities will require the development of shared purpose and buy-in from all actors: individual researchers; university leaders and management; funders; individual policy professionals; and policy organisations. This shared purpose can help to make the case for dedicated and specialist resources to support researchers to engage with public policy and to more explicitly articulate the full breadth of policy impacts from research.

Our ambition is for academic–policy engagement to become a mainstream activity for universities, funders and policy stakeholders – no longer a specialist or additional activity, but something which is valued and rewarded by institutions, resourced by funders and an established part of the policy process. Building shared purpose can help all parties to negotiate the evolving landscape of academic–policy engagement and progress beyond linear concepts of knowledge exchange towards closer collaboration and co-production. Perhaps the question we should be seeking to answer is less 'What do policymakers want from researchers?' but rather, 'How can researchers and policymakers work together to co-create policy questions and solutions?'

ACKNOWLEDGEMENTS

We are very grateful to the many individuals quoted throughout this chapter for their time, thoughtfulness and candour in speaking to us. We have made every effort to reflect their views accurately and in context, but any errors or omissions are our responsibility alone.

NOTES

1. The first CSA was Solly Zuckerman, who had previously held the Ministry of Defence advisory role.
2. The authors are respectively a co-investigator on CAPE and chair of the CAPE Advisory Board.
3. More than two-thirds of the 6,600 impact case studies in Research Excellence Framework 2014 included references to impact upon public policy (Kings College, 2015).
4. See, for example: Institute for Government, 2019.
5. See, for example: House of Commons Liaison Committee, 2017–19.

REFERENCES

Bothwell, E., 2015. Science is only one lens policy makers look through. Accessed May 2021 at https://www.timeshighereducation.com/content/science-is-only-one -lens-policymakers-look-through

Campaign for Science and Engineering, 2017. *Improving the Use of Evidence in UK Government Policymaking.* Accessed May 2021 at https://www.sciencecampaign .org. uk/static/uploaded/5da82e8c-4344-4c3c-9412bf3b37a67244.pdf

Geddes, M., 2018. Committee hearings of the UK parliament: Who gives evidence and does this matter? *Parliamentary Affairs.* 71(2): 283–304. https://doi.org/10.1093/pa/ gsx026

Government Office for Science, 2019. *A Review of Government Science Capability.* Accessed May 2021 at https://www.gov.uk/government/publications/government -science-capability-review, May 2021

Heckels, N., Giles, G., Marsh, M., Peters, C., Renberg-Fawcett, K., and Stevenson, O., 2020. Engaging with UK government areas of research interest: Learning and insights from the Universities Policy Engagement Network. UPEN. February. Accessed May 2020 at https://www.upen.ac.uk/what_we_offer/reports/ARI_Report%20WEB%20SINGLE%20PAGES.pdf

House of Commons Liaison Committee, 2019. Fourth Report. *The Effectiveness and Influence of the Select Committee System.* Accessed May 2020 at https://publications.parliament.uk/pa/cm201719/cmselect/cmliaisn/1860/1860.pdf

House of Lords Science and Technology Committee, 2012. Fourth Report. The role and functions of departmental Chief Scientific Advisers. Accessed May 2021 at https://publications.parliament.uk/pa/ld201012/ldselect/ldsctech/264/26402.htm

Kenny, C., Rose, D.C., Hobbs, A., Tyler, C., Blackstock, J. 2017. The use of research evidence in the UK Parliament. London, UK, Houses of Parliament.

King's College London and Digital Science. 2015. *The Nature, Scale and Beneficiaries of Research Impact: An Initial Analysis of Research Excellence Framework (REF) 2014 Impact Case Studies.* Bristol, United Kingdom: HEFCE. Accessed May 2020 at https://webarchive.nationalarchives.gov.uk/20170712123928/http://www.hefce.ac.uk/pubs/rereports/Year/2015/analysisREFimpact/

Leyser, O., 2020. CaSE Annual Lecture 2020. Accessed May 2021 at https://www.sciencecampaign.org.uk/engaging-with-policy/events/case-annual-lecture-2020.html

Nice, A., 2012. Explainer: Government Chief Scientific Adviser. Institute for Government. Accessed April 2021 at https://www.instituteforgovernment.org.uk/explainers/government-chief-scientific-adviser

Penn, A. 2021. Personal interview with Alan Penn, Chief Scientific Adviser, Ministry of Housing, Communities and Local Government. Spring 2021.

Pook, C. 2021. Personal interview with Chris Pook, Deputy Director, Science and Innovation, Systems and Capability, Government Office for Science. Spring 2021.

Policy Officer. 2021. Personal interview with Policy Officer from a Mayoral Combined Authority. Spring 2021.

Sasse, T. and Haddon, C., 2018. How government can work with academia. Institute for Government. Accessed at https://www.instituteforgovernment.org.uk/publications/how-government-can-work-academia

Sasse, T. and Haddon, C., 2019. How academia can work with government. Institute for Government. Accessed May 2020 at https://www.instituteforgovernment.org.uk/publications/how-academia-can-work-government

Sasse, T. and Norris, E., 2019. Moving on: The cost of high staff turnover in the civil service. Institute for Government. Accessed May 2020 at https://www.instituteforgovernment.org.uk/publications/moving-on-staff-turnover-civil-service

Sharkey, Lord. 2021. Personal interview with Lord Sharkey, Liberal Democrat peer. Spring 2021.

Stevenson, O. and Tan, A., 2020. Greater support for underrepresented groups is vital in overcoming barriers to academic-policy engagement. UCL Policy Postings. Accessed May 2020 at https://medium.com/policy-postings/greater-support-for-underrepresented-groups-is-vital-in-overcoming-barriers-to-academic-policy-d6da71b1c093

3.   The value of research evidence for policy

David Christian Rose and Chris Tyler

3.1   INTRODUCTION

In this chapter, we explore the value of research evidence to policy-makers and provide a number of suggestions to researchers about how to engage productively with them. We understand that policy-makers engaging with academics can provide a rewarding experience for both groups, as indicated by the following quote:

> When you connect with the academic world, it really is oxygenating, you feel invigorated because it exposes you to a whole other world out there that is thinking in different ways. (Dr Gemma Harper, Deputy Director, Marine, Defra – testimony, Centre for Science and Policy (CSaP) Policy Fellows scheme)

However, defining the term 'research evidence' is not straightforward. In this chapter, we refer to research evidence in a way that academics traditionally would, associating it with knowledge generated through a rigorous, scientific methodology, encompassing the natural and social sciences and the humanities. We recognise that the boundary between 'research evidence' and other forms of knowledge is blurry and we do not seek to place academic ways of knowing on a pedestal. But, other forms of knowledge, such as anecdotal or experience-based evidence, are not usually generated using a robust scientific methodology (Alliance for Useful Evidence, 2016; Kenny et al., 2017).

With reference to a study of research use in the UK Parliament and four initiatives to bring research and policy together, we start by outlining why policy-makers want to use research evidence to make decisions. We then provide some top tips for how researchers can improve the chances that their research evidence is used by policy-makers.

3.2　WHY DO POLICY-MAKERS WANT TO USE RESEARCH EVIDENCE?

Critical scholars frequently refer to the myth of evidence-based policy-making, arguing that policy-makers do not utilise research evidence to its full potential (Nutley et al., 2007). However, in a survey of over 2,000 policy officials in Australia by Newman et al. (2015), the majority of respondents (58 per cent) said that they used databases to download academic research and more than 60 per cent reported using research evidence in written reports. Though the Institute for Government (2018) in the UK noted problems with the way research evidence was used, it did highlight a number of examples of where it was being useful to policy-makers.

A collaborative study between University College London (UCL) and the Parliamentary Office of Science and Technology asked UK parliamentarians and the staff supporting them if they valued research evidence in their work, and if so, why? This study engaged 157 people in Parliament, including MPs, Peers and parliamentary staff, through a mixed methods approach (Kenny et al., 2017; Rose et al., 2020a). In a survey used for this study, 98 per cent of respondents strongly agreed or agreed that research of all kinds was useful to them and over half reported that they used it daily. Parliamentarians and staff found research evidence useful for a number of reasons, including:

- To make more robust and credible policy decisions
- To provide background knowledge, helping them to understand an issue
- To provide balance
- To learn lessons from other countries
- For political purposes, scoring points over opponents.

Though we know that research evidence can be used politically (Cairney, 2016), studies have shown its value in making policies more robust and credible (see e.g. Phoenix et al., 2019). Credibility was the number one factor determining the use of evidence in the study of the UK Parliament (Rose et al., 2020a). Parliamentary staff said that they wanted to make sure they were 'only using authoritative sources'. MPs' staff spoke of the need to illustrate points 'credibly' with 'killer facts' (Kenny et al., 2017). Credible research evidence was seen as important to scrutinise existing policies to see how they could be made more effective, and evidence from academics tended to be perceived as credible (Kenny et al., 2017; Rose et al., 2020a).

The example of the Conservation Evidence initiative, shown in Box 3.1, highlights how research evidence can be vital in creating credible policies and avoiding mistakes.

BOX 3.1   USING RESEARCH EVIDENCE TO AVOID MISTAKES – CONSERVATION EVIDENCE

The Conservation Evidence initiative (see www.conservationevidence.com) summarises the evidence on the effectiveness of conservation interventions from the academic literature and provides lay summaries in an accessible form for policy-makers. In 2019, an average of 29,000 pages were viewed each month by an average of 9,000 people and it has been cited in multiple policy documents in the UK and New Zealand. A number of organisations, such as Froglife and regional branches of the Wildlife Trust, have signed up to be evidence champions, which partially involves making a pledge to check Conservation Evidence for information on whether a proposed intervention or policy is likely to work or not. There are many testimonies of how useful the collated evidence has been to policy-makers, with the Head of Planning and Environment at Forest Enterprise England saying that they use it 'to ensure that our limited funds stretch as far as possible'.

Policy-makers can use this resource to make sure that they do not make decisions that are unlikely to work. For example, Norfolk County Council have been criticised for spending £1 million on bat gantries, designed to guide bats to fly over roads at a high level to avoid collisions with cars (Crowley, 2020). However, a simple check of Conservation Evidence would have shown, based on the research evidence, that such a policy was unlikely to work. A check of the synthesised evidence could have saved money for the taxpayer and helped Norfolk Council to find alternative approaches that were more likely to work (such as installing underpasses or overpasses).

Policy-makers also value research evidence as a means to broaden their horizons and to spot emerging threats and opportunities. The Policy Fellows programme at the CSaP in Cambridge (UK) is a good example of where policy-makers have been exposed to the latest cutting-edge research evidence (see Box 3.2).

BOX 3.2   USING RESEARCH EVIDENCE TO BROADEN HORIZONS – CSAP POLICY FELLOWS SCHEME

The CSaP (UK) has run a Policy Fellows scheme since 2011. This invites policy-makers from a range of governmental departments and beyond on a two-year programme to connect them with researchers in Cambridge. Each bespoke programme begins with a few days at the University of Cambridge, with a series of meetings with academics who have been carefully selected to meet the research evidence needs of each policy-maker. The remainder of the two years sees a wide variety of engagement opportunities between policy-makers and researchers. Since its launch in 2011, more than 450 Fellows have been recruited and meetings have been set up with them and over 1,700 academics. In 2019/20, 833 meetings were held between Policy Fellows and researchers.

The scheme has been helpful to researchers interested in the application of their research to policy, even prompting new lines of research enquiry. It has also been valuable to those policy-makers who have taken part. Two of the major impediments policy-makers face in engaging with research evidence is time and access (Kenny et al., 2017). By taking policy-makers out of Whitehall (and other government centres) and embedding them (primarily) in the University of Cambridge for a week, they have the time and access they need to explore both their broad and particular evidence needs. Policy Fellows report that their horizons have been broadened by having the time to make contact with a number of researchers from different disciplines who each have their own unique take on solving a problem. The quote from Dr Gemma Harper (Defra) at the start of this chapter argued that Policy Fellows felt 'invigorated' by discussions held with researchers. Claire Moriarty (Permanent Secretary, Department for Exiting the European Union) said of the Policy Fellows scheme:

> *Connecting things together will always give you access to a wider range of solutions that anyone could get in their own minds, no matter how fantastically brilliant they are.*

Siddharth Varma, who was a Policy Fellow while he was a Policy Adviser at the National Infrastructure Commission, said:

> *The day-to-day of working in the centre of government, invariably on a procession of urgent things, is exciting but isolating. Policymaking is done best when its practitioners are genuinely open to new ideas and the latest evidence, acting with confidence about what they know and humility about what they do not. My time in Cambridge gave me plenty of time to practice the latter in an environment conducive to debate and reflection.*

These comments show that research evidence is valued by policy-makers, as are the opportunities to engage with researchers on a deeper level with more time.[a]

Note: [a] For more information please see https://www.csap.cam.ac.uk/policy-fellowships/policy-fellows/

We also know that policy-makers like to learn from international evidence of what works. In the study of the UK Parliament, one Peer said that having international evidence in public policy is like 'gold dust', a 'hugely powerful resource to back up your recommendations' (Kenny et al., 2017). The International Public Policy Observatory is a recent example of the mobilisation of global research evidence to address the social impacts of COVID-19. Indeed, the way that research evidence has been used across the world to inform policy responses to the pandemic has illustrated the significant value of research to policy-makers. Our response to the pandemic from lockdowns, to vaccine development and eventually to recovery would not have been possible without research evidence. One of the enduring memories from the pandemic across the world will be of politicians and scientific advisers standing on podiums to give press conferences, pointing to various graphs filled with research evidence. An example of how research evidence has been used to inform policy-makers during the pandemic can be seen in Box 3.3.

BOX 3.3   IPPO – MOBILISING GLOBAL EVIDENCE TO INFORM POLICY-MAKERS

The International Public Policy Observatory (IPPO)[a] is a collaboration between UCL, Cardiff University, Queen's University Belfast, the University of Auckland and the University of Oxford, along with partners such as the Scottish Policy and Research Exchange, Pivotal, the International Network for Government Science Advice (INGSA) and academic news publisher *The Conversation*. IPPO aims to be more demand-led than some past observatories, engaging directly with decision makers to understand their evidence needs and then synthesising answers they can use, including examples from global practice as well as formal syntheses of research evidence. As such it places a high premium on relationships and conversational engagement with policy-makers.

The various research partners work with policy partners across England, Scotland, Wales and Northern Ireland to offer insights, evidence and analysis of global policy responses to COVID-19 to enable them to address the immediate social, economic and public health impacts and help communities to recover. IPPO focuses on social issues relating to COVID-19, such as education, mental health, living online, care homes and adult social care, housing, vulnerable communities, and addressing the disproportionate impacts on Black, Asian and minority ethnic groups. In each area, evidence from wide sources – including many international sources – is synthesised, analysed and communicated to policy-makers, local leaders and frontline workers to help improve the outcomes of the difficult decisions they have to take.

Funded by the Economic and Social Research Council (ESRC), IPPO is one of a number of novel approaches to making the most of academic research in public policy. Whereas most major investments by research funders focus primarily on novel research, this ESRC investment focuses largely on research synthesis (led by UCL's EPPI-Centre) and policy engagement (led from UCL STEaPP along with all the other partners). We know from our own research that policy-makers value evidence synthesis and international evidence (Kenny et al., 2017; Rose et al., 2020b), and in this respect IPPO is a timely and important innovation.

Note: ª For more information please see https://covidandsociety.com

Studies have also shown the value of research evidence to policy-makers if it is synthesised in an accessible form, which is one of the aims of the Parliamentary Office of Science and Technology (POST) Fellowship scheme, described in Box 3.4.

BOX 3.4   POST FELLOWSHIPS – LEARNING HOW TO PRESENT RESEARCH EVIDENCE TO POLICY-MAKERS

The Parliamentary Office of Science and Technology (POST) is the UK Parliament's in-house source of science and technology advice. For nearly 30 years, POST has been running a Fellowships programme bringing PhD students from a wide range of disciplines into Parliament to work on briefings for parliamentarians. This is valuable for Parliament for two reasons. First, the more than 20 PhD students joining the team for three months at a time is funded externally to Parliament, which means that politicians and their staff are getting great value for money. Second, the influx of external enthusiasm and expertise is invaluable. Some of the PhD students work with select committees and occasionally elsewhere in Parliament, but most of them spend their time with POST, each researching and drafting a four-page briefing document called a POSTnote.

POSTnotes are internationally recognised as a gold standard for parliamentary briefings. Today they are widely imitated around the world as parliamentary science advisers slowly move away from a primary reliance on long and weighty reports. Our research showed that a lack of time is a major barrier for politicians and their staff to access research evidence (Kenny et al., 2017; Rose et al., 2020b). This is one reason why the relatively short and focused POSTnotes are so popular in Parliament. Another reason is that they are designed to place science and technology in a policy context, providing the link between policy options and available evidence for politicians. Finally, they are widely respected as non-partisan and accurate, which is a function of the expertise of POST, the training they provide the PhD Fellows and the importance of extensive peer review as part of their production.

Parliament is not the only beneficiary of this programme. During their time in Parliament, the PhD students learn how Parliament works, how to translate evidence into parliamentary briefings (both written and oral) and the importance of bringing the best of academic research to bear on parliamentary debate, scrutiny of government and legislative activity. At the end of the fellowship, the students take this knowledge with them back into academia. Many of them go on to successful academic careers and very often to stay close to POST, and their experience in Parliament influences their research activities, making them more relevant to public policy. Another subset of the fellows leave academia but go into policy roles, for example in scientific institutions and academies. The POST Fellowships are similar to PhD Internships, which are covered in more detail in Chapter 13 of this book.

Policy-makers do, therefore, value the use of research evidence. However, the impact is not always quick. Owens (2015) has shown that examples of 'direct hits' between the provision of research evidence and policies informed by that evidence are rare. Rather, impact is slower and more diffuse. A key message for academics then is not to get disheartened if policy-makers do not appear to be influenced by research evidence immediately. We make some further recommendations below about how academics can improve the chances that their research evidence is valued by policy-makers.

3.3   COMMUNICATING RESEARCH EVIDENCE TO POLICY-MAKERS

There are plenty of excellent guides for academics about how to communicate with policy-makers so that their research evidence is more impactful. Oliver and Cairney (2019), for example, offer a series of 'dos and don'ts' of influencing policy based on a systematic review. Phoenix et al. (2019) also provide an interesting perspective as a group of social researchers in the Department for Environment, Food and Rural Affairs (UK) about what type of communication strategies are most valued. They argued that research evidence needs to be relevant to policy-makers, presented at the right time to seize on policy windows, as well as being tailored to the audience in terms of presentation style. Good forms of communication include preparing policy briefs and slide-packs written in non-academic language. These tips are valuable because policy-makers in the study of research use in the UK Parliament criticised academic research evidence for sometimes lacking relevance, being too difficult for a non-specialist to understand, as well as being inaccessible due to paywalls and not being presented at the right time (Rose et al., 2020a). Advice for academics on how to engage with legislatures has been combined into a blog based on several studies (Tyler et al., 2020).

Below we draw on personal experience, for example as Director of POST and CSaP (Tyler), as well as on academic and our study of the UK Parliament, to outline five top tips for researchers seeking to improve the chances that their evidence is used by policy-makers. We recognise that there are institutional barriers, such as lack of time and incentives for academics, to putting some of them into practice.

Synthesise evidence and communicate succinctly: the examples of Conservation Evidence and the POSTnotes produced through the POST Fellowships highlight the importance of synthesising evidence and putting it into an accessible form for policy-makers. Policy-makers generally want to learn what the body of evidence says about an issue, rather than reading individual studies. If efforts can also be made to synthesise global evidence, as in the IPPO example, then this can be hugely valuable to policy-makers. Synthesised evidence provided in an accessible form can be easier to use in a fast-paced, time-poor policy-making environment. Writing a good policy brief, or preparing an engaging slide-pack or infographic, is an important skill for researchers to learn (Phoenix et al., 2019). In addition to doing evidence synthesis, academics should work with research funders and their own institutions to establish systems that fund and reward the time, expertise and impact of these efforts. ESRC's investment and UCL's leadership of the IPPO are a good recent example of the value of prioritising evidence synthesis and policy collaboration.

Establish two-way channels of knowledge exchange: the examples of the CSaP and POST Fellowships show the value of bringing policy-makers and researchers together. Many of the most productive relationships between the two occur as a result of sustained efforts over a long period of time to establish a connection and build trust, even re-establishing contact with new staff who take on policy roles. Listening to policy needs and investing time in building a relationship, rather than looking for immediate impact, is important. Ideally, over time, public policy will be influenced by good research and the research projects will be influenced by current and future policy needs.

Understand how policy-making timescales work: in the study of research use in the UK Parliament, parliamentarians and their staff criticised academic researchers for missing key policy windows; for example, calls for evidence. Knowing how policy-making timescales work, seizing on windows of opportunities (easier if trusting relationships are already formed) and presenting research evidence in a timely fashion is vital (Rose et al., 2020b). In the absence of available time to conduct fresh research, making use of the best available evidence, both locally and internationally, is still valuable.

Spend time enhancing your credibility: a key part of developing trusted relationships with policy-makers is the establishment of a credible research profile. Policy-makers are generally wary of individuals who have an axe to grind, perhaps from a specific political viewpoint. Building a credible scientific reputation and public persona is an important step to being invited to engage with policy-makers in windows of opportunity. Networks of researchers, policy-makers and intermediaries evolve over time, and the foundational relationships that fuel these important networks require effort. A shared cup of tea today may yield important results in a few months' time.

Make research open access where possible: policy-makers regularly complain that they are unable to access research evidence that appears to be useful from a title. This is rarely the fault of the individual researcher, but rather the fault of academic publishing models. Where possible, academics should ensure that their research is open access, or if it is not, time should be spent undertaking more accessible forms of dissemination, such as writing blogs or policy briefs, and making these available publicly.

Undertaking the steps above can ultimately help boost the credibility, relevance, iterativity and legitimacy of academic engagement at science–policy interfaces, which are key hallmarks of success (Sarkki et al., 2015).

3.4   CONCLUSION

Academic research evidence is valued by policy-makers to make better policies and avoid mistakes, to inform scrutiny of existing policies and to broaden horizons and knowledge on issues of societal importance. If research evidence is accessible to policy-makers, free from paywalls and scientific jargon, synthesised and summarised for speedy digestion, as well as being available on time to meet deadlines, then it is much more likely to be used. Initiatives described in this chapter, including academic-led evidence synthesis, partnerships designed to bring together multidisciplinary experience on a specific issue and knowledge brokering organisations who link science and policy, are well-placed to inspire or assist readers to enhance the policy impact of their own work.

REFERENCES

Alliance for Useful Evidence (2016). Using research evidence: A practice guide, Alliance for Useful Evidence, NESTA, London, UK.

Cairney, P. (2016). The politics of evidence-based policy making, The Politics of Evidence-Based Policy Making. 1–137. https://doi.org/10.1057/978-1-137-51781-4

Crowley, J. (2020). Norwich NDR bat bridges 'are not working'. Accessed 3 August 2021 at https://www.bbc.co.uk/news/uk-england-norfolk-51193389

Institute for Government (2018). *How Government can Work with Academia*. Accessed at https://www.instituteforgovernment.org.uk/publications/how-government-can -work-academia

Kenny, C., Rose, D.C., Hobbs, A., Tyler, C., Blackstock, J. (2017). The role of research in the UK Parliament. Accessed at https://www.parliament.uk/globalassets/ documents/post/The-Role-of-Research-in-the-UK-Parliament.pdf

Moriarty, C. (2019). Clare Moriarty: Case Study at Department for Exiting the European Union. Accessed August 2021 at https://www.csap.cam.ac.uk/network/ clare-moriarty-case-study-two/

Newman, J., Cherney, A., Head, B.W. (2015). Do policy makers use academic research? Reexamining the 'two communities' theory of research utilization. *Public Administration Review*, 76(1), 24–32.

Nutley, S., Walter, I., Davies, H.T.O. (2007). *Using Evidence: How Research Can Inform Public Services*. Policy Press, Bristol, UK.

Oliver, K., Cairney, P. (2019). The dos and don'ts of influencing policy: A systematic review of advice to academics. *Palgrave Communications*, 5, 21.

Owens, S. (2015). *Knowledge, Policy, and Expertise: The UK Royal Commission on Environmental Pollution 1970–2011*. Oxford University Press, Oxford, UK.

Phoenix, J.H., Atkinson, L.G., and Baker, H. (2019). Creating and communicating social research for policymakers in government. *Palgrave Communications*, 5, 98.

Rose, D.C., Kenny, C., Hobbs, A., Tyler, C. (2020a). Improving the use of evidence in legislatures: The case of the UK Parliament. *Evidence & Policy*, 16(4), 619–38.

Rose, D.C., Mukherjee, N., Simmons, B.I., Tew, E.R., Robertson, R.J. et al. (2020b). Policy windows for the environment: Tips for improving the uptake of scientific knowledge. *Environmental Science & Policy*, 113, 47–54.

Sarkki, S., Tinch, R., Niemelä, J., Heink, U., Waylen, K. et al. (2015). Adding 'itera-tivity' to the credibility, relevance, legitimacy: A novel scheme to highlight dynamic aspects of science-policy interfaces. *Environmental Science & Policy*, 54, 505–12.

Tyler, C., Beswick, D., Foxen, S., Geddes, M., Hobbes, A., Rose, D. (2020). How universities can improve parliamentary engagement: A 12 point plan. Accessed 1 September 2021 at https://transforming-evidence.org/blog/heres-how-universities -can-improve-parliamentary-engagement

Varma, S. (2019) Siddharth Varma: Case study at HM Treasury, Accessed August 2021 at https://www.csap.cam.ac.uk/network/siddharth-varma-case-study/

4. Speaking a shared language

Sarah Foxen and Rowena Bermingham

4.1 INTRODUCTION

We could begin this chapter with any number of quotations from eminent individuals about the importance of language for spreading ideas, uniting communities and understanding cultures. Instead, we would like to invite you to reflect on how you use language every day. Rather than thinking about the language used in famous speeches, we want to marvel at the feats of communication found in daily life; the same building blocks of communication that are used when a world-famous activist gives a rousing speech to inspire global change are also used when someone asks a checkout assistant to double-bag their groceries.

When communication is working well, we tend not to reflect on what is making it work. When it fails, we are suddenly made aware of how vital good communication is for everything to function efficiently. As we will explore in this chapter, humans are highly skilled at adapting their communication styles depending on context. In our personal lives, we adapt as a matter of course; gesturing the desire for another pint to a friend in a noisy pub, trying to give clear directions to a famous landmark to someone who speaks very little English, or attempting to explain a complicated social issue to a primary school child. However, in our professional lives, we can become inflexible, and sometimes even uncooperative, in our language.

It is sometimes suggested that academics and policymakers speak two different languages, making it harder for these groups to work together to achieve shared goals, including the generation of evidence-informed policy. Over the past few years, both academia and policy have given increasing attention to the notion of working together to generate evidence-informed policy. However, this has led to the emergence of a new set of jargon (such as 'knowledge mobilisation' or 'impact') which, ironically, now makes some of the information written about working across research and policy unintelligible to researchers or policymakers who are not themselves experts in this interface!

What stops us from recognising that we have slipped into jargon is our familiarity with the language. For many researchers and policymakers, years of experience have made it difficult to distinguish between language or concepts that are generally known and those that are specialist. This can create significant challenges to communication between research and policy.

In this chapter we draw on our linguistics backgrounds to help you understand why academia and policy have developed different 'languages', how this creates a barrier to working together and what is needed to enable mutual understanding. Combining knowledge from our time spent in academia with insights gained from working as policy practitioners, we suggest techniques that you can use for more effective dialogue.

One of the principles of good communication that we touch on is brevity. Accordingly, we have included a short summary of this chapter to close the chapter.

4.2 THE POLICY–ACADEMIA LANGUAGE BARRIER THROUGH THE LENS OF COMMUNICATION STUDIES

4.2.1 What is the Point of Language?

Language is our primary means of communicating meaning, be it through words, writing or gesture. However, language does not just convey meaning; it can also communicate information about the background of an individual (Bucholtz and Hall, 2005). In spoken language, for example, we are likely to infer that a person with a discernible Manchester accent has spent a certain amount of time in that region. In written language, we can also make inferences about the writer and presumed audience. For example, it is often said that you can tell the power dynamic between two people from the length of their emails, with the more senior person generally sending shorter emails. Thus, it is not just *what* is communicated, but also the *manner* of communication that reveals information about the communicator *as well as* their relationship with the receiver of the communication.

Just as identity can be inferred from language, language can also be used to construct identity and signal group belonging. For example, a seminal linguistics study in the 1980s showed how language was used by teenagers in Detroit to signal belonging to one of two distinct groups, or 'communities of practice': 'jocks' and 'burnouts' (Eckert, 2006). A community of practice is a group of people with similar interests and/or objectives, who share similar practices and who use a common language (Eckert, 2006; Lave and Wenger, 1991). It is a concept which can help us understand why those from the policy world and researchers may struggle to communicate with one another.

4.2.2 Why the Struggle in Mutual Understanding?

If we consider researchers and those working in policy as belonging to different communities of practice, we can understand how their development and use of language might mean they struggle to communicate effectively. To give an example, microbiologists are a broad group of people with a common interest who are likely to share similar objectives (such as conducting research to advance understanding of aspects of the human body). Crucially, they also all use a common language, specific to their community of practice. Having a common language enables the community to communicate more effectively. For example, 'pharmacogenomics' takes much less time for a microbiologist to read and comprehend than 'the science concerned with understanding how genetic differences among individuals cause varied responses to the same drug and with developing drug therapies to compensate for these differences' (Merriam-Webster, n.d.). Similarly, in the policy world, the term 'green paper' can save a policymaker having to write out 'a document containing ideas about a particular subject that is published by the Government so that people can discuss them before any decisions are made' (Collins, n.d.). However, what acts as useful shorthand for one discipline may act as a barrier to those outside that field.

You may have experienced this feeling of exclusion when travelling to a foreign country where you do not speak the language or even when passing a group of young adults using lots of slang that you are not familiar with. The good news is that humans have a wealth of tools at their disposal to overcome 'language barriers', many of which we use subconsciously.

4.2.3 How Do Different Communities Overcome Language Barriers?

For as long as different speech communities have existed and come into contact with each other, they have needed to overcome language barriers to be able to communicate. This might be through one community shifting to speak the language of the other, convergence between the two, or the evolution of a new language born out of the original two (as seen with many of the Creole languages that emerged in colonial settings between the 15th and 19th centuries (Winford, 2007)). Another way we overcome linguistic barriers is by looking for a shared language or a 'lingua franca'. This may not be the first language of anyone in a particular conversation, but is one that all parties understand. A current example is the use of English in the majority of international journals and conferences. While these are linguistic choices that we are usually conscious of, we also adapt our communication in many subconscious ways.

Linguists have identified that individuals change the way they speak according to context – be it word choice, sentence structure or accent feature. This is known as 'style shifting'. One example of this is where speakers temporarily modify their speech to more closely match that of the person they are speaking with (Mesthrie et al., 2011). The linguist Allan Bell analysed speech on New Zealand radio stations and reported that not only do speakers modify their style of speech to reflect their addressee (the individual they were directly speaking to) but also that of presumed listeners who might be hearing the conversation (Bell, 1984).

4.2.4   What Do We Do to Make Ourselves Understood?

We have established that humans are extremely skilled at communicating. By recognising the underlying principles that we subconsciously follow when successfully adapting our conversation for others, we can apply these principles consciously to all our communication. In the 1970s, the philosopher Paul Grice developed a set of statements (or 'maxims') as hallmarks of productive conversations:

1. The maxim of quality: Contributions are truthful.
2. The maxim of quantity: Contributions are informative.
3. The maxim of relevance: Contributions are relevant.
4. The maxim of manner: Contributions are clear and brief. (Grice, 1975)

Conversations that abide by these maxims are said to follow the cooperative principle, meaning that the people involved are adapting the way that they talk to be understood by others.

These maxims may seem easy enough to abide by during a conversation and, thankfully, most interactions follow the cooperative principle. However, people do break these maxims, whether accidentally or purposefully (for example, by lying or by flouting a maxim for comic effect). Almost every poor conversation you have ever had will have included someone breaking one or more of these maxims. Speaking to a friend at a dinner party about their work and being left feeling utterly confused about what they actually do for a living may have been caused by your friend not giving you enough information to understand the content (therefore not abiding by the maxim of quantity). The reason for avoiding a conversation with a particular neighbour may be that you know from experience that your neighbour will talk at you endlessly about the bin collections for no clear reason (therefore not abiding by the maxims of relevance or manner).

When the maxims are applied correctly, we are able to bring our conversational partners along with us. However, if we break the maxims, we risk confusing, and perhaps even annoying, the person we are talking with. If you want to reflect more on how we abide by these maxims in our everyday interactions without even realising it, see Box 4.1.

In the next section we will talk about how to apply some of the principles that we have outlined in this section to adapt communication to enhance understanding. While recognising the need for those in both policy and academia to reflect on how they communicate with the other, we focus on what academics can do to enhance the effectiveness of their communication with those in policy.

BOX 4.1 THE MAXIMS AT WORK IN AN EVERYDAY CONVERSATION

Good conversations rely on people being cooperative and interpreting the statements of other people through the lens of the maxims above. For example, look at the interaction below:

Hannah: I take my tea with milk.

Thomas: In the fridge on the middle shelf.

Read entirely literally, these two sentences can be seen as two unrelated, random statements. However, because they form part of a conversation, we know that they must relate in some way. Both statements are examples of conversational implicature. This is where the meaning of a statement is not actually said explicitly, but can be inferred. Most of the time we talk, we are using and interpreting these conversational implicatures. In the example above, Hannah's statement about how she takes her tea is an indirect request for milk and Thomas's response giving the location of the milk is an indirect offer. We understand these meanings because we assume that this conversation follows the cooperative principle and therefore their statements must be relevant. Hannah and Thomas do not need to explicitly state their meaning because they can rely on each other to apply the maxims of relevance and quantity to infer what the other person means. By using these brief statements, instead of stating the explicit underlying meaning at length, they are abiding by the maxim of manner.

Even the simplest interaction that humans have, like the one above, requires a difficult but vital ability; being able to make correct assumptions about what other people know. In his reply, Thomas assumes that Hannah knows where the fridge is; perhaps they are flatmates. However, if the context were different then Thomas would not be able to use this same response. Imagine that Jane is a potential flatmate having a cup of tea while viewing Thomas and Hannah's flat. Thomas would have to adapt and give a different response to the same statement to be cooperative:

Jane: I take my tea with milk.

Thomas: I've got some milk that you can have. It's on the middle shelf of the fridge in the kitchen. The kitchen is through the door at the end of the hallway.

Ignoring that he is being somewhat rude by not fetching the milk himself, Thomas has been a cooperative conversational partner. He has considered that Jane does not know where the kitchen is and his response reflects this. If he had used the same response to Jane as he did with Hannah, he would be breaking the maxim of quantity by not providing her with enough information to make his statement useful.

4.3   HOW TO SPEAK THE SAME LANGUAGE

As discussed above, professionals operate in communities of practice where they can communicate extremely effectively with those who are also part of that community. However, many people struggle when having to talk about their specialist fields to non-specialists. We suggest that good communication requires taking it back to basics and employing the conversational skills we use every day (as outlined in Grice's maxims). In conversations we are usually trying to achieve something by engaging with another person. Productive conversations require knowing what you want to achieve, understanding the person you are talking with and adapting your style to suit the context. Therefore, when considering engaging and communicating with someone working in policy, be it a civil servant, member of parliamentary staff, Member of Parliament or Government minister, consideration of three simple questions may be helpful:

1. What do you want to achieve?
2. Who are you communicating with?
3. How are you communicating with them?

The answers to these questions are interlinked and you will likely circle round, visiting them more than once. However, the start of your engagement is likely to be because there is something specific you want to achieve (question 1) or you have the opportunity to communicate with someone (question 2). Here we explore each question in turn and reflect on how you can apply the maxims outlined above to ensure your communication is as cooperative as possible. We have not been prescriptive about modes or styles of communication in the following section, as there are many appropriate ways. However, we have put together 'top tips' in Box 4.2 based on effective ways we have seen people talk across the policy–academia divide.

4.3.1   Ask Yourself What You Want to Achieve

Before even thinking about how to adapt your language, or who to engage with, think about what it is you want to achieve. For example, do you think there is a need for new or updated legislation? Do you want your research findings to feed into the development of Government policy? Do you want to raise awareness among decision-makers about your research findings? If so, why? Has an opportunity arisen to respond to a call for evidence or consultation? What do you want to achieve by responding? Reflection on these questions will help you determine who you need to engage with and how to achieve your aim, including how to communicate.

4.3.2   Ask Yourself Who You Are Communicating With

Sometimes an opportunity arises to communicate with someone in the policy world. For example, you have been invited to a roundtable or you have a meeting lined up with your local MP. However, often there is no specific opportunity but you have identified that there is something you want to achieve and you need to engage with a particular person to make that happen. Once you have determined who you will be communicating with, consider what you know about that person.

Some questions you might ask yourself include: What does their role involve and how can your work help them? What knowledge are they likely to have about your field in general and your specialism in particular? It is better not to assume that the person you are talking with has in-depth knowledge of your specialism. Remember that many civil servants are considered generalists (someone with a broad range of knowledge on a variety of subjects) rather than specialists (someone with a deep level of knowledge of one subject in particular). Members of Parliament are also required to engage with a breadth of policy issues so, although they are likely to have their own specific specialisms and interests, it is not possible for them to be specialists in all fields.

You can use your awareness about what that person is likely to know to inform the way you 'design' your communication. You can make sure your contribution is *informative* by providing the right amount of detail for the receiver to understand it. You can make sure your contribution is *relevant* to the person and their role by thinking about their needs. While a detailed explanation of your research methods may be necessary and interesting for your peers, is this useful for a policymaker?

4.3.3 Ask Yourself How You Are Communicating

A reflection on the mode of communication will help you ensure that your means of communication is appropriate, as you will need to change the content and length of your communication depending on context. For example, if you are planning on emailing a request to a Member of Parliament, consider that their inbox receives hundreds of emails a day, so they (or more likely their staff) will have limited time to consider your email. Therefore, ensure that your communication is *clear and brief.* If you are responding to a Government consultation or select committee call for evidence, then it is important to be sure to respond to the questions or terms of reference posed. Remember that to make your contribution *relevant* and usable, you will need to produce something bespoke. Field-specific modes of communication (such as academic journal articles) have a particular style and are written for set purposes, usually making them inappropriate for a policy audience. For example, journals often have a prescriptive writing style for their publications and authors often write articles with a certain purpose in mind. These styles and purposes are unlikely to match with those of a reader who is more interested in how results can be applied in a policy context. Therefore, you will need to take time to consider how best to summarise your research for a general audience.

When submitting something in writing, you have time to reflect and edit. But what if you find yourself standing next to a civil servant in a relevant Government department at a buffet? In the precious few minutes where you may be able to capitalise on their attention, remember that communication allows for a two-way exchange of knowledge and ideas. Rather than trying to squeeze as much of your 30-minute conference paper as possible into a 3-minute chat, you might like to build rapport with them and find out more about their role. Not only is this more likely to lead to future conversations than giving them an unsolicited lecture, it will also give you the knowledge you need to identify what information you can share with them which is *informative* and *relevant* for their role (allowing further reflection on question 2 'who are you communicating with?').

4.3.4 Ask Yourself *Again* What You Want to Achieve

As mentioned above, these three questions are all interlinked. However, it is always useful to return to the purpose of your communication. It is likely that ultimately what you want to achieve falls into one or both of two broad categories: (1) change or (2) relationship building. As described elsewhere in this book, to achieve either of these, trust is essential. Therefore, finally, when communicating with those in policy, it is important, above all, to be *truthful.* For example, when presenting research findings, explain if there is consensus in the field or not, and be honest about limitations and unknowns in data and your own knowledge.

BOX 4.2   TOP TIPS FOR EFFECTIVE COMMUNICATION WITH POLICYMAKERS

Stating your purpose upfront: It may sound obvious, but being clear about what you want someone to do with the information you are giving them makes it more likely that they will do it. If you expect your conversation partner to infer what you want, there is always a chance they will reach an incorrect conclusion. For example, as part of our training for academics in engaging with Parliament, we had an activity where we asked participants to imagine they were talking to an MP and to explain their research and indicate what they wanted the MP to do in three minutes. On many occasions their time was up before they had mentioned what they wanted the MP to do and we found ourselves asking at the end: 'So what? What do you want me to do?' We have now changed the framing and ask them to state what they want their MP to do, underpinning their suggestions with research findings. Try to do the same yourself: look at your research, say to yourself: 'So what?' and start there.

Swapping out jargon: Making language as accessible as possible allows people to engage more effectively with your work. If someone can understand what you are talking about, they will find it easier to engage. Reflect on your terminology, and prepare non-specialist alternatives where necessary. For example, in 2019 the Commons Science and Technology Committee conducted an inquiry into Japanese knotweed (a plant that causes damage to properties). Part of the problem is due to the plant's rhizomes. Since this term is not understood by many, the second line of the introduction to the report states '[Japanese Knotweed] has distinctive rhizomes (underground structures that resemble roots) ...' (UK Parliament, 2019).

Asking for the possible: When listening to specialists, policymakers are usually seeking answers, often in the form of recommendations. However, policymakers often note that academics feel comfortable communicating their research and findings, but less comfortable making recommendations based on those findings, even when invited to do so. While it may feel intimidating presenting policy options, we encourage you to do so; policymakers and shapers have to get their ideas from somewhere, so make sure you contribute to their options. A common pitfall that many academics fall into is making their key recommendation a call for more research. Although undoubtedly true that more research is often needed, this is not something policymakers can act on. Therefore, try to avoid making that your principal or only recommendation.

Including case studies: Stories, case studies or narrative structure can bring information to life and help the reader or listener to imagine the information you are trying to convey. Relatedly, it is for this reason that select committees will often try to go on visits as part of their inquiries: to explore case studies and engage with lived experience and stories. Narrative structures can be used very effectively in policy communication (Deserai and Jones, 2018), so do not shy away from using these devices if appropriate.

4.4 SUMMARY

In this last section, we draw out the key points from the chapter to help the reader enhance their communication with policy audiences. If you have skipped straight to this section from the introduction then we welcome you here without judgement; we understand that you are busy and we hope this summary is useful. Remember that policy professionals are also very busy people, so we hope that you always include summaries in your work for them! We have laid out our summary in one structure (see Box 4.3) that policy professionals suggest academic researchers consider using in their communications: a problem/solutions structure.

BOX 4.3 SUMMARY OF OUR CHAPTER

Problem: Academics and policymakers do not speak the same language

Academics and policymakers have their own separate jargons. This prevents effective communication between the two worlds. A lack of effective communication means that opportunities to work together can be hindered or missed.

Solution: Adapt your language to be understood by policymakers

Below we make some recommendations for bridging the language divide between academia and policy. These are drawn from linguistic theory that explains why groups use different languages and how humans adapt their language to be more cooperative when talking with others. (You will notice that we have not included an in-depth exploration of the theory here because, if you were interested in that, you would probably have read the previous sections. Consider whether policymakers reading work in your field may feel the same way; it is likely that they are more interested in the solutions presented by the research rather than the specifics of the research itself.)

Recommendation 1: Think about what you want to achieve in your communication

All communication should have a purpose. What is yours? Do you want to build a relationship or make a specific change? What are the steps to making that happen? Reflection on these questions will help you determine what you need to do and who you need to engage with to achieve your aim. Above all, be honest about what your work can actually do for policymakers.

Recommendation 2: Think about who you are communicating with

Consider the role and knowledge of the person you are communicating with. Adapt the information you include and the language you use based on their needs and knowledge. Give them the right quantity of information (neither too much nor too little) and make sure it is relevant to their work.

Recommendation 3: Think about how you are communicating

You may be sending an email, responding to a Government consultation or talking to a policymaker over a cup of tea. All of these modes of communication will require a different style and different content. Keep in mind the manner of communication and remember to be clear and brief whatever mode you are using.

Recommendation 4: Learn from what has worked previously

Look at academic blogs or reports from outside your field that you found easy to read. Consider how the writer made their work understandable and engaging to non-specialists. It is likely that they will have employed one or more of the following techniques:

• Hooking the reader early with a clear purpose or interesting introduction
• Using an easy-to-follow structure (like problem/solution)
• Providing a summary upfront
• Using headings and subheadings to make it easier to skim and identify relevant information
• Avoiding (or explaining) jargon
• Using case studies or an engaging narrative structure

> • Making recommendations or giving policy options (not just calling for more research in an area!).

REFERENCES

Bell, A (1984) 'Language style as audience design'. *Language in Society*, 13(2), 145–204.

Bucholtz, M and Hall, K (2005) 'Identity and interaction: a sociocultural linguistic approach'. *Discourse Studies*, 7(4/5), 585–614. https://doi.org/10.1177/1461445605054407

Collins (n.d.) 'Green Paper'. https://www.collinsdictionary.com/dictionary/english/green-paper. Accessed 8 January 2021.

Deserai, C and Jones, M (2018) 'Narratives as tools for influencing policy change'. *Policy & Politics*, 46(2), 217–34.

Eckert, P and Brown, K (2006) 'Communities of practice', in *Encyclopedia of Language and Linguistics* ed K Brown (2nd edn, Amsterdam: Elsevier), 683–5. https://doi.org/10.1016/B0-08-044854-2/01276-1

Grice, H P (1975) 'Logic and conversation', in *Syntax and Semantics 3: Speech Acts*, eds P Cole and J J Morgan (New York, NY: Academic Press), 41–58.

Lave, J and Wenger, E (1991) *Situated Learning: Legitimate Peripheral Participation.* Learning in Doing: Social, Cognitive and Computational Perspectives (Cambridge: Cambridge University Press). https://doi.org/10.1017/CBO9780511815355

Merriam-Webster (n.d.) 'Pharmacogenomics'.https://www.merriam-webster.com/dictionary/pharmacogenomics. Accessed 8 January 2021.

Mesthrie, R, Swann, J, Deumert, A and Leap, W (2011) *Introducing Sociolinguistics* (Edinburgh: Edinburgh University Press).

UK Parliament (2019) 'Introduction'. *Japanese Knotweed and the Built Environment.* https://publications.parliament.uk/pa/cm201719/cmselect/cmsctech/1702/170204.htm. Accessed 8 January 2021.

Winford, D (2007) *An Introduction to Contact Linguistics* (Oxford: Blackwell Publishing).

5.   From broadcast to engagement: moving beyond traditional mechanisms

Anand Menon and Jill Rutter

5.1   INTRODUCTION

The prominence of the 2014 Scottish Independence referendum and the 2016 referendum on the UK's European Union (EU) membership have reinforced interest among politicians and media, including foreign media, who are keen to try to understand the ultimate question: 'What is going on in the UK?' In more recent times, the COVID-19 pandemic has amplified interest by policy stakeholders to gain informed expertise and in-depth, nuanced research evidence to better understand the complex nature of public debates as well as policy.

On the back of these important turns in our history, the Economic and Social Research Council (ESRC) has set up and funded the UK in a Changing Europe initiative ('UKICE' or 'the Initiative'), designed to promote a greater understanding of the complex and ever-changing relationship between the UK and the EU through high-quality, independent research. This chapter will draw on our experiences working at UKICE to demonstrate that a holistic approach to impact can be gained by considering all stakeholders and using dissemination mechanisms beyond conventional means.

5.2   PRESENTING THE CHANGING EUROPE INITIATIVE

The history of the UKICE initiative began in earnest with the Conservative election victory in the 2015 UK General Election which cleared the way for a referendum on EU membership. The ESRC funded UKICE with the objective of ensuring that academic research made its way into the referendum debate to come. This in turn meant finding a way to take research to non-academic audiences, with identified key stakeholders to include politicians, civil servants, businesses groups, third sector organisations and the general public. The decision was taken to staff an office and to advertise for a number of Senior Research Fellows to work with the Initiative. From the start, we focused on building close and collaborative relationships with key user groups, particularly staff on the campaigns we were involved in and journalists.

The inception of UKICE presents an opportunity to develop a better understanding of the intricacies of knowledge exchange between academics and policy makers and innovative ways to manoeuvre through this complex landscape. The Initiative in itself is a unique approach to engagement, not least because it was created with the sole and explicit objective of achieving impact and effective knowledge exchange. While the principal aim of UKICE is to provide independent, critical, social science research into UK–EU relations, the remit of the research network was not restricted to policy makers. Given the context during the early years of the Initiative's activity (with our research focusing on a national referendum on the Europe question), our ambitions included an intention to impact on public debates as well as policy. Serendipitously, the two agendas have dovetailed, with the higher profile achieved via media channels used to communicate with the public serving a standard in the minds of policy makers with a subsequent increase in access and engagement.

The UKICE model changed over time (see Box 5.1). Moreover, UKICE was not created without learning from prior experience in similar contexts. The UKICE model was based on the experience of the Future of the UK and Scotland initiative,[1] which was created to provide research-based evidence and information during the Scottish independence referendum campaign in 2014. Both the UKICE model *and* the Future of the UK and Scotland initiative were designed to address the sense that social sciences had a useful contribution to make, but that relying on conventional dissemination mechanisms meant they had so far failed to contribute enough to key national debates. By outlining our experience with UKICE, we highlight that a holistic approach to impact through consideration of all stakeholders can be particularly meaningful, especially when working with policy makers.

BOX 5.1   UKICE'S STAGED APPROACH

It is useful to discuss the UKICE project as having two phases, the time prior to the EU referendum and the period after the EU referendum as the context necessitated a different approach. During the referendum campaign, while we engaged privately with the campaign groups, our focus was on communicating with the public. We did this using a number of techniques ranging from events held around the country, at which members of the public were encouraged to ask questions, to engagement via the media (with an emphasis on more popular outlets such as 5 Live, Breakfast TV, local stations and the tabloids) to partnerships with organisations such as Mumsnet that provided us with access to groups that otherwise would have been difficult to reach.

After the referendum, the focus of our work shifted. We have spent more time engaging with decision makers in the civil service and parliament, which has been achieved largely through regular meetings with MPs and officials, along with briefing sessions for groups of MPs and a regular series of masterclasses for civil servants. Much of this was focused not just on working through how to take forward the referendum result, but on filling in gaps in basic understanding on how the EU worked and what EU membership meant for the UK in practical terms.

That meant tapping into the reserves of academic knowledge in fields such as EU law, trade policy (where the UK had very little trade policy capacity as it was an EU competence) and economics. When designing a project which aims to impact disparate groups of stakeholders, we feel it is important to consider at what stage it is most impactful to engage with each group. This is not only for efficiency's sake, but also to ensure that the academic knowledge reaches key areas of influence at the correct time.

As mentioned above, we have engaged with a number of non-academic audiences ranging from the general public to civil servants, businesses and business organisations and third sector organisations (trade unions, charities and voluntary associations).

5.3   UKICE'S HOLISTIC APPROACH OF ENGAGING WITH POLICY STAKEHOLDERS

5.3.1   Create a Platform for Engagement and Raise Awareness on Your Expertise

A platform built by one research project can be used to highlight, promote and raise awareness on the many sources of academic evidence which can be used by policy makers. Using UKICE as an example, the work built by the Initiative has certainly helped to enhance the profile of social science evidence, not only among policy makers but also the general public via frequent interactions with national, local and indeed international media.

The broad remit of UKICE was to provide research-based evidence on the UK–EU relationship as well as on the Brexit process and its implications. For the majority of the researchers who have been involved in the Initiative, the key motivation was a desire to engage more effectively with key stakeholders. While UKICE provided some funding for research, much of the funding was used to promote engagement with non-academic audiences via UKICE's website, social media, videos, official events and other dissemination and engagement methods. In this way, UKICE served as a resource platform beyond the academics directly funded by the scheme to social scientists in general, assisting them in gaining a larger audience for their research findings and in engaging directly with key user groups.

Building a platform to create awareness of your expertise depends largely on your source of funding. For UKICE, it had been important from its inception to use the generous ESRC funding to build not just a research network, but rather an *infrastructure*. While we set aside funding for staffing an office, launching and maintaining our website, and launching events, we also prioritised the creation of a communications team. A communications team was crucial in allowing UKICE to start engagement, build trust *and* maintain relations with key external stakeholders. It is important to identify who your key external stakeholders would be, based on the potential of repeated engagement and communication activities. For UKICE, this group is formed by journalists, politicians, civil servants, business groups and third sector organisations.

The importance of having a communications team is also to spread awareness of a group's or project's strength and expertise as researchers. Therefore, projects which aim to work in this way should consider costing a communications team into their budget. Taking UKICE for example, a main goal was to ensure that social science research should be perceived as having something to contribute to important national debates. The point of UKICE, therefore, was not to achieve impact for specific pieces of research but, rather, to enhance the reputation of the social sciences as a whole in terms of their ability to engage with and provide knowledge to not only policy makers but also (given the context of referendums in Scotland and the UK) the public as a whole. One of the key insights from the UKICE project was that research projects can serve as a resource to promote the use of social science evidence itself, as well as promoting individual pieces of social science research.

5.3.2   Leverage a Broadcast and Media Profile

The prominence of a specific news agenda can have an important role to play in reinforcing interest among the general public and politicians (domestically and internationally) to pay attention to your research if it is responding to the same topic. One insight we gained is that building a broadcast and media profile (that is, a reputation for appearing on radio or television, among other media methods) raises the potential for more media engagement. It is therefore important to locate opportunities for expert opinion on a popular news agenda.

Appearances on media (local, national and/or international) not only provided opportunities to meet and forge relationships with politicians, but also served in their minds a kind of standards in testifying the reliability of the researchers they are engaging with.

At UKICE, the prominence of Brexit as a media topic has been extremely helpful in building our broadcast profile. This was most evident after appearances by our researchers Professor Barnard and Professor Menon on *Question Time*, the BBC's most viewed political programme. This appearance led to a significant increase in approaches from politicians for meetings and briefings as well as subsequent opportunities. For example, evidence from our network of fellows was regularly used in Parliamentary Select Committees and UKICE's Senior Fellow, Professor Katy Hayward at Queen's University, Belfast, won the Political Studies Association award for communicator of the year for her work on Brexit and Northern Ireland.

During the Brexit referendum campaign, UKICE also worked closely with a number of journalists and media organisations to provide background and information about the nature of the UK–EU relationship and the key issues being debated in the campaign. UKICE built a reputation for impartiality, which became particularly advantageous when discussing the UK–EU relationship with the press. Unlike other organisations (such as think tanks), UKICE remained neutral on the positions of the referendum, making it more free to comment on evidence from both sides of the debate. While collaborations with journalists provided UKICE with significant reach, initially there was limited engagement with policy makers and with campaign groups. However, as the profile of the Initiative grew, the willingness of policy makers (civil servants and politicians) to engage increased notably. Members of parliament in particular proved more willing to engage with us once our reputation was established.

Top Tip

Academic work can be useful to journalists due to greater perceived impartiality and journalists can in turn provide significant reach and a gateway to policy makers.

Considerable effort has been made in building UKICE's broadcast profile. From the start, we aimed to address two key challenges of engaging via media. Firstly, we realised that there is a critical and well-identified barrier to the media, the government and policy makers, which is the inability to identify academics beyond a shortlist of 'usual suspects'. The formation of UKICE as a resource platform in providing connections to diverse academic expertise had been deliberately set up in overcoming this challenge. Secondly, research engagement with media often requires a rapid turnaround, a challenge when considering academics' availability, differing timescales and multiple responsibilities. Having a full-time team who could respond at short notice to media and other requests was also crucial in this regard, as was the creation of a team of Senior Fellows who could devote a significant part of their time to the work of the Initiative. This meant that UKICE were frequently able to offer a contributor, which created a virtuous circle of broadcast profile and influence.

It is worth adding that all UKICE project members benefited from a high-quality media training course. This both provided the skills necessary but also worked as a powerful way of bonding together a group of academics working in institutions across the country, many of whom had never had any contact before.

As mentioned above, having a communications team is invaluable in forging relationships with external stakeholders. In building our broadcast profile, the team had been useful in carrying out briefings for groups of journalists from multiple newspapers and broadcast organisations. A communications team is also helpful in maintaining an active social media presence, which, in today's age, is invaluable in capturing ad hoc media opportunities. UKICE's communications team also works hard in maintaining our official website to ensure that it constantly hosts a lot of new content. The success of our engagement reach can be seen when we take a peek into our website's hit during the COVID-19 pandemic, which reached two million views by November 2020.

5.3.3 Embedding Flexibility, Adaptability and Dynamism as an Engagement Mechanism

A key strength of the UKICE approach has been the ability and willingness to use different ways of communicating with the dynamic sets of audiences we want to reach.[2] We know by now that, to non-academics, academic expertise can mean a variety of things. Through a more traditional perspective, academics can be experts of their research area. However, more broadly, researchers can also act as experts representing the academic community as a whole. As such, the opportunities to engage with media can be endless. For example, UKICE's relationship with the Governance After Brexit programme (also funded by the ESRC) exemplifies the way we have represented as champions for traditional social science research projects.

Similarly, the types of research findings used in engagement with media can shift depending on the need of the media engagement, as well as the reputation and profile of the research project. On one hand, we have used findings from long-term research projects in various ways, to feed into discussions and presentations using dynamic methods. On the other hand, we have also drawn on more 'reactive' research, such as economic analyses of the Brexit deals negotiated by Theresa May and Boris Johnson, which we released within days of the texts being published.

Top Tip

Often the motivations of key stakeholders can shift with contextual changes; researchers engaged in this type of work must be able to adapt and work with these changes.

To know how best to engage with different audiences is to continue experimenting with your research findings and your expertise as academics. At a policy level, direct engagement with policy makers and senior politicians via events has proven a useful means not only to build links with these individuals, but also to drive interest to academic work among a broader audience. MPs nevertheless still tend to prefer private briefings in small groups of like-minded colleagues. For other types of stakeholders, formal conferences and seminars have worked well for some audiences. For other audiences, deploying short videos explaining key issues, even using light-hearted social media (TikTok) based communications could work better. At UKICE, we have not shied away from the potential of engaging using all these mechanisms to see what works best.

Top Tip

Tailoring engagement to your audience, recognising their different needs, preferred communication methods and interests is beneficial.

When organising conferences as impact events, it is important to deliberately differentiate them from academic conferences by putting together panels comprising a mixture of academics, journalists and policy makers. The aim is to both encourage knowledge exchange between these different groups and to show a wider audience how those different perspectives can shed useful light on contested and controversial issues. Streaming events and making them available online also helps increase audiences significantly. At UKICE, we moved our events entirely online and rebadged them 'isolation insights' during the COVID-19 lockdown. Surveys suggest our reach has broadened with 25 per cent of attendees have never attended one of our events before.[3]

Written outputs are also important, and it is vital these are produced in a range of formats tailored to circumstances. At UKICE, we have noticed that, in response to requests from MPs, short (one page) explanations of the key issues confronting the country are useful. There is also a big public appetite for explanatory pieces: a piece posted on the UKICE website on the new Immigration Bill by Peter Walsh of the Migration Observatory has had 27,000 views since its posting in June 2020. Similarly, an explainer on what an 'Australian-style deal' – the government's preferred term for no deal – would mean had 18,000 views in two months.

While experimenting with various methods of engagement, it is also worthwhile to note that reports remain a popular engagement tool, due to their flexibility of being produced in various sizes and to prove depth on a breadth of research topics. It is important that academic groups who wish to stay relevant with policy makers try to continuously provide written outputs. For example, at UKICE we frequently write short discussion pieces on popular emerging issues related to our research expertise, such as on the impact of Brexit on manufacturing, to the potential implications of no deal, to issues at stake in the negotiations over fisheries. Periodically, we will also publish large publications made up of short contributions from a range of academics that are intended to provide more exhaustive summaries of key social, political and economic developments and to showcase the contribution that social scientists can make in helping non-academic stakeholders understand these developments.

Across all the written work, it is vital that all outputs are clear and concise, avoiding unnecessary jargon and written with a non-specialist audience in mind. That means helping academics learn how to write in a style that is far removed from the style that works for academic audiences, which in turn has opened up opportunities to contribute writing to other outlets. This can often be quite labour intensive work, as reports often go through a series of iterations and numerous edits before being released to ensure that complicated ideas are expressed clearly. It can be useful therefore to publish two sets of reports on the same issue. One could be a longer, exhaustive version, aimed at a more specialist audience. The other one could be a shorter summary version intended for a general audience.

Top Tip

Adapting your writing style to a policy audience is an important skill; see Chapter 4 in this book for guidance.

The strength of academic engagement with policy makers lies on the characteristic that academics can be much more independent and impartial than research think tanks. As we have mentioned earlier, UKICE's strength is to demonstrate a non-partisan view on the Brexit decision, emphasising instead research-based evidence to understand the consequences that flow from the decision to leave. Impartiality extends beyond simply stating that one is of a certain opinion or not. As academics engaging the media, impartiality also involves the careful use of language when providing an informed opinion. For UKICE, it is crucial that our written and spoken discussions avoid language that implies a preference to Brexit outcomes (for example, 'happily', 'sadly', etc.). During the development of the referendum, we also used the tag line 'providing the evidence you need to decide for yourself'.

Demonstrating sensitivity to what politicians and policy makers need from their stakeholders is important in building long-term relationships based on trust. While the reputation and work of UKICE helped attract interest, working closely with policy makers requires them to know not only that the outputs will be of a high quality, but also that the individuals involved can be trusted and that the confidentiality around conversations will be respected.

Building such relationships inevitably takes time, experimentation, persistence and entails repeated interactions. Nonetheless, the outcome of effort placed at maintaining engagement can be extremely invaluable. At UKICE, we realise that the more we work on bridging the gap we have with our stakeholders and to keep our relationships closer, the more that the people we engage with will turn to us requesting our expertise, inevitably leading to a virtuous cycle of mutual benefits.

5.4   LESSONS LEARNED

Working collaboratively with different institutions can emphasise and extend the profile of a research project and subsequent impact. Our work has benefited not only individual researchers, but also from collaborating with other Higher Education institutions and the ESRC. In turn, by helping to raise the profile of individual social scientists, their reputations, and those of their home institution and of the research council, have been enhanced.

Perhaps the key element allowing for the success of the Initiative has been the creation of a group of scholars committed to effective communication and engagement and willing to work together as a team to achieve it and with the financial support provided by the ESRC to enable them to do it. It is hard to overstate the degree to which the success of UKICE has hinged on the willingness of these colleagues to respond to requests at short notice, to travel to media studios and various events around the country and to contribute to publications.

In concluding our chapter, we draw on several lessons learned. Firstly, engagement matters. It is never too early to start building relations with potential users of research. But doing so is time-consuming and difficult. It is unreasonable for universities or research councils to expect individual researchers to go out and 'do' impact on their own. Get in touch with those few organisations that can help – consider your own university communications department and indeed your research council itself or even UKICE. These and other institutions might be able to help you in getting in touch with the right people and in securing a decent non-academic audience for your research.

Secondly, UKICE has shown it is possible to create a virtuous circle between broadcast and engagement – posting rapid and authoritative commentary opens up doors to engagement opportunities – to brief or present new research to decision makers. But it is vital that those undertaking this activity are able to adapt to the needs of different audiences without compromising their academic integrity.

Thirdly, one of our key learnings is that many academic colleagues both find it hard to communicate to non-academic audiences but are also not aware that what seems to them to be statements of objective fact contain a lot of implicit biases which risk alienating audiences who do not share the same world view. This has the potential to limit the ability to engage.

There is no getting away from the fact that the incentive structure in place in universities does not always reward those who choose to spend time on communication and engagement. While the Research Excellence Framework (REF) has moved towards placing more emphasis on 'impact' (its particular definition of the term is not necessarily helpful for social scientists), it is still the case that promotion, particularly the top-ranked departments, depends almost exclusively on publication records rather than on 'impact'-related activities. As long as this is the case, the danger is that such activities are something done on the side rather than being seen as core to a career in social science.

This being said, the experience of our team has shown that effective engagement is both immensely rewarding and potentially important. Without wanting to exaggerate the role that UKICE has played in the Brexit debates of the last few years, it remains the case that we have helped to inform not only key decision makers but also the public on a variety of complex issues that have confronted the country since the referendum of 2016. In so doing we have helped individual academics build networks among non-academic communities that will form the basis of future partnerships and that will help promote the research of these colleagues well beyond academe.

NOTES

1. For more information, see: https://www.centreonconstitutionalchange.ac.uk/opinions/welcome-future-uk-and-scotland-website (accessed 8 April 2022).
2. See Chapter 4 for more information on how to communicate with different sets of audiences.
3. Chapter 11 in this book expands on in-person and online events as engagement methods and the ways in which they can be designed to encourage impactful discussions.

BIBLIOGRAPHY

UKICE (April 2016). Leave/remain: the facts behind the claims. Available at: https://ukandeu.ac.uk/partner-reports/leave-remain-the-facts-behind-the-claims/ (accessed 27 August 2021).

UKICE (June 2016). SWOT: strengths, weaknesses, opportunities and threats of EU membership. Available at: https://ukandeu.ac.uk/wp-content/uploads/2016/06/SWOTS.pdf (accessed 27 August 2021).

UKICE (January 2017). A successful Brexit: four economic tests. Available at: https://ukandeu.ac.uk/partner-reports/a-successful-brexit-four-economic-tests/ (accessed 27 August 2021).

UKICE (September 2018). The Brexit endgame. Available at: https://ukandeu.ac. uk/partner-reports/the-brexit-endgame-a-guide-to-the-parliamentary-process-of-withdrawal-from-the-european-union/ (accessed 27 August 2021).

UKICE (September 2020). What would no deal mean. Available at: https://ukandeu.ac.uk/research-papers/what-would-no-deal-mean/ (accessed 27 August 2021).

UKICE (January 2021). Brexit and beyond. Available at: https://ukandeu.ac.uk/research-papers/brexit-and-beyond/ (accessed 27 August 2021).

6. Between disciplines and perspectives: ACT as a PERIpatetic researcher

Matjaz Vidmar

6.1 INTRODUCTION

Where new research is driven by a combination of practitioners' concerns and scholars' ambition to systematise and integrate the state-of-the-art insights and methodologies into a coherent set of tools and practices, an increasingly close analytical relationship between partners is required. This is embodied in the context of academic–policy relations, where one of the core challenges of academics engaging with policymakers is creating and maintaining connections across complex systems. The PERIpatetic approach to research allows academics to engage with industry and policymakers to generate insight in a responsive manner. The PERIpatetic approach is closely associated with innovation studies but has a wider application across academia, industry and policy.

Within the field of innovation studies, there persists an acute lack of integration of the current (micro-level) literature on innovation process, the (meso-level) literature on (regional and sectoral) Innovation Systems and capacity building within the (macro-level) innovation policy context (Flanagan et al., 2011). In particular, the interconnection between micro-level organisational behaviours, meso-level inter-organisational interaction and macro-level policy interventions and support has been unclear. The particular emerging concern is the notion of 'transition' towards Open Innovation, i.e. how do organisations adopt/change these processes (from meso- to micro-level) and how are the individual changes built upon a systemic level (meso- to macro-level and the reverse)? These questions are especially pertinent in the context of the small and medium-sized enterprises (SMEs) who form a significant part of the innovation landscape and are becoming the focus of innovation policy in many countries, including the UK (Bodas Freitas and von Tunzelmann, 2008).

Hence, in order to both meaningfully research as well as co-shape the best practices in managing and supporting innovation through policymaking, a new approach of closer embeddedness of researchers within the field is required. This chapter puts forward a perspective on such an approach based on ACT principles: Analyse, Challenge, Translate. Starting from a closer embeddedness in the field, it outlines the PERIpatetic epistemological framework. Secondly, it examines the researcher's positioning within the field as an 'uninformed insider', and the potential (ethical) pitfalls of collaboration with your research subjects, as well as how to engage with them by developing a 'challenge function' (Kattirtzi, 2016). Finally, it looks at translating research across different policy domains by scaling and layering frameworks and findings, before concluding with some avenues for further exploration and practical questions for any researcher to answer.

6.2   APPLYING THE ACT PRINCIPLES

6.2.1   Analyse

Building on personal experiences in the field (see Box 6.1) the Practical Epistemology for Researching Innovation was developed, subsequently called the PERIpatetic approach. Its conceptual origins come from the ancient Greek schools of Philosophy, where some lead thinkers (in particular Aristotle) developed their thoughts by 'walking about' and speaking with their followers. In fact, the word 'peripatetic' itself is derived from ancient Greek, directly merging the meanings of the walking or treading ('patetic') with 'going about' ('peri').

Firstly, the PERIpatetic approach aims to describe multiple perspectives on a particular subject matter by recording and analysing narratives, developing concepts and integrating individual accounts into community-wide trends and nested multi-layered contexts. Secondly, the researcher is an active co-creator of the studied environment and empathises with (though not necessarily shares) the practitioners' concerns, focusing on what is at stake within different perspectives. Thirdly, the explanations are developed with an abductive epistemological position, i.e. deriving theoretical models from interrogating empirical data through a real-life problem-solving process. This is a pragmatic, critical realist position, which accepts that knowledge claims validity through its application rather than derivation. Fourthly, understanding of positional challenges and intellectual biases is tackled by sticking to a rigorous ethics framework, engaging in constant reflection and (publicly) acknowledging the participatory action nature of such work.

BOX 6.1   EMBEDDING A PHD: WORKING WITH GATEKEEPERS

The research design I adopted in my PhD project researching the development of the New Space Sector in Scotland (Vidmar, 2019a) was developed on the back of my pre-existing familiarity with the Astrophysics community through my first degree. In particular, I built on my close links and significant interest in the work carried out at a particular institution and their desire for furthering the impact of this work, which led to the creation of a new technology/knowledge transfer and business development facility. Here, the organisation's lack of theoretical and practical understanding of the key mechanisms to build strategies and work within a multi-level policy environment to deliver the impact desired of the new centre became a key driver of my research.

The scope of the research partnership covered the support provided by the organisation, though there were no formal expectations placed on me as the researcher, beyond the exploration of the critical questions of how is the Scottish Space Sector policy developing and what would be the most beneficial intervention a new innovation intermediary could deploy. Based on this partnership, I became embedded in the organisation's Innovation team, who were my main gatekeepers. This meant I was physically located there (desk space, IT support, etc.), and participated in their meetings, helped organise and deliver their activities and attended third-party events (conferences, meetings, etc.) as part of their delegation.

This enabled significantly easier access to the field and led to the direct and tangible application of my findings – in particular, the critical contribution to knowledge through a systematisation of literature on innovation intermediation by focusing on interventions (instead of functions) and developing a more comprehensive classification and typology of roles (Vidmar, 2020). In addition, my interaction with colleagues at the organisation meant that I was consulted on a variety of state-of-the-art social science insights to do with emerging policy as well as organisational behaviour and community development. For instance, I helped develop a reference library in innovation management literature for use in centre, supported a Horizon 2020 research project they were involved with, as well as providing input into various discussions of new studies, reports and white papers.

6.2.2   Challenge

Being in close proximity to the field of study can raise its own challenges; being embedded within the policy(making) context even more so, as the direct impact of interaction with the field can be particularly visible and politically sensitive. On one hand the 'embeddedness' allows for easy access to both (ethnographic) data about the landscape, as well as introductions to potential informants. On the other hand, close collaboration with a particular player leads to potential exposure to conflicts of interest jeopardising academic independence as well as reputational risks to the collaborating organisation. Even if those big challenges are successfully dealt with, there is also the issue of maintaining good personal relationships whilst posing challenging questions and examining individuals' expertise and work practices, which can prove difficult (Ostrander, 1993).

This is the crux of the insider-outside positioning, though these are more of a part of a continuum, with relative and fluid perspectives (Darwin Holmes, 2020). Past studies have identified researcher positionality in close collaboration and professional environment as 'concerned foreign friend' or 'informed outsider' (Welch et al., 2002). However, my personal experience led me to consider a perspective from the opposite end of the spectrum as an 'uninformed insider' (Vidmar, 2019a). Being an 'uninformed insider' involves skilful role playing, where you become an insider through embeddedness with collaborators, but also stress your lack of 'insider' understanding during data collection. Facets of such role play have long been established as key principles in interviewing professional elites (Platt, 1981), as well as in anthropological and increasingly also other (auto)ethnographic research (Naaeke et al., 2012).

However, the bigger challenge is the potential for academic partiality with the 'insiders' concerns, introducing (unconscious) bias as well as reinforcing dominant narratives. Though 'reflexivity', i.e. examining and acknowledging the context of the researcher's position within the field, is often cited as the key response (Berger, 2015), there are more proactive options to consider. Two particular strategies resonate with the author's experiences – extending embeddedness to multiple gatekeepers and embracing the 'challenge function' within the field. On the former, personal experience (see Box 6.2) shows that embedding within multiple additional stakeholders, in particular those situated in different contexts and with different agendas and organisational cultures, allows for more community-driven perspectives and identification of research questions. This experience also chimes with the role of social scientist within the field as providing a 'challenge function', described as 'social researchers [...] hav[ing] aided policy officials to rethink their understandings' (Kattirtzi, 2016, p. 1). Unlike formal (external) evidence-gathering and knowledge exchange structures, this refers more to informal everyday interactions in meetings, inputting and commenting on documents, providing advice and structuring and presenting evidence as part of the policy and implementation drafting process.

BOX 6.2   COMMUNITY-DRIVEN: THE EXTRA-CURRICULAR PERIPATETIC ENGAGEMENT

It is very important to reach beyond the gatekeepers and the policy context in order to find and include alternative perspectives and voices in policy research. With the core ambition of reflexively engaging with an industry, the PERIpatetic approach to research includes a broad engagement with the field, beyond the research agenda and field site(s), and this often serendipitously leads to new research questions and projects.

For instance, as part of my research of the Space Sector, I participated in several R&D, business and social development initiatives. For example, I engaged with both mapping out the state of progress in the development of the Slovenian Space Sector (a joint project with the University of Ljubljana), as well as developing a series of events with the Slovenian Science Foundation, as part of the annual science festival and wider. In particular, working with colleagues in Slovenia alerted me to an excellent opportunity for a comparative case study between flagship innovation intermediaries in the two countries – the Scottish Higgs Centre for Innovation and the Slovenian Centre for Excellence Space-SI (Vidmar, 2019b).

Beyond research, I also served as the National Point of Contact for Slovenia at the Space Generation Advisory Council, where I started a programme of social activities and a project to connect the space people in Slovenia and the wider region. This enabled me to uniquely access the high-level policy debates about the development of the global Space Sector, as well as allowing for the dissemination of the results of my research directly to key stakeholders (in particular space agencies).

As part of these endeavours, and since there seemed to be an acute lack of integration of disciplinary perspectives, I co-founded two interdisciplinary research networks – the global sociology-driven Social Studies of Outer Space (SSOS) and the local (Scottish) interdisciplinary Social Dimensions of Outer Space (SDOS). This engagement critically illuminated the near-dichotomous split between the ethnographic take on innovation and technology development and the econometric and bibliometric one. Attempts to bring these closer together led me to deploy mixed-methods social-network analysis (SNA), experiment with these methods, as well share ideas, new practices and results.

To expand on the discourse about the future of these fields, I also engaged in a project to speculatively design a new international space station in geostationary orbit (Gateway Earth Development Group) as well as taking part in the *Scotland in Space* (Scott and Malpas, 2019) edited volume exploring the future of Space Exploration using science fiction.

This series of activities allowed for an intellectual as well as participatory journey to integrate perspectives, theories, projects and strategies, which allowed for a comprehensive and structured understanding of the studied phenomena, leading to both exciting new theoretical frameworks, as well as their practical applications.

6.2.3   Translate

Having developed a research programme and established oneself as a contributor to stakeholders' activities, a critical function is to translate both general principles and findings across different domains and scales. In particular, there may be obvious policy and strategy implications of answering participant-inspired questions such as on allocation of resources, inclusion/exclusion of stakeholders and geographical and temporal scoping of activities. For instance, one of the first questions asked, working with the case outlined in Box 6.1, was: how far (geographically) will the new innovation centre reach? At which distance will the partners disengage? This is hard, if not impossible, to answer! It is important that any answers given are framed in an understandable way, whilst retaining the theoretical nuance and reflecting the complexity of the examined context, all the time staying true to the objective evidence collected. Often, this is best done using visual tools – i.e. designing tables, diagrams/schematics and maps (see Box 6.3) – which not only translate findings, but can be used as heuristic frameworks for future research as well as policy and strategy development.

BOX 6.3   POLICY OF SCALE: TRANSLATING FINDINGS AND TOOLS FROM SMALL TEAMS TO LARGE ORGANISATIONS (AND VICE VERSA!)

The PERIpatetic approach was developed through a series of internships, research projects and consultancies. It aided in the development of a framework for mapping and analysing evolutionary trends within innovation systems and helped form discussions with innovation intermediaries and policymakers at different levels, from advising a couple of innovation intermediary managers, as in the case outlined in Box 6.1, to examining opportunities to develop a more entrepreneurial higher education sector in Romania, on behalf of the Organisation for Economic Co-operation and Development (OECD).

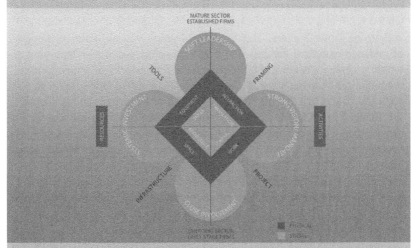

Source: Vidmar, 2020.

Figure 6.1   A schematic outline combining core innovation intermediaries' interventions systematisation (eight classes of possible activities), embedded within the contextual environment of their deployment, highlighting the nature of interventions (inner vs outer diamond), the evolutionary trajectory (bottom-top) and the associated organisational frameworks (outside circles).

For example, working with the Innovation Caucus, we produced a series of briefing notes to systematise possible innovation intermediation interventions and a conceptual logic model for UK policy stakeholders. These notes were building on my past extensive literature review and survey, and led to an iterated framework which I subsequently used as a heuristic tool to collect and analyse data in order to advise stakeholders in the Scottish New Space Sector regarding both the overall provision of support (Vidmar, 2021) as well as specific operational programmes (Vidmar, 2019b). Using a schematic representation of the new systematisation and typology of possible intermediaries' interventions (see Figure 6.1) allowed for explaining its complexity to policy stakeholders who adopted it for their strategy design.

I was also involved in drafting strategic documents, in particular within the Data-Driven Innovation Programme, which is part of Edinburgh and South-East Scotland City Region Deal. Here a new iteration of the synthesis of the above was contextualised with particular policy objectives, intended for senior university management, development agencies and local authorities' policymakers. This contextualisation was an iterative process of turning theoretical insights into a generalisable toolkit and deploying it within a series of studies. Starting with the frameworks of innovation intermediation I had designed, I co-developed a mapping Opportunity Areas Analysis Tool (OAAT), outlined in Figure 6.2, to scope gaps and opportunities for further R&D and innovation support based on empirical data about past economic performance and socio-political context. This was deployed to prepare strategic visions, policy evidence and logic models for potential interventions, both in the sectoral context (i.e. Space and Satellite), as well as in regional industrial and entrepreneurial ecosystems in the participating local authorities. It was recently commented that this approach was the most significant City Region Deal achievement to date in linking local authorities' policy with the R&D and industrial renewal agenda.

Finally, I used the skills and tools I developed for mapping innovation dynamics to help deliver analysis of higher education innovation framework conditions in Romania as part of the OECD's HEInnovate programme.[a] The translation here was more subtle, identifying challenges for development of entrepreneurial ecosystems and framing opportunities for policy interventions, based on the pre-existing innovation intermediation functions classification, reinterpreted in the context of the HEInnovate framework.

OAAT Dimensions	Key "Change Agents"	Attributes and Actions	Empirical Evidence	
TRENDS	Policy and Investment attitudes (trans-regional)	Developmental priorities and strategies (political, societal and economic) Scientific evidence Public opinion	Geographical, demographic and socio-economic data Local economic strategies Regional skills assessments Research organisations' strategies Government/corporate investment	Creation of the Opportunity Space based on the articulation across the dimensions
CAPABILITIES	Organisations and consortia (inter-organisational, regional)	Existing innovation and economic activity Inter-institutional relationships	Resources and facilities Organisational structures Network analysis Stakeholder groupings	
CAPACITIES	Individual actors, small groups and clusters (within organisations or partnerships)	Experimentation and discovery Knowledge and technology recombination New/additional innovation and entrepreneurial ideas	R&D projects (Re-)development projects Company formation (start-ups/spin-offs/ community enterprise)	

Source: Development Opportunities in the Scottish Borders Study (Kitagawa and Vidmar, 2022).

Figure 6.2   *The OAAT tool integrates the need to align multi-level perspectives that integrate policy trends, organisational capabilities and emerging niche capacity. This is more easily explained as a table, linking dimensions with the contexts of 'change agents', the dimensions of 'attributes and actions' and the evidence collected in the mapping process.*

The core takeaway of this journey in scaling up frameworks alongside policymakers and industry is that it is an iterative process that needs to be translated within (and for) each new policy context.

Source: [a] See Vidmar and Rosiello (2019).

6.3   CONCLUSION

In summary, the impact principles of Analysing, Challenging and Translating through doing PERIpatetic research can help develop a research agenda that can scale from a doctoral thesis, through small-scale strategies towards national policymaking and international consultancy. Whilst the approach I have outlined is somewhat context specific, its building blocks can be applied in any immersive research practice, in particular those concerning professional (work) environments.

Here, particular attention when working with policymakers should be on establishing truly cooperative research partnerships, where the academic analysis actively responds to practitioners' concerns, whilst research can be supported and to a degree facilitated by the policymakers. Whilst doing so, researchers need to involve themselves in activities beyond the gatekeeper organisation in order to ensure multiple and varied perspectives and voices are included, as well as introduce these voices to the practitioners. Finally, using different didactical methods, in particular visual tools, the researchers need to ensure their insights and (theoretical) concepts translate iteratively in a way that is accessible to non-academic audiences, without compromising the integrity of the scientific work.

In addition, these approaches should be examined further, in particular with reference to abductivist research epistemology, maintaining the dynamic researcher positionality, as well as formalising the design of research translation.

Some reflection questions central to this approach are:

- Analyse: How can research inform bottom-up change?
  - Perspective: What is your background and (how) does it relate to the studied field?
  - Embedded: Who are the stakeholders and what are their concerns?
  - Responsive: What are the main knowledge areas and sites of problem-solving?
  - Introspective: What is my position and ethics (at any given time)?
- Challenge: Can I be part of multiple stakeholders? Do I (freely) challenge my stakeholders' views?
- Translate: Who holds the levers of decision-making and how are your findings relevant to them? How is it best to present them (visually)?

ACKNOWLEDGEMENTS

This chapter is largely based on work within my doctoral thesis 'Scottish Space Sector and Innovation: A PERIpatetic study of an emerging innovation system and the roles of innovation intermediaries' funded through the Scottish Graduate School of Social Science on behalf of the Economic and Social Research Council (grant number: ES/J500136/1).

This work greatly benefited from constructive feedback and suggestions from many colleagues, in particular my doctoral mentors: Dr Alessandro Rosiello, Dr Niki Vermeulen, Prof. Robin Williams and Dr Julian Dines; as well as Prof. Tim Vorley, Prof. Franc Mali, Prof. Jamie Fleck and many other colleagues. Last but not least, I am very grateful to all participants in the study for their valuable time and expertise and many others who have assisted me with my enquiries, as well as the project manager, Phil Wallace; the Edward Elgar editorial team; and the thorough and helpful anonymous reviewers.

REFERENCES

Berger, R. (2015). Now I see it, now I don't: Researcher's position and reflexivity in qualitative research. Qual. Res. 15(2), 219–34.

Bodas Freitas, I.M. and von Tunzelmann, N. (2008). Mapping public support for innovation: A comparison of policy alignment in the UK and France. Res. Policy 37, 1446–64.

Darwin Holmes, A.G. (2020). Researcher positionality: A consideration of its influence and place in qualitative research – A new researcher guide. Shanlax Int. J. Educ. 8(4), 1–10.

Flanagan, K., Uyarra, E. and Laranja, M. (2011). Reconceptualising the 'policy mix' for innovation. Res. Policy 40(5), 702–13.

Kattirtzi, M. (2016). Providing a 'challenge function': Government social researchers in the UK's Department of Energy and Climate Change (2010–2015). Palgrave Commun. 2. https://doi.org/10.1057/palcomms.2016.64

Kitagawa, F. and Vidmar, M. (2022). Strategic intelligence for the future of places: enabling inclusive economic growth through the Opportunity Areas Analysis Tool. Regional Studies. https://doi.org/10.1080/00343404.2022.2045267

Naaeke, A., Kurylo, A., Grabowski, M., Linton, D. and Radford, M. (2012). Insider and outsider perspective in ethnographic research. Proc. New York State Commun. Assoc. 2010.

Ostrander, S.A. (1993). 'Surely you're not in this just to be helpful': Access, rapport, and interviews in three studies of elites. Journal of Contemporary Ethnography. 22(1), 7–27. https://doi.org/10.1177/089124193022001002

Platt, J. (1981). On interviewing one's peers. Br. J. Sociol. 32(1), 75–91.

Scott, D. and Malpas, S. (eds) (2019). *Scotland in Space: Creative Visions and Critical Reflections on Scotland's Space Futures* (Edinburgh: Shoreline of Infinity).

Swann, G.M.P. (2009). *The Economics of Innovation: An Introduction* (Cheltenham, UK and Northampton, MA, USA: Edward Elgar Publishing). doi: https://doi.org/10.1556/AOecon.60.2010.4.6

Vidmar, M. (2019a). Scottish Space Sector and Innovation: A PERIpatetic study of an emerging innovation system and the roles of innovation intermediaries (Thesis, The University of Edinburgh).

Vidmar, M. (2019b). The ten million euro question: How do innovation intermediaries support smart specialization? Croat. Econ. Surv. 21(2), 37–84.

Vidmar, M. (2020). Innovation intermediaries and the 'final frontier' of the New Space Sector in Scotland, in Vidmar, M., *Innovation Intermediaries and (Final) Frontiers of High-Tech* 39–61 (London: Springer International Publishing). doi: https://doi.org/10.1007/978-3-030-60642-8_3

Vidmar, M. (2021). Enablers, equippers, shapers and movers: A typology of innovation intermediaries' interventions and the development of an emergent innovation system. Acta Astronaut. 179, 280–89.

Vidmar, M. and Rosiello, A. (2019). Preparing and supporting entrepreneurs, in *Supporting Entrepreneurship and Innovation in Higher Education in Romania* (Paris: OECD/EC).

Welch, C., Marschan-Piekkari, R., Penttinen, H. and Tahvanainen, M. (2002). Corporate elites as informants in qualitative international business research. Int. Bus. Rev. 11(5), 611–28.

7. Co-producing policy relevant research

Clementine Hill O'Connor, Lucy Gavens, Dan Chedgzoy and Mary Gogarty

7.1 INTRODUCTION

The production of policy relevant research is a key principle in and of itself for many researchers. The importance of this aim should also be understood within the context of an increased focus on academic 'research impact'. In the UK changes to applications for major funders and the implementation of the Research Excellence Framework (REF) mean that research funding is now 'strongly dependent on researchers' abilities to respond adequately to questions about the broader (non-academic) value of their work' (Smith and Stewart 2016, p. 110). This shift is reflective of international trends towards research funders placing increased emphasis on research utilisation (Tetroe 2007) and societal impact (Phipps 2011).

Nevertheless, the creation of impactful research is complex (see Smith et al. 2020 for full discussion) and in the transfer of knowledge from academia to policy there are some key issues that have been highlighted in the extensive literature that explores this question:

- There is a poor fit between research findings and policy context
- Research outputs do not include clear and actionable messages
- Research evidence is not created in the places that the findings will be used.

In order to address some of these issues there has been increasing interest in the role of researchers who work between academia and policy in order to support the development of policy relevant research (Cheetham et al. 2018).

SIPHER is a multi-disciplinary programme of work consisting of eight interconnected workstrands designed to support public policy design and decision-making (see Box 7.1 for more information). A key feature of the programme is the use of embedded researchers (ERs) who are co-funded by the research funding and the policy organisations. SIPHER has two full-time ERs, one each working in the Scottish Government and Greater Manchester

Combined Authority (GMCA), and two ERs in Sheffield City Council who split their time equally between SIPHER and their data analyst roles.

In this chapter we introduce the concept of co-produced research and the role of ERs and then illustrate the way that this approach was established within SIPHER. We finish with some reflections on the process and a series of questions for those considering the use of this approach in their own work. Box 7.1 introduces and provides content to the SIPHER project.

BOX 7.1   SYSTEMS SCIENCE IN PUBLIC HEALTH AND HEALTH ECONOMICS RESEARCH – THE SIPHER CONSORTIUM

SIPHER is a large UK Prevention Research Partnership (UKPRP)-funded national research collaboration that is developing systems science methods to support public policy design, with a focus on improving the health and wellbeing of the population and reducing inequalities. The consortium is a partnership between seven academic institutions and local, regional and national government organisations. The research involves eight intertwined strands of work drawing upon a range of academic disciplines including social policy, public health, geography, economics and engineering. The research is methodologically diverse, combining qualitative interviews, ethnography, system dynamics modelling, participatory systems mapping and the development of decision support tools. At the time of writing, the research is 18 months in to a five-year funding period.

7.2   CO-PRODUCTION AND THE ROLE OF EMBEDDED RESEARCHERS

A range of terms are used to describe the role of ERs. One such term is 'knowledge brokers', which is used to describe those working within health services research to support the 'mobilisation of research evidence into clinical practice and policy making' (Kislov et al. 2017, p. 107). This role requires information management, linkage and exchange and capacity building skills (ibid.). Other studies have described a 'researcher-in-residence' model which stems from participatory approaches to research (Bussu et al. 2021; Marshall et al. 2016). This has an explicit focus on the creation of new knowledge alongside the mobilisation of established knowledge and, as such, can be understood as a mechanism for co-produced research (Bussu et al. 2020). In addition, in a 'researcher-in-residence' model the role is (1) embedded within a non-academic institution, (2) brings new expertise to the team, and (3) able to negotiate and build upon different forms of knowledge (ibid.). Arguably, an umbrella term for these roles is 'embedded researcher'. This term has been used more generally as 'individuals who are either university based, or employed with the purpose of implementing a collaborative jointly owned research agenda in a host organisation in a mutually beneficial relationship' (Cheetham et al. 2018, p. 65). Even more simply, it has been described as someone doing research as a member of the team that is central to the focus of the research (Lewis and Russell 2011).

Whilst co-production is most often associated with the creation, planning and/or delivery of services through direct user involvement (Bovaird 2007; Bussu and Tullia Galanti 2018), it is used differently within the context of research and knowledge exchange. Within this context it is used to describe how research and policy can be produced in relation to one another, and through interactions across the 'boundary' (Wehrens 2014). It is then the role of ERs to work across this boundary and, in doing so, they support the co-production of knowledge and its translation into practice (Bussu et al. 2020) through acting as a 'facilitator, interlocutor, capacity developer and advocate' (Genat 2009, p. 114).

7.3 SIPHER'S APPROACH TO EMBEDDED RESEARCH AND CO-PRODUCTION

Within SIPHER the ER model differs from the 'researcher-in-residence' approach outlined above in that the role is undertaken by people directly employed by the policy organisation, either an existing employee or a new recruit, rather than by an academic on secondment or placement. As an employee of the policy organisation ERs have access to resources, people (through networks and existing relationships) and institutional insight that it is often impossible to achieve as an outsider. Whilst there are many benefits to taking this approach, which will be outlined in subsequent sections, it is important to highlight here that one of the limitations of this approach is that there is little to no control over the recruitment process. It can also limit the extent to which the academic institutions involved can shape the role on a day-to-day basis.

Although ERs are not the only mechanism through which co-produced research can be achieved, they play a crucial role in facilitating policy relevant research. They are able to support the translation and dissemination of knowledge through their understanding of the structures, processes and personalities within a policy organisation. This supports academic researchers to understand the routes through which to access the expertise necessary to ensure meaningful and useful knowledge creation and dissemination.

7.3.1   Motivations and Rationale for this Approach

The starting point for engaging in this form of co-produced research is to generate findings that are relevant and useful for policy. Working directly with the intended users of the research allows space to build shared knowledge and to explore and refine findings as they emerge. In the process of working across the policy/academic boundary ERs support colleagues in their own organisations to better understand research processes and methods. As policy organisations have played a role in the creation of the research it is hoped that there is greater confidence to share and use the findings in practice.

For academic institutions ERs offer insights into organisational culture, priorities and processes that can be difficult to access unless you are a member of that organisation. ERs – when defined as academic researchers 'in residence' – allow for an assessment and understanding of the 'worldview' of the organisation in the context of academic knowledge and literature (Lewis and Russell 2011). When this understanding is co-produced in dialogue between embedded and academic researchers there is a mutual understanding that develops as both sets of researchers gain access, insight and understanding of the context in which they are each working. This process can start to address some of the challenges of generating research impact and therefore is a key motivation for both academic and policy organisations. Whilst this role is not a panacea, it is one way to generate shared knowledge across the perceived boundaries between academia and policy.

A further motivation for using this approach is the potential for a reciprocal exchange of expertise. In the interactions between academia and policy the ER gains an insight into research methods, literature and research discussions which they can start to apply within their own organisations. This creates capacity within organisations, an important part of a co-produced research (Vindrola-Padros et al. 2019) and a motivating factor for policy organisations to support this approach. Policy organisations have significant ambitions but can be limited by the lack of resources. Being involved in multi-disciplinary collaborative research offers access to a wide range of academic knowledge and expertise.

7.3.2   Establishing and Developing the Role of Embedded Researcher

In establishing the role of an ER there are a number of practical considerations. Firstly, it is important to find institutional buy-in from the right level within the policy organisation. With senior support for partnering with academia it becomes easier to navigate the relevant processes and structures required to create and establish ERs. Secondly, the funder plays an important role in ensuring that this approach is practical and feasible. Policy organisations are often stretched to capacity and the idea of utilising limited resources solely for the purpose of an academic research project is not necessarily an attractive proposition. A co-funding approach (where the policy organisations match the research funding equally) can create a win–win situation. However, this remains an unusual approach and so it is advisable to negotiate on what is possible. From the perspective of the funders, this makes for a stronger bid as the policy commitment to the research is clear.

At the outset of the project, it is important to develop a clear understanding of the range of responsibilities the ER is expected to fulfil. A role description is useful, however agreement on this may be a challenge and can result in a long list of diverse responsibilities. Each ER will also bring their own expertise and experience and so retaining some flexibility in the role responsibilities is important to enable the team to make best use of these skills. The needs of policymakers and academics may also evolve over the duration of a project, and may be affected by exogenous factors (e.g. a pandemic), further highlighting the value in flexibility to role success.

Management of the ER role requires regular conversations between the ER(s), their line manager (who, in a policy organisation, is often not directly engaged in the research) and the academic research team. Day-to-day management of the ER may be the responsibility of someone outside of or with only very limited involvement in the project. This can create multiple, potentially competing, demands on an ER's time as they seek to balance requirements of the policy organisation and requests from across the academic research teams. A practical approach to managing this is to produce a work plan in the early stages of the project. This requires engagement across the research team to understand upcoming tasks and priorities. It is necessary for this to be a process of continual reflection and engagement with both academic and policy colleagues to ensure tasks are accurately prioritised and key opportunities or activities are not missed.

A further ongoing discussion that is required in developing the ER role is related to the forms of technical knowledge that are needed over the course of a project. On a multi-disciplinary project ERs are not expected to be expert in all of the methods. However work is required to enable ERs to understand the general concepts that underpin the approaches taken and the purpose they serve. This allows ERs to assess how they align with the goals of the policy organisation and how to support academic and policy colleagues to work together.

In some circumstances, ERs may need to develop specific technical skills and, as previously highlighted, this is part of the motivation for policy organisations to get involved. In the context of SIPHER there are ample opportunities for ERs to develop their own skills in areas such as systems mapping, evidence synthesis and approaches to policy ethnography. There is flexibility across the project so that ERs can work in ways that build on their own skills and ensure that they are relevant for their policy organisation. Specifically, SIPHER's ERs have undertaken training on policy ethnography and qualitative analysis. This has brought valuable insights to outputs and broader thinking across the research programme (see subsequent sections for more detail). As the project develops there will be increased scope for ERs to utilise their existing research skills and add to research outputs in this way.

7.3.3   Being an Embedded Researcher

Fundamental to the ER role is the building of relationships both *within* the policy organisation and *between* the academic researchers and the organisation, which contributes to ensuring that the project's research and outputs are effectively co-produced and land well within the policy organisation. In acting in this brokerage role between academic researchers and colleagues in policy organisations ERs work to bridge gaps in understanding between the two sides. In one direction this has involved making colleagues in policy organisations aware of what it is possible for academic researchers to achieve with the tools and expertise available, and in the other it has involved clearly setting out for researchers the specific questions that the policy organisations are grappling with. However, within this role there are challenges on both sides which can result in circular conversations as both academics and policy partners seek to find ways to convey their requirements and expectations within the context of co-production. For example, in working to develop a decision support tool for a policy organisation, academics sought input from policy partners to outline their needs. However, without the expertise to understand the possibilities and options it was hard for policy partners to articulate this. On both sides there is a desire to understand and accommodate the other and a clear commitment to co-producing knowledge and research outputs. Nevertheless, it requires a significant amount of discussion and reflection on the part of both academic and policy researchers to find a way to meet in the middle in order to get past the circularity of academics asking 'what do you need?' and policy partners responding 'what is possible?'.

There are a series of practical tasks that SIPHER ERs have been engaged in during the project so far. In the early stages a significant amount of time was required for background reading, orientation and knowledge sharing between academics and policy partners. This was to ensure there is a good understanding of each other's roles from the start. There is also a bureaucratic aspect to the ER role which involved organising and facilitating meetings, workshops or similar in order to meet the needs of particular workstrands. These tasks are also part of the process of co-production as ERs are required to provide regular updates in both directions across the boundary. Pragmatically, this requires

ERs to retain a significant amount of information and also necessitates some translation and co-creation of shared language to enable effective working (see Chapter 4: on Speaking a Shared Language in this book for more top tips on communicating with policymakers).

Specific research tasks that SIPHER ERs have been involved in are qualitative analysis of interviews and ongoing ethnographic work. ERs were provided with initial training and take part in monthly meetings to reflect on the organisational developments related to the research topic, the wider policy landscape and organisational perceptions of the larger research project. ERs keep a personal diary which forms the basis of written and verbal summaries that are shared in monthly meetings. To allow the meeting conversations to feel unconstrained, ERs signal where the information they are sharing should be treated confidentially. This has been a useful process throughout the research as it offers space to formally reflect on the co-production process and is a key mechanism through which the academic and embedded researchers build shared knowledge.

7.3.4   Reflecting on Experiences so Far

The ERs have facilitated both individual and organisational buy-in to and credibility of the research. The experience in SIPHER has been that ERs often know, or are able to identify quickly, the key stakeholders to engage with the research. They are evidence of an organisational commitment to the research and there is a sense that policy colleagues have engaged with the research to a greater extent than with previous projects. This is reflected in the academic researchers' experience as they have seen greater responses to requests for participation in interviews and workshops.

Through the ERs there has been direct dialogue between researchers and users of research, vital to bringing the creation of research into the context in which it will be used. This is described as a key predictor in the application of research in policy settings (Lomas 2000). It also addresses concerns that a challenge of bringing evidence into policy is that there is a disconnection between evidence producers and users (Marshall et al. 2016; Walshe and Davies 2013).

The strong relationships that have been developed across academic and policy organisations have grown to extend beyond the original project. The consortium has been able to take advantage of further funding opportunities (sometimes at short notice), particularly where the funder requires partnership with policy organisations. The development of further projects, which include components of co-production, is also evidence of the confidence that policy partners have in the approach.

The approach of direct employment within policy organisations has been particularly beneficial in the context of the Covid-19 pandemic. As secondees it would have been likely that researchers would be pulled back into research institutions; in this instance, although ERs were required to take on more tasks related to policy organisations' vital Covid responses, important lines of communication have remained open in a way that may not have been possible otherwise. Box 7.2 outlines practical ways to apply this approach.

BOX 7.2   HOW TO APPLY THE EMBEDDED RESEARCHER APPROACH

There are a number of questions to consider when developing ER roles within research projects. Addressing the following questions in the design of the project will help ensure that the expectations of both the academic and policy organisation can be met and that the collaboration is successful.

What is the role of the ER within the project?
In practice it can be any combination of facilitating research, designing and/or conducting research, brokering knowledge and evaluating existing knowledge in the context it is being used.

Will the ER be employed by a policy organisation or will they be an academic seconded to a policy organisation?
In SIPHER ERs are employed by policy organisations which requires consideration of the following (1) how the ER will be managed day to day to best support the research project, (2) how the academic partners can play a role in recruitment to identify a good fit for the wider team, and (3) development of a plan for how the ER will engage in the research project in the case of exogenous shocks to their organisation (e.g. Covid-19).

What skills are required for the role? Do you need an analyst or a policy officer?
Identifying the key roles and responsibilities will be important here, as well as reflecting on how realistic it is that one individual will be able to fulfil the role if your expectations are diverse. Particularly in a multi-disciplinary project, it is easy to ask too much of ERs, expecting them to get involved in developing, facilitating, analysing and disseminating the work of different academic disciplines in a way that we would not expect of an academic.

Do we need one full-time or two part-time ERs, with each person bringing a different skillset to the role? What skills are important at the outset of the project and how might those needs change over time?

Each of these considerations will have implications for the kind of skills and characteristics the team will look for when recruiting the ER.

What kinds of training might the ER need to fulfil their role in the project, and how will this be delivered?
Some training might need to be formal courses, but in other situations work-based placements and the opportunity to work side by side with an academic researcher can be beneficial.

7.4 CONCLUSION

Whilst the success of the ER approach we are using has not yet been assessed, indications so far suggest that positive steps are being taken to achieve meaningful impact. As we have discussed, there are some challenges in establishing a clear role description and around the potential circularity of conversations. However, ongoing reflection and discussion has identified a number of benefits in this ER approach. ERs have supported timely and more nuanced communications between academics and policy stakeholders throughout the research process. This has been achieved, in part, through ERs acting as a bridge between academic researchers and the policy context in which the research may be used. In SIPHER, we have used this to adapt the research approach and the communication of plans and findings. Where the ER role is seen as the start of a co-production relationship this can also bring wider benefits in terms of applying for further collaborative funding opportunities. Some of the initial rationale for the approach stems from achieving research impact from an academic perspective, but it is clear that policy partners are also invested in working differently with academia to achieve change.

REFERENCES

Bovaird, T., 2007. Beyond engagement and participation: user and community coproduction of public services. *Public Administration Review*, 67(4), 846–60.

Bussu, S. and Tullia Galanti, M., 2018. Facilitating coproduction: the role of leadership in coproduction initiatives in the UK. *Policy and Society*, 37(3), 347–67.

Bussu, S., Lalani, M., Pattison, S. and Marshall, M., 2021. Engaging with care: ethical issues in participatory research. *Qualitative Research*, 21(5), 667–85.

Cheetham, M., Wiseman, A., Khazaeli, B., Gibson, E., Gray, P., Van der Graaf, P. and Rushmer, R., 2018. Embedded research: a promising way to create evidence-informed impact in public health? *Journal of Public Health*, 40(1), 64–70.

Genat, B., 2009. Building emergent situated knowledges in participatory action research. *Action Research*, 7(1), 101–15.

Kislov, R., Wilson, P. and Boaden, R., 2017. The 'dark side' of knowledge brokering. *Journal of Health Services Research and Policy*, 22(2), 107–12.

Lewis, S.J. and Russell, A.J., 2011. Being embedded: a way forward for ethnographic research. *Ethnography*, 12(3), 398–416.

Lomas, J., 2000. Using 'linkage and exchange' to move research into policy at a Canadian foundation. *Health Affairs*, 19(3), 236–40.

Marshall, M., Eyre, M., Lalani, S., Khan, S., de Silva, D. and Shapiro, J., 2016. Increasing the impact of health services research on service improvement: the researcher-in-residence model. *Journal of the Royal Society of Medicine*, 109(6), 220–25.

Phipps, D., 2011. A report detailing the development of a university-based knowledge mobilization unit that enhances research outreach and engagement. *Scholarly and Research Communication*, 2(2), 1–13.

Smith, K. and Stewart, E., 2016. We need to talk about impact: why social policy academics need to engage with the UK's research impact agenda. *Journal of Social Policy*, 46(1), 109–27.

Smith, K., Bandola-Gill, J., Meer, N., Stewart, E. and Watermeyer, R., 2020. *The Impact Agenda: Controversies, Consequences and Challenges.* Bristol: Policy Press.

Tetroe, J., 2007. Knowledge translation at the Canadian Institutes of Health Research: a primer. *FOCUS Technical Brief No.18.*

Vindrola-Padros, C., Eyre, L., Baxter, H., Cramer, H., George, B., Wye, L., Fulop, N.J., Utley, M., Phillips, N., Brindle, P. and Marshall, M., 2019. Addressing the challenges of knowledge co-production in quality improvement: learning from the implementation of the researcher-in-residence model. *BMJ Quality and Safety*, 28(1), 1–7.

Walshe, K. and Davies, H.T., 2013. Health research, development and innovation in England from 1988 to 2013: from research production to knowledge mobilization. *Journal of Health Services Research and Policy*, 18(3), 1–12.

Wehrens, R., 2014. Beyond two communities: from research utilization and knowledge translation to co-production? *Public Health*, 128(6), 545–51.

8.   Developing and delivering university consortia

Annette Bramley

8.1   INTRODUCTION

According to Reid (2020), regional research collaborations, alliances, partnerships and networks can bring incredible intangible benefits to member institutions. They help raise the profile of research within the region the research is in and help funders, policymakers, governments and regional organisations to find a single point of conversation for future opportunities. They also provide a forum through which participants can learn from one another's experiences in securing funding. They also help shape the balance between collaborations and competition among the research community, in order to place more emphasis on the benefits of collaborations. At the university level, they also help university research teams to increase their competitiveness in securing bidding partnerships, and sharing infrastructures and risks and burdens of bidding for funding.

The UK now has a number of strategic university research and innovation alliances, often regionally based. These include, but are not limited to, the N8 Research Partnership (the N8; see Box 8.1), Midlands Innovation,[1] GW4,[2] Eastern Arc[3] and Yorkshire Universities,[4] as well as the subject-specific Scottish Research Pools. These consortia have a different purpose from the so-called 'mission groups', like the Russell Group or Universities UK, existing primarily to facilitate research collaboration between the member universities. More broadly, these types of cross-faculty, single or multi-university collaborations, sometimes called 'institutes', are becoming an increasingly common feature of the research landscape in the UK and globally. They are one way to evolve long-established organisational structures so that they are able to encompass both the needs of teaching and 21st century research.

In this chapter, I provide insights and suggestions, using examples from the N8, where I work, on how to build a university consortium successfully. To do so, I have compiled my suggestions based on the 'why', the 'how', the 'who' and the 'what'. Firstly, I speak about knowing the reasons for starting a university consortium. Then I will talk about the good practices that have helped us at the N8 become a successful example of a university consortium. Due to the broader relevance of university consortia to the current conversations around research culture and people management, I discuss in length the important actors who are responsible in managing these networks of people, leaders and the role of partnership brokers, facilitators and project managers. Lastly, I look at what the impacts of university consortia can be and their relevance to policy.

BOX 8.1   INTRODUCING THE N8

This chapter was written in reflection of my experiences working with the N8. The N8 Research Partnership is the oldest and most powerful strategic research alliance in the UK, with all eight of its members in the top 25 universities in the UK (N8 Research Partnership, 2021). Established in 2006, our vision is to be an exceptionally effective cluster of research innovation and training excellence, delivering benefits to the economy and communities in the North of England and beyond. The N8 provides a means for its members, the eight most research-intensive universities in the North of England (Durham, Lancaster, Leeds, Liverpool, Manchester, Newcastle, Sheffield and York), to speak with one voice on policy issues related to research and innovation in their region, to share both resources and risk, and to develop collaborations around their research strengths (N8 Research Partnership, 2021). The N8 has championed new ways of working in the sector, helping to shape policy in equipment sharing (Georghiou, 2006), efficiency (Jackson, 2013) and the economic contributions of the N8 universities to the Northern Powerhouse (Kelly, 2015). The alliance's research programmes also support the development of evidence-based policy and practice in Policing, Food Systems, Decarbonisation of Transport and more.

The N8's *raison d'être* has evolved over 15 years of collaborative activity. For example, in 2011 the N8 instigated a programme to provide a focus for the more intensive use of capital equipment through sharing across the partnership, establishing the N8 Shared Equipment Inventory System (N8 Equipment, 2011). More recently, its focus has been on collaborative multidisciplinary research programmes such as the N8 Policing Research Partnership (2021), which embeds co-production with the users of research and stakeholders into its research culture; and Net Zero North, a research and innovation initiative that will lead the Northern Powerhouse in its transition to a net-zero economy by harnessing the unique mix of industry, science and research capabilities in the region.

8.2   LOOKING FOR THE 'SWEET SPOT' IN A UNIVERSITY CONSORTIUM

Just like any collaboration, starting a university consortium must begin with the question of 'why are we doing this?'. A university consortium can only succeed where there are benefits to all the participants from taking part, which outweigh the opportunity and financial costs of the collaboration. At the N8, we sum this up as, 'where we are stronger together, we go together', whether the activity is research and innovation, speaking to policymakers or raising our profile. Identifying this 'sweet spot' for research collaboration (i.e., the area that meets the interest of all stakeholders involved) is the major challenge for partnership brokers in the N8 and other strategic research alliances. Some common features of sweet spots for the N8 include areas where there is:

- a complex challenge or issue that a university could not tackle on its own;
- a clearly defined, shared purpose;
- a sense of urgency which might be driven by a societal challenge, a funding opportunity or another deadline;
- sufficient scale to enable the universities to have freedom to operate as separate entities as well as a collaborative partnership;
- an opportunity, or need, for focus and leadership in evidence-based policy development at a regional or national level;
- the potential to establish new international collaborations and relationships based on a critical mass of research excellence;
- support from the highest levels of university leadership – for the N8 this is the Vice Chancellors and Pro-Vice Chancellors for research (or their equivalent);
- a joint commitment to long-term investment in relationship and community building.

There are two main ways in which research consortia tend to be formed around these 'sweet spots':

- 'bottom-up': via ideas from the research base and/or collaborating partners. Our Engineering and Physical Sciences Research Council (EPSRC)-funded network in the decarbonisation of transport, DecarboN8, was initiated this way.
- 'top-down': through a strategic analysis of challenge opportunities, research strengths and assets and their alignment to individual university priorities. Our N8AgriFood programme was established via this route.

In both cases, successful strategic collaborations can only come together where the top-down, strategic perspective of the senior teams and the enthusiasm, ideas and commitment of individual researchers meet. This alignment tends to come around a set of shared values. When you do something that is aligned to your values, you have an intrinsic drive which enables you to prioritise this activity and to make time for the things that need to be done. It enables you to see the picture beyond your own university and expand from your own interests to understand the interests of the consortium and what it is trying to achieve.

Top Tip

Every collaboration is about bringing together a group of individuals in pursuit of a common purpose with a desire to be successful. The purpose might be, for example, 'to tackle climate change'. While individuals or universities may share the same purpose, they may have different reasons for doing so. Aligning different agendas and priorities is crucial for strategic organisational partnerships. Often people will be able to agree that there is a problem, an opportunity for research or a need to influence policy, even where their motivations are different. Finding the 'why' for collaboration and using this as the focus for the diverse perspectives of the partnership is the first step to success.

8.3   BUILDING A SUCCESSFUL UNIVERSITY CONSORTIUM

For a seed to grow, it needs to be planted into fertile soil and subjected to favourable conditions. It may take time, sometimes years, for seeds to germinate and for seedlings to poke their leaves above the soil surface. Even then they are particularly susceptible to being critically damaged by adverse environmental conditions or other external forces. It is not until they are well established that they can fend for themselves, withstand more severe fluctuations in their environment and bear fruit.

Collaborations are similar to our tiny seed, but are built on relationships and trust. Whether that is the overall partnership or an individual project, the partners in a collaboration will need time and space to understand each other's viewpoints and how each of them thinks about an issue. There can be friction between partners that needs to be harnessed for its creative power rather than its destructive power. They have to work together to create a climate and a culture where they can disagree well and have enjoyably robust discussions. This is preparing the fertile soil into which the seed of collaboration can be planted; the productive space between individuals where relationships get built and collaborations are formed. Like a seed, an embryonic collaboration will benefit from nutrients in the form of resources, whether that is internal (e.g. buy-out of time) or external (e.g. grant funding). For example, GW4's 'Generator Fund' recognises this issue and provides resources for new collaborations and ideas emerging from their existing communities, to help them become viable.

Conducting collaborative research, particularly as part of a consortium that spans multiple universities, comes with an opportunity cost for researchers and universities. These costs may be personal, for example travelling to other universities may mean that a researcher is unable to pick their child up from school or miss their weekly choir practice. They may also be professional, for example the papers that are not being written while they are participating in a multi-university partnership. There are huge personal and professional benefits too, but these cannot be realised unless these opportunity costs are overcome.

Through this lens, a university consortium simply comprises groups of people who have come together to realise shared value, while taking risks in doing so. These communities of people seeking to reach a common goal form what can be called 'tribes', which I will expand on further next.

8.3.1 The Tribal Nature of Collaboration

When we establish a new collaboration from within a strategic university consortium we are effectively developing a new social and academic 'tribe' associated with the collaboration. Everyone taking part in the partnership will already be a member of several other tribes, associated with their own organisation, their own discipline or specialisation or their other interests. We naturally 'hang out' with people that have similar interests and speak similar languages. We understand the vocabularies of these groups including the terminology, jargon, acronyms, slang and even banter and 'in' jokes. This helps us to form bonds and establish relationships quickly.

When we bring people together under the guise of a strategic university partnership, or a research collaboration, we need to form a common language and make sure that we do not exclude people by how we talk to each other. Professor Mark Pagel, Professor of Evolutionary Biology at the University of Reading, explains in his 2010 TEDGlobal talk:

> *It seems that we use our language, not just to cooperate, but to draw rings around our cooperative groups and to establish identities, and perhaps to protect our knowledge and wisdom and skills from eavesdropping from outside. And we know this because when we study different language groups and associate them with their cultures, we see that different languages slow the flow of ideas between groups. They slow the flow of technologies.* (Pagel, 2011)

Building collaboration has to be based on creating a common and inclusive language. Jargon and acronyms are gremlins to look out for. It is also important to be precise about the meaning of words, because many words have different meanings in different contexts or in different disciplines.

Take for example the word 'goal'. What image does that conjure up for you? A target? A football (soccer) goal? Rugby posts? If you want to score a goal in football or rugby it will help to know which side of the crossbar you have to place the ball to score (or miss)! Any misunderstanding about a football goal compared to a rugby goal could be quickly resolved if the conversation was accompanied by a picture of the goal you are trying to score into. There are lots of words like this with double meanings that often come up in conversations about research.

If you are a researcher, talking to a policymaker, it is quite likely that you might stumble on some of these language gremlins, so it is worthwhile spending some time to be very intentional and precise with your use of vocabulary, defining terms more than you might usually do. Taking part in multidisciplinary consortia or attending webinars not related to your own discipline are good ways of expanding your awareness of these gremlins and for practising how to best get your message across to non-experts.

Top Tip

Five tips for clearer communication for researchers wanting to collaborate:

1. Build a diverse network and have lots of conversations with different people.
2. Use pictures and diagrams to help clarify meanings.
3. Identify role models and study them.
4. Learn from your mistakes!
5. Think about words you use which might have double meanings, or mean something else in a different context. Some examples are: *Normal, Mean, Solution, Chaos, Network, Sensitivity, Viral, Virtual, Common, Slip, Noise, Observation, Marker, Power, Culture, Relative, Equal.*

8.4   MANAGING AND FACILITATING PEOPLE IN A UNIVERSITY CONSORTIUM

Developing a successful university consortium is largely about the successful management of different types of people. At the N8, we have identified two important sets of actors who are essential to a university consortium: leaders; and partnership brokers, facilitators and project managers.

8.4.1 Leaders

Once you have identified the purpose of the particular collaboration, identifying one or more individuals with the interest, time and skills to lead the developing consortium is essential. They need to be able to manage relationships and politics, solve problems and motivate and inspire the whole team. Being a research leader in a collaborative team, particularly a cross-institutional, multidisciplinary partnership, is far more demanding on the time of an academic than conventional research. While the temptation is to nominate the 'star' researcher to lead a consortium, it might not always be in the consortium's best interests to have a world-leading researcher in that position.

In their *Research Culture: Embedding Inclusive Excellence* report, the Royal Society (2018, p. 13) makes a distinction between the skills associated with being scientific leaders and being leading scientists:

> *Leading scientists were described in terms of individuals pushing the boundaries of research in academia and industry. [...] By contrast, scientific leaders of research groups, programmes and institutions were identified as having a responsibility to advocate for the researchers of the future and develop the talents and skills of their research teams.*

Star researchers *can* be leading researchers *and* research leaders, but there is not always a correlation, and sometimes the opposite is true. World-leading researchers already have many pressures on their time, and have a high degree of power and status arising from their research track record. Others will defer to them and this may not lead to the best decisions being made, or the most creative avenues being pursued.

Top Tip

If you are trying to put together a research collaboration, here is a mental checklist to run through when thinking about who the individual(s) are that are best placed to take the leadership position(s).

Are they ...? *Curious, Generous, Inspiring, Inclusive, Appreciative, Tactful, Intellectually tolerant, Able to bring people together, Committed to the purpose and to the partnership*

Do they ...? *Act with integrity, Share power, Listen to understand, Build and maintain relationships, Have enough time, Share the values of the other partners*

A collaborative project depends on its leadership for success. Similarly, the success of a strategic university alliance like the N8 depends critically on the leaders of our member organisations; the Vice Chancellors and the Pro-Vice Chancellors of Research (or their equivalent) and their colleagues on their own senior leadership teams. The senior teams and the way that they lead their own university will define its culture. Leaders weave their values into the decisions they take, the things that they say, what they prioritise, and the incentives and accommodations for collaborative practice which will be needed for the aims of the partnership to be realised. Neither 'top-down', nor 'bottom-up' consortium building will be successful without buy-in from and the explicit support of the senior leaders.

8.4.2   Partnership Brokers, Facilitators and Project Managers

Many large strategic university consortia have a core team, or secretariat. The precise functions of these teams vary, depending on their focus. The N8 Directorate team is a partnership broker, and exists to provide leadership to the strategic research collaboration between our partner universities. We are there to act as a catalyst for collaboration, for convening and facilitating partners and other stakeholders. We do this by:

- seeding ideas for areas where there might be the potential for N8 collaboration to add value to the universities' individual research strengths;
- creating opportunities for people across the partnership to come together and explore ideas and challenges from different perspectives;
- ensuring the partnership is agile and able to respond to new opportunities and changes in the research policy and economic environments;
- acting as an honest broker in partnering relationships between N8 universities and with other stakeholders;
- articulating a single voice for the partnership on research and innovation policy issues with a regional dimension.

Part of the role of a partnership broker is to act as a facilitator; that is, to create the open atmosphere that encourages people to take part, build trust and share their thoughts. The N8 Directorate has project management capabilities, but we do not manage the operational aspects of research consortia. Professional project management is a specialist function which is essential for university research collaborations to fulfil their potential. Research consortia need people that can manage multiple tasks, from organising a conference to organising a visa. They keep track of reporting to funders, exactly who is doing what, oversight of the financial status of the project, and tracking outcomes and outputs. A good project manager will free up researchers at all levels to do what they do best in the interests of the consortium.

8.5   IDENTIFYING AND MEASURING THE IMPACT OF UNIVERSITY CONSORTIA

While we all want to have great outcomes from university consortia, it is not only the outcomes in isolation that we need to shift the dial on to create successful university partnerships. We tend to measure the *results* of collaboration, which are highly visible, and not the *process* of collaboration, which is often unseen and with significant opportunity costs. This is especially true where the participants come from diverse backgrounds and the 'germination time' of the consortium is longer than for single discipline or single university collaborations.

Too often organisations and funders use 'lagging metrics', like publications, to evaluate the performance of long-term collaborative processes. Collaboration is about relationships, and relationships are an ongoing practice, not a goal or an outcome. So that we do not strangle collaborations before they have had an opportunity to flourish, it is important to identify 'leading metrics' which will help us to see whether the activity is moving forward. Leading metrics will measure change in the system and processes, lagging metrics will measure whether a target, outcome or goal is reached. Unfortunately, it is hard to measure change in the process and systems in a simple, quantitative way because they deal with changes in 'intangible outcomes', that is, outcomes which are not physical in nature. Papers and other publications, or conferences, are 'tangible outcomes'. Goodwill, understanding, trust and a common vocabulary are 'intangible outcomes' and need more qualitative approaches.

Leaders and funders of university consortia need to agree on metrics which are meaningful in the context of collaboration, and that incentivise the processes and behaviours that, over time, will deliver the desired outcomes. Put simply, if we look after the system, the outcomes will take care of themselves.

8.5.1   Return on Investment, or 'What's in It for Me?'

When smart people from a singular background are placed into a decision-making group, he suggests, they are likely to become collectively blind. And that can have horribly destructive effects. (Syed, 2019)

It has been shown again and again that diverse leadership teams and diverse workforces are proven to bring the best returns on investment when they are well led. The N8 Research Partnership attracts income more than four to five times our subscription level, but this is likely to be the tip of the iceberg of the benefits of our partnership. Our N8AgriFood programme alone has generated more than £150 million of research income, on the back of a £15 million joint investment by the university partners and the Higher Education Funding Council for England. N8AgriFood researchers have produced policy briefs, commissioned analysis and provided input into specific food-related policy. Publications have arisen from pump-priming projects funded by the consortium, and researchers have prepared oral and written evidence for a range of House of Commons select committees, House of Lords Food and Farming inquiries and for the National Food Strategy.

While we can measure publications, reports, appearances at select committees and funding won, how might we value the networks, connections, trust and learning that have been deposited in the banks of social capital of both individuals and our member organisations, which are there for the future? As time goes on it becomes harder and harder to keep track of all the tangible outcomes and outputs that have been generated by a particular consortium or activity because the intangible benefits are hard or impossible to track. Without a doubt, these benefits are compounded by and integrated with the intangible *and* invaluable outputs from other activities and networks.

8.6   CONCLUSION

Coming to the end of our chapter, we conclude by saying that influential organisations are made up of influential individuals who tend to have large networks. A large, diverse network actually makes you luckier and more innovative in your approach to research and policymaking. Serendipitous encounters are more likely to happen where you have looser connections to others in your network because this opens you up to new perspectives, opportunities, information and resources. Serendipity is luck combined with some wisdom, openness to opportunity and tenacity. You can encourage serendipity into your attempts to influence policy by expanding your networks and preparing yourself to be ready for the opportunities when they present themselves.

As such, university consortia can be powerful vehicles for research, innovation and policy influence. Long-term investment is needed on the part of individuals and universities to overcome the opportunity and financial costs of collaboration. Emergent consortia and the researchers taking part in them need to be nurtured and supported; in return, the returns on investment for universities and academics can be significant and, in some cases, transformative.

NOTES

1. Midlands Innovation is a research alliance formed by eight partner universities in the Midlands, UK (Aston University, University of Birmingham, University of Leicester, Keele University, Loughborough University, University of Nottingham, University of Warwick and Cranfield University).
2. The GW4 Alliance brings together four of the most research-intensive universities in the South West, UK (University of Bath, University of Bristol, Cardiff University and University of Exeter).
3. The Eastern Arc comprises three universities: the University of East Anglia, the University of Essex and the University of Kent.
4. Yorkshire Universities (YU) has been the regional voice for higher education (HE) in Yorkshire. YU represents 11 universities and one specialist higher education institution (Bradford, Huddersfield, Hull, Leeds, Leeds Beckett, Leeds Trinity, Leeds Arts, Sheffield, Sheffield Hallam, York and York St John, as well as the Leeds Conservatoire).

REFERENCES

Georghiou, L. (2006). Synthesis Report: Professor Luke Georghiou on behalf of the N8 Research Partnership. N8 Research Partnership. Available at: https://www.n8research.org.uk/view/3472/14137-N8-Sharing-for-Excellence-and-Growth-Report_web.pdf (accessed 1 December 2020).

Jackson, S. (2013). Making the Best Better. Available at: http://www.n8research.org.uk/media/EfficiencyReportFinal.pdf (accessed 1 December 2020).

Kelly, U. (2015). The Power of 8: Knowledge, Innovation and Growth for the North. N8 Research Partnership. Available at: https://www.n8research.org.uk/view/6189/ThePowerof8.pdf (accessed 5 January 2021).

N8 Equipment (2011). *Welcome to the N8 Shared Equipment Inventory System.* Available at: https://www.n8equipment.org.uk/ (accessed 15 December 2020).

N8 Policing Research Partnership (2021). *About Us.* Available at: https://n8prp.org.uk/about_us/ (accessed 3 January 2021).

N8 Research Partnership (2021). *The N8 Research Partnership.* Available at: https://www.n8research.org.uk/ (accessed 2 June 2021).

Pagel, M. (2011). How Language Transformed Humanity. TEDGlobal. Available at: https://www.ted.com/talks/mark_pagel_how_language_transformed_humanity (accessed 15 February 2021).

Reid, G. (2020). Strength in Diversity. Available at: https://uniswales.ac.uk/media/Strength-in-Diversity-Professor-Graeme-Reid-FINAL.pdf (accessed 15 December 2020).

Syed, M. (2019). *Rebel Ideas: The Power of Diverse Thinking.* John Murray Press. London.

The Royal Society (2018). *Research Culture: Embedding Inclusive Excellence Insights on the Future Culture of Research.* Available at: https://royalsociety.org/-/media/policy/Publications/2018/research-culture-workshop-report.pdf (accessed 2 February 2021).

9. When worlds collide: the role of the funder in connecting research and policy

Melanie Knetsch and Lauren Tuckerman

9.1 INTRODUCTION

As in many other countries, the UK research funding landscape is rich and complex. It consists of a mixture of public funding which can be provided through vehicles such as UK Research and Innovation (UKRI), the Academies or provided directly through government departments. There are also private trusts, charities and other associations who provide funding for research which feeds into their core themes and activities. Similarly, the policymaking context is complex, with international, national, devolved, regional and local governance systems all interacting with research evidence. To add to the complexity, policymakers are not a homogeneous group: policymaking is a process with many actors at different levels, from different fields with a variety of perspectives.

The traditional perception of a research funder can conjure the image of a grant-giving body who invites, assesses and awards grants. While a main function is to undertake this activity, there has been a shift in the role of contemporary funders that extends beyond this single purpose. Traditionally, there was less of a role for funders once the funding decision had been made. Similarly, funders had perhaps focused on the linear element of impact (dissemination and communication) but are now taking a more holistic view of supporting impact, which includes the relational (fostering relationships for 'useable' knowledge) and the systemic (looking at building impact infrastructure) (Hopkins et al., 2021).

Funders also have a key facilitation and brokering role beyond these traditional activities (Brantnell et al., 2015). They often play a vital link between users and researchers or research institutions, for example bringing policymakers and academic researchers together to share insights under a specific theme or area to not only shape the research questions or funding call, but also

Table 9.1   *Role of the funder in stimulating an 'impact environment'*

Role of the Funder	Researcher Lens	Policy Lens
Facilitating connections	Helping to bring research and researchers to policymakers (fellowships, placements, people exchanges, etc.) Enable spaces for engagement to build their knowledge into activities funded	Helping to bring policymakers to researchers (fellowships, placements, people exchanges, etc.) Helping policymakers to identify opportunities to build relationships with researchers and integrate research into policymaking
Building capability	Supporting academics with understanding and skills to help them to engage with policy	Supporting policymakers with skills to absorb research and researcher insights into policymaking
Creating capacity	Building grants which are impact led, ring fenced for partnerships (rather than single applicants) and funding professional knowledge exchange activities Encouraging institutions to build capacity for policy impact by supporting knowledge exchange professional service staff	Viewing the policy landscape to understand where collaborations can add capacity in policymaking Creating access points to research and researchers
Understanding the need and articulating the offer	Helping researchers to form policy-relevant questions and understand how to pitch research for policy impact	Working with policymakers to understand and articulate the evidence gaps Helping policymakers understand how to get research insight that meets their needs
Incentivising impact	Creating the right conditions for research policy impact through funding calls and grants which encourage collaboration between researchers and policymakers and focus on gaps in evidence Supporting reviewers to critically assess impact components in applications	
Rewarding best practice	Recognising and celebrating research impact through activities such as further funding, prizes and awards	
Evidencing the impact	Working with researchers and policymakers to gather evidence of research impact, to understand the ways in which it can be facilitated	

to maximise the research impact on policymaking. Funders are often involved in the stimulation of outcomes which can help lead to impact and support far more than calls for proposals. They have a role in creating an environment which encourages impact in different forms and often play a role as a catalyst to incentivise and influence behaviours of both academics and practitioners. This includes activities funders undertake before applications to catalyse research impact (to influence applications for funding), activities taken as part of the application and awarding process, and activities undertaken after the award has been given to facilitate research impact.

Some of the key areas that take funders beyond their traditional roles are presented in Table 9.1. The remainder of this chapter will discuss the ways in which funders work with academics and practitioners to create a research environment which is conducive to policy impact, looking at both the traditional and new roles for funders.

This chapter will provide an overview of the role the funder can have in connecting research and policy, beginning with how funders can work with academics and policymakers and concluding with what happens when these worlds collide. It concludes with some key lessons on how funders can think about their role as a facilitator, bringing policymakers together with academic research and researchers and vice versa.

9.2   WORKING WITH ACADEMICS

Research funders who provide significant resources to academic institutions have a role to play in encouraging and facilitating ways in which researchers can create policy impact. Funders themselves cannot make impact happen, however they can set the parameters and influence the environment to ensure it has the best possible chance of happening. From a traditional perspective, funders have four key stages in which they can create an environment to encourage policy impact; these are: (1) scoping and setting an area to fund, (2) the application and decision-making process, (3) after awarding a grant, and (4) evaluating research. Within these stages the new roles for funders come into play.

Firstly, when *scoping and setting an area to fund*, it is important for funders to engage with policymakers. Funders often engage with a broad group of stakeholders to ensure the issues, gaps in knowledge, context and opportunities can be considered around an area. This also can have an added benefit of stimulating new networks between policymakers and researchers. Depending on the topic or area, funders may partner with a government department to co-fund an area or programme. This enables the overarching aims and questions to be tailored towards their interests and needs and ensures that they are invested in making use of the insights. Engagement before setting an area is a key first step the funder has in creating an environment for impact.

Secondly, funders can also create opportunities for policy impact throughout the *application and decision-making process*. In the funding call itself, funders can make it mandatory for applicants to have partnerships with policymakers or government agencies in their proposal. Applicants should also check that calls which encourage non-academic partnerships also enable applicants to cost for knowledge exchange and impact-focused activities within their proposal, as this is often the case. It may also be possible to include 'impact expertise' such as a knowledge exchange professional.

Many funders also include user voices in their peer review and funding panel meetings. This ensures that assumptions and assertions made in an application can be assessed from different lenses. While it can be tempting for applicants to focus on previous experience of successful policy impact in applications, and this is important to highlight, the focus should be on impact realisation within the proposed project (National Co-ordinating Centre for Public Engagement, n.d.). Panel members often value when plans for impact are tied to key project milestones (National Co-ordinating Centre for Public Engagement, n.d.).

Reviewers often look at how policy impact is considered from the start of the research, including partners and engagement activities, such as outlining the ways in which an applicant intends to reach and engage with policymakers, rather than bolted on at the end through post research dissemination only. The applicant needs to evidence the best methods of engagement. Tried and tested methods are valued as much as creative and innovative approaches. Reviewers often look for evidenced approaches that are well thought out and appropriate to all partners (some ideas for engagement methods are given in Part II of this book). Considering the policy impacts at the planning and application stage strengthens an application and gives the funder and the reviewers confidence in the ability to deliver changes. Although there is a growing fear that funders value impact over the quality of research (Grove, 2017), funders generally use a complex set of considerations or criteria to evaluate applications, and impact is one aspect of these. As a rule, different types of impacts are not prioritised over others, as reviewers and funders are more concerned with ways in which research can achieve impact.

After awarding a grant, funders can provide on-going engagement and support with the award holder. This process can enable insights from the funded investment to be shared with the funder who can then share these across their networks, or bring new networks to the grant holder. Funders often play a role in convening and catalysing, bringing together new groups, users and researchers who may not otherwise meet. In this way funders can often act as a knowledge broker. Support, guidance and training in policy impact can also take many forms and help to demystify the policy process. Fellowships, placements and internships (see Part II of this book for some engagement examples) can provide experience which allows a flow of knowledge between researchers and policymakers, which funders often enable.

Funders *close the feedback loop* by evaluating and evidencing if the funding has made any difference. Research funders such as the UK's research councils can use evidence of impact to justify current investment and make the case for further investment. A key challenge when demonstrating policy impact is evidencing the link between the research and a policy development or change. This can be done through a policy document citing the research, but often this does not happen. However, when government departments and policymakers are partners in a grant, testimonials of the difference the research or methods made in the policy formation or delivery can often be drawn out. Building in policy engagement from the start makes this more likely to happen (National Co-ordinating Centre for Public Engagement, n.d.).

The funding process is a central part of how funders can encourage researchers to have a policy impact. However, they also have an important role to play in supporting an *impact culture* within universities as well as building skills and understanding of policymaking processes within academia. Funders can also support the 'infrastructure' and capacity for creating different impacts. In the UK there are a number of drivers such as the Research Excellence Framework (REF) that financially reward Higher Education Institutions whose researchers achieve research impact. There are also funds that support professional services such as knowledge exchange roles, technology transfer and impact support administrators, and a key element of these roles includes connecting with non-academics. Developing partnerships takes time, and funders can also support local seed funding and networking events which help create the time and space for initial meetings and the sharing and developing of ideas. Funding can also create new relationships and collaborations through connecting people, using engagement methods such as people exchange, fellowships, secondments, placements and internships. In this way funders can stimulate the wider connecting system in order to bring groups together, which can encourage policy impact.

It is also important for funders to recognise, reward and celebrate impacts. The Economic and Social Research Council (ESRC) has an annual Celebrating Impact Prize, which offers a cash prize to further impact-focused activities, a high profile awards ceremony and options to further disseminate the impact through case studies and videos (ESRC 2, n.d.).

9.3   WORKING WITH POLICYMAKERS

Most government departments (national, devolved, local and many international ones) seek independent evidence to shape policy development and implementation. Funders often develop strong networks across the policymaking, landscape and not only have a role in advocating for the use of academic evidence in policymaking, but also in creating opportunities for interactions between policymakers and researchers. A key activity many funders undertake is building relationships across government departments to understand how they use evidence, what their evidence needs are, and how they are (or are not) able to connect with the research, researchers and Higher Education sector.

Funders also work in collaboration with policymakers to create opportunities to share ideas and insights, for example through round tables, seminars and discussion sessions, or suggesting researchers to support their governance and advisory structures. The advocacy role that funders can take is an important one as well, as funders often have cross-departmental links with people within the policymaking sphere which could support researchers to either develop new partnerships or communicate their work in front of the right people.

Many government departments need access to a breadth of different data to provide an evidence base. In ESRC we have invested in key areas to support policymakers to access insights. We support a number of different data infrastructure, including collecting new data and building new data sets to give new insights (for example, Understanding Society), to providing access to a vast archive of social science data through our UK Data Service. In partnership with the UK's Office of National Statistics, we support the linking and joining up of existing administrative data to provide new insights[1] and also encourage academic/non-academic partners to reuse existing data via funding through our Secondary Data Analysis Call.[2] With an increase of the breadth and type of data comes the need to support policymakers in their ability to understand, absorb and use the results of research and data. This could include training for more advanced data skills within government, as they seek to understand even more complex information provided to them, or enabling access to researcher collected data sets.[3] Funders can provide and/or encourage uptake of advanced training for policymakers. This enables policymakers to continue to be intelligent consumers of research and data.

We have also partnered with government departments to co-fund investments that target research with a focus to generate new insights (for example, the Enterprise Research Centre[4]) and linking up with policy communities and government departments to understand what the existing insights are, such as through the What Works Centres.[5] Finally, we have also invested in a number of activities that have a key driver of providing insights for government, including a high element of funding for engagement and communications (such as our Productivity Institute, the Economics Observatory and the International Public Policy Observatory[6]).

BOX 9.1   ESRC IMPACT ACCELERATION ACCOUNTS (IAAS)

The ESRC funds Impact Acceleration Accounts (IAAs) to allow universities to be more in control of how they invest in and support impact. They are part of the ESRC's portfolio of supporting more responsive and creative approaches to impact. The IAAs build capacity for social sciences to take a cross-disciplinary approach to impact, encouraging them to seek out new audiences for their research, including policymakers. The IAAs are flexible, allowing universities to focus on areas of strategic need and academics to tailor their impact work towards their institutional priorities and opportunities which arise.

Building connections and creating networks is often a key activity in IAAs that will lead to researchers proactively engaging with different stakeholders. They cultivate culture change and build capacity through skills development for knowledge exchange. The IAAs can support the development of outputs and outcomes for projects that can help enable impact to occur and the funding can help enable an institution, department or academic to leverage additional funding to progress these further.

Learning from the ESRC's first funded round of IAAs highlights the need for dedicated professional services staff, as they are essential to developing an impact culture in an institution.

9.4   CONCLUSION – WHEN WORLDS COLLIDE

As with any engagement between researchers and consumers of knowledge, bringing together policymakers and academics with funders as facilitators can enable inspiring and exciting new opportunities for all parties. The facilitation of engagement such as through seed funding, placements and collaborative research (see Part II for examples) by funders creates three key positives: (1) the creation of real world solutions and innovation as a result of collaborations, (2) the generation of impact on the world, and (3) new and untapped avenues for future research opportunities.

Firstly, bringing together people from two different worlds can often generate new ideas and provide fertile ground for creativity. When academics and policymakers work together, research questions that are mutually beneficial, but also highly important, can be brought out through discussion. This leads to the second of the key positives, that these relationships can generate insights that can have ramifications in the real world. Funding alone cannot make research impact happen, but funders can share understanding of best practices for researchers to have research impact with policymakers and vice versa. For example, funders are acutely aware that the earlier researchers engage with potential users of their research, and the earlier those users are involved in the research process, the more likely it is that insights will be used. Thirdly, that the relationship with policymakers has a great benefit to researchers as they are able to work on new challenges, access new data, be challenged on their assumptions and build capacity to work in a more collaborative way. These three benefits are central to what we often try to achieve as funders.

To conclude, in addition to the traditional funding role, funders are also catalysts in creating the environment for policy impact to happen. Their strength lies in facilitating connections, building capability and creating capacity. These roles are important to consider from both sides: academic and policymakers. It is important to remember that research impact is an evolving area, and that everyone is still learning. Some key lessons are provided in Box 9.2.

BOX 9.2 KEY LESSONS

- Earlier engagement between researchers and policymakers increases the likelihood that the research is asking the right questions and is able to consider the policy driven evidence gaps and therefore it is more likely to be used.
- Earlier engagement also means that policymakers can be made aware of existing knowledge and research before initiating new calls for evidence.
- Impacting policy is complex, and funders can play a key role in navigating and building relationships between policymakers and academics, and not to forget the key (often hidden role) funders can have in stimulating and supporting new partnerships.
- There is a need to continue to support the systems to enable impact such as brokers and connectors, the institutions and people who support impact; reward and recognition drivers; researcher training, skills development and methodologies to support knowledge exchange.

NOTES

1. See, for example, Administrative Data Research UK (ADRUK) (https://www.adruk.org).
2. For more information on the Secondary Data Analysis Call, see website https://www.ukri.org/opportunity/secondary-data-analysis-initiative.
3. See, for example, https://ukdataservice.ac.uk.

4.   For more information on the Enterprise Research Centre, see https://www
      .enterpriseresearch.ac.uk.
5.   For more information on What Works Centres see https://www.gov.uk/guidance/
      what-works-network.
6.   For more information see the following links: Productivity Institute (https://
      www.productivity.ac.uk), Economics Observatory (https://www.economicso
      bservatory.com), International Public Policy Observatory (https://covidandsociety
      .com).

REFERENCES

Brantnell, A., Baraldi, E., van Achterberg, T. et al., 2015. Research funders' roles
    and perceived responsibilities in relation to the implementation of clinical research
    results: a multiple case study of Swedish research funders. *Implementation Science*,
    10(100). https://doi.org/10.1186/s13012-015-0290-5
ESRC 1, n.d., *Influencing Policymakers*. Accessed at https://esrc.ukri.org/research/
    impact-toolkit/influencing-policymakers/
ESRC 2, n.d. *Celebrating Impact Prize*. Accessed 4 April 2022 at https://www.ukri.org/
    what-we-offer/esrc-celebrating-impact-prize/
Grove, L., 2018. The effects of funding policies on academic research. Accessed at
    https://eprints.lse.ac.uk/88207/1/Grove_Thesis_2017.pdf
Hopkins, A., Oliver, K., Boaz, A., Guillot-Wright, S., and Cairney, P., 2021. Are
    research-policy engagement activities informed by policy theory and evidence? 7
    challenges to the UK impact agenda. *Policy Design and Practice*, 4(3), 341–56.
National Co-ordinating Centre for Public Engagement, n.d. *Pathways to Impact*.
    Accessed   at   https://www.publicengagement.ac.uk/do-engagement/funding/
    pathways-impact

PART II

Modes of engagement

10. Critical friends – real time insights for shaping strategy

Debbie Johnson, Geeta Nathan and Syahirah Abdul Rahman

10.1 INTRODUCTION

The concept of 'critical friends' has been prevalent in academia for a number of decades (Stenhouse, 1975). It stems from the idea that, without criticism of existing work, progression in knowledge would not be possible (Handal, 1999). Critique, as in the originally French term, is an important dimension of academia, as without the learning from criticism, academics will not be able to evaluate their current practices and make improvements.

In a similar vein, the concept of critical friends and its usage were birthed in the educational development literature to facilitate mutual learning among academics and practitioners (Simons, 1987). As Lawrence Stenhouse, a British educational theorist, suggested, a 'critical friend' or 'critical colleague' should be thought of as a partner who is able to give mutual advice and feedback to facilitate the process of research and reflective learning by the two parties involved in the friendship in a cooperative manner (Kember et al., 1997). Since then, the usage of critical friendships for collaborative activities has been prevalent in academia. Critical friends could be found whether through academic–academic, academic–business, academic–community and even academic–policy maker collaborations.

Nonetheless, the purpose of this book is to provide lessons on fostering successful academic–policy maker relationships and, as such, this chapter focuses on the usage of critical friends for this purpose. In writing this chapter, the authors, policy maker *and* academic by background, take note of the often taken-for-granted nature of critical friends. Therefore, we begin by going back to the foundation of critical friendships, identifying what constitutes a critical friend and what their value can be to both policy makers and the research community.

10.2   THE VALUE OF CRITICAL FRIENDS FOR POLICY MAKERS AND RESEARCHERS

Increasingly, the usage of critical friends has been beneficial in policymaking as there is an acceptance that policy makers might not possess all the knowledge on a given issue needing policy attention. For policy makers, a critical friend assists in the effective articulation of the question that needs answering. Academic experts provide insights and evidence to inform the policy maker integral to the delivery of credible policy proposals. It creates a virtuous circle that assists policy makers to ensure that their proposals and policy discussions are backed by academic rigour. More importantly, there is a desire in the government to address gaps in knowledge in policymaking, backed by the growth of evidence-based policymaking. In Jill Rutter's report *Evidence and Evaluation in Policy Making*, the author found that many government officers saw real potential value in engaging with academics who could contribute directly to the policymaking process (Rutter, 2012).

For policy makers, the starting point of any policy begins with a problem. A policy maker might not always have subject expertise or wider views on this problem and how to find solutions for it. A critical friend thus helps to sense-test the policy maker's knowledge on this problem, providing different lenses through which this idea may develop and its potential impacts to policy design. The wider the consultation of a problem, the more refined a policy will become and, in turn, increase credibility for the policy maker's proposal. This further assists policy makers to provide high quality evidence and justification to their policy design.

Similarly, the benefits of critical friendships to researchers is in the development of a problem, although usually this idea stems from an academic inquiry. Academics may learn from policy makers on what types of discussions are relevant and what translations of evidence are needed to influence policy, thus improving the relevance of the academics' research. In addition, being a critical friend allows an academic to use their in-depth knowledge of a particular policy area to inform and guide policy officials who may not themselves be subject specialists. It is a role which can make a real difference to effective policymaking. As one of our academic critical friends has said, 'Being a critical friend helps keep you real!' This may be beneficial to academics who might want to see their research having real-life outcomes in the form of policy impacts. The academic critical friend can also involve early career researchers (ECRs) in aiding and providing feedback to policy makers, assisting ECRs' career developments by linking their research to policy agendas and helping them to build their own networks. Lastly, being a critical friend can also illuminate academics to new research areas and academic inquiry, thus supporting the virtuous circle of learning.

10.3   HOW DO CRITICAL FRIENDSHIPS DEVELOP?

For the policy maker, there are several reasons for engaging externally. It could be that the policy maker is unable to move forward with a policy development due to resistance from stakeholders. It could be that there is a lack of solutions found through existing consultation, and as such, there might be a desire for independent critique of work or an alternative perspective. Policy makers could also have insufficient subject matter expertise, or insufficient internal capacity to undertake the work. To whom the policy maker turns for engagement or what has initiated the challenge to the policy maker's thinking is most telling and may help steer the approach of the critical friend. Sometimes seeking out a critical friend will be serendipity. A policy maker might have seen an article, hear someone speak on a webinar or at a conference, or given a recommendation.

There is no standard template to what a critical friend looks like: they can be from another public body, business or academic field, either local or global. In particular academics can provide a non-politicised lens to the discussion and academic critical friends, due to the nature of their profession, often enabling a broader perspective to the subject matter.

Top Tip

It is likely the working arrangements with a critical friend will begin informally, most likely as ideas and tasks are set in motion. It is therefore a necessary consideration as to when more formal arrangements should be set out. This is essential in maintaining the trust and respect which underpin the arrangement.

Often, critical friendships begin when a policy maker knows that there is value to be gained from an academic expert. These academic experts may have been identified through the policy maker's existing networks or a direct request based on the policy need in which the academic's expertise can add value. Identifying the need for a critical friendship usually starts by happenstance.

It is recognised from the policy makers' perspective that they are not always experts in the subject matter discussed in policy and that they may need input from external sources to credibly shape policy. The policy maker may have found themselves at a position in which they are struggling to articulate a policy question that needs answering, for example, and through this, the policy maker may decide that seeking academic rigour would help in building confidence and credibility in their policy discussions. At other times, the identification of a critical friendship may have happened through the academic's own initiative to network with policy makers and show them opportunities to develop policy discussions backed by academic research, in which they may be experts in.

Navigating the best route to identify academic expertise is critical. Some policy makers may use academic facilitators to bridge the gap between policy makers and academics. For example, as we will discuss later on in this chapter, our experiences with Innovation Caucus, an academic network of innovation experts, have been integral in learning about the different types of academic experts we could approach to meet our various policy needs.

At the initial stage of a critical friendship, the time may be spent by the critical friend playing the role of a facilitator to the policy maker. This means that they may need to engage in what we can term as a 'knowledge translation' activity. Knowledge translation here refers to assisting the policy maker with how to articulate the policy problem that they want to develop into a more formalised discussion. Often, policy makers may have a vague proposal on what that problem may be. The critical friend, however, would help to shape this problem into a more concrete discussion, using academic evidence and practices to support the policy maker's thinking.

Thus, the essential starting point for both the policy maker and the researcher is to have a common understanding of the policy problem to be addressed. Discussions should start early on to identify constraints and dilemmas in the way both the policy maker and the researcher operate. It is integral for both parties to understand the expectations of what types of outputs will be generated from the services provided by the critical friend. For example, the policy maker must inform the critical friend of the reality of the political landscape, which will not allow every recommendation to move forward. Changing economic and/or political environments can often limit the policy makers' ability to influence radical change. Similarly, critical friends must inform the policy makers of the nature of their roles as academics, for example, the need to reach academic rigour in order to produce outputs such as academic journals. An appreciation of the reality of the way both parties operate can help expectations to be managed, potentially leading to the most realistic, rather than ideal, outcome.

Whilst critical friendships could be long-lasting, the strength of the critical friendship will be tested based on its resilience. Both policy makers and academics must be aware that no matter how successful a critical friendship may have started, the relationship could face various unexpected challenges. Policy discussions may fizzle out, for example, only to be picked up months or years later. Setting expectations early on in the likelihood of critical friendships abruptly ending or fizzling out is recommended, as it would give both parties resilience in their management of the critical friendship.

10.4   EXPECTATIONS FROM A CRITICAL FRIENDSHIP

Working as a critical friend or engaging with critical friends can often be difficult to scope, and formal protocols and processes mean it is often necessary to work with a larger degree of flexibility than both policy makers and the researchers are used to. For example, both the policy maker and the critical friend must be able to define the desired output, which can be more challenging when neither the policy maker nor critical friend know the path which will be adopted. In these instances it may be necessary to agree on the scope of the role of the critical friends and the desired physical outputs from the engagement, for example, a presentation or a report, rather than the full detail of how this output will be obtained.

It is helpful to understand who will be impacted as a result of the work. This will help the critical friend to have a better understanding of the research carried out, thus enabling an overall perspective to be gained. A critical friend needs to challenge policy makers constructively, and to this end there may be broader organisational considerations affecting the policy holder which need to be understood and, as appropriate, unpicked. This may involve the policy maker facilitating conversations with both internal and external stakeholders to support the critical friend in understanding how policy proposals may impact decision makers, other activities and dependencies.

It is not always the case that work goes according to an agreed schedule. In the case where policy partners are aspiring to improve their policy positions, critical friends may become involved in additional and ad hoc work. These situations may be known as 'thought leadership', instances in which critical friends act as valuable advisors to the policy makers. These unplanned activities often focus on having the critical friend challenge the policy maker's existing thoughts and assumptions on a potential policy problem that needs solutions. This may result in a more in-depth commissioning of evidence and insights of the critical friend which likely need to be more formally procured.

To make the most effective use of a critical friendship, policy makers should appreciate the breadth of critical friends' experience and knowledge. Whilst much of this can be gleaned from a CV or publications, the underpinning of trust is most likely to be the route to begin a conversation which extends into a formalised relationship. It is likely through academic and/or research networks that there will be interest in particular areas of work, and in this way it is the interest of the critical friend which is of necessity. If the area of policy is not of interest to a researcher there may not be the curiosity needed to best meet the needs of the policy maker.

There is a second reality for the critical friend to be mindful of – that of rejection when the research outputs presented do not align with the policy maker's priorities. No matter how robust and thought-provoking the insights provided, sometimes, the academic finding is simply not palatable to the policy maker. It could also be that the discussion had not come at the right time, given the current political and/or economic climate. For the critical friend, even though their role is to give input, there is an importance of accepting that the listener may not take on board what is being said. There has to be an accept-ance that some decisions will not align with advice. Not only this, there will be other critical friends with alternative views, and at times offering critical friendship to others within the same policy context. In the case of influencing the policy makers, critical friends need to accept that, even though their evi-dence and research may be compelling, there will be occasions where policy makers are dictated by political considerations that prevent an application of the critical friends' evidence.

10.5   THE CRITICAL FRIENDSHIP OF INNOVATE UK AND INNOVATION CAUCUS

For government agencies such as Innovate UK, which strategises for business innovation involving multiple dimensional policy domains, the need for crit-ical friendships is integral. These friendships are invaluable in assisting the knowledge development of our policymaking. Critical friends provide us with the latest academic insights, evidence and wider perspective of the actors in the UK Innovation system. Policy makers often lack such nuanced, qualitative insights, in which case social scientists, such as the academic network of Innovation Caucus, can often contribute.

The engagement between Innovate UK and Innovation Caucus initially came from the latter. Innovation Caucus was originally in the periphery of Innovate UK's vision. However, their networking activities with Innovate UK was done with the intent to develop a more long-lasting relationship with Innovate UK. Through various, smaller works that Innovation Caucus had done for Innovate UK, the academic network's value was quickly recognised. The critical friendship was eventually built after a long course of continuous, regular and reciprocated conversations.

Although Innovate UK typically consults with various external stake-holders, the choice to continue a relationship with critical friends such as Innovation Caucus is based on the need to have deeper relationships with stra-tegic stakeholders that are underpinned by longer-term, focused conversations and insights. Prolonged dialogues that can be obtained through critical friends would give both the critical friend and the policy maker meaningful time to explore a certain issue, which most of the time may lead to explorations on other key areas in policy.

Additionally, Innovate UK recognised that whilst it was appropriate for a relationship to be established with a critical friend, the 'friendship' must be welcomed and encouraged by internal stakeholders in the organisation, in order for outputs to be meaningfully considered. To an extent the same is true for the critical friend. Whilst the behaviours are inherent in the ability to be a critical friend, it is less likely that the expertise to advise on all matters will be present in one individual. It is therefore essential that there is an underpinning network which can be called on as and when appropriate.

The Innovation Caucus' contribution to Innovate UK is most evident in their active participation to organise strategic dialogues between academics and policy makers at Innovate UK. One such channel of dialogue was delivered through a webinar series, a platform for live, face-to-face discussions between social science academic experts and Innovate UK's policy leads. Innovation Caucus was able to provide their expertise in identifying academics with the most cutting-edge or up-to-date academic insights on a particular innovation matter and, in response, policy makers at Innovate UK were able to provide insights into which types of academic research could inform policy discussions in a more effective way. The discussions of these webinars were so engaging that they have led to deep dive round tables and subsequent strategic policy discussions in Innovate UK.

Beyond these webinars, Innovation Caucus' main contribution to Innovate UK as a critical friend is to provide a platform for a virtuous and mutual circle of learning. To the academics in Innovation Caucus, having a close contact with Innovate UK and facilitating their policy discussions also meant that they were able to gain insights into the priorities and dilemmas facing policy makers, to shape future academic research and refine the skills needed to become critical friends.

10.6   CONCLUSION: WHAT CONSTITUTES A SUCCESSFUL CRITICAL FRIENDSHIP?

The effectiveness of a critical friend requires an open mindset, from the policy maker's perspective to be challenged and for the critical friend to be recognised that they will be heard but may not see policy changes as a result of evidence and research presented. Without these mindsets at the outset, critical friendships are unlikely to lead to impactful collaboration.

An important lesson that we had from our own experiences is to bring in academic critical friends at the earliest stage of brainstorming to ensure policy makers understand what the evidence is providing them. To be an evidence-led policy organisation, a top-down buy-in with a bottom-up approach is needed. This takes a lot of time, patience, resilience and a relationship of mutual respect. Some of the greatest challenges come from unexpected quarters, therefore both policy makers and critical friends must prepare for as many 'knowns' as you can to ensure you have time for the 'unknowns'.

In an ideal situation, the two parties – the critical friend and the policy maker – will create a virtuous circle, whereby critical friends understand the need and communicate their evidence in an effective style to policy makers. Policy makers will see the virtue of what is provided and in turn will help them to position their policy solutions, in the context of getting endorsement from senior decision makers or on how the policy should be delivered.

In the context of Innovation Caucus and Innovate UK, the policy dialogue webinars provide a good example of one type of a successful outcome. The initial objective of this dialogue activity was to support Innovate UK's thinking on a strategy for UK business innovation. When these webinars were set up by Innovation Caucus, a specific outcome had not been identified, apart from simply providing the policy partner with a forum for debate. However, what has materialised are programmes of further research and analyses. Through this activity, several key policy areas emerged as requiring further policy development, thus illustrating the value of critical friendships.

From the perspective of Innovate UK, the outcome of these series of dialogues is a widening appreciation of the benefits of engaging critical friends. A further unexpected outcome has been the importance and need for a platform for internal debate, as the series of webinars illuminated how much internal debates in the organisation could reap positive outputs. A key lesson learned from this experience is that there is a need to bring critical friends into policy formulation at the earliest stage in order to understand what evidence is available and the gaps identified from the existing evidence which provide a valuable starting point for policy discussion.

At the earlier stages of building a model for collaboration between policy makers and critical friends, it is important that both parties encourage some form of review or evaluation process. This would help to identify the value of the critical friendship for both sides of the party, to measure the progress made in the relationship, and learn from past experiences. A risk to a successful critical friendship is that without a right mindset and transparent expectation in place, there is potential for disappointment on either side or lack of enthusiasm for future collaborations. Lastly, to continue developing successful critical friendships, the success of existing critical friendships should be widely communicated to the organisations that both parties are involved in. Increasing appreciation of the value of critical friendships would help both policy makers and academic researchers to find opportunities in working together as critical friends.

REFERENCES

Handal, G. (1999) 'Consultation using critical friends.' *New Directions for Teaching and Learning*, 79, 59–70.

Kember, D., Ha, T.S., Lam, B.H., Lee, A., Ng, S., Yan, L. and Yum, J.C. (1997) 'The diverse role of the critical friend in supporting educational action research projects.' *Educational Action Research*, 5(3), 463–81.

Rutter, J. (2012) *Evidence and Evaluation in Policy Making.* London: Institute for Government. Available at: https://www.instituteforgovernment.org.uk/sites/default/files/publications/evidence%20and%20evaluation%20in%20template_final_0.pdf (accessed: 23 January 2021).

Simons, H. (1987) *Getting to Know Schools in a Democracy: The Politics and Process of Evaluation* (vol. 5). London: Psychology Press.

Stenhouse, L. (1975) *An Introduction to Curriculum Research and Development.* London: Heinemann.

11. Designing and delivering targeted policy engagement events

Sarah Weakley

11.1 INTRODUCTION

Targeted policy engagement events are opportunities for researchers and policy actors to come together in both in-person and virtual spaces to influence the design, implementation, and evaluation of policy. Engagement events are held at all stages of research and policy development and implementation to explore these common interests in practice. Common event types include day-long conferences, short seminars or discussions, or a discussion/seminar 'series' that builds on one another with a group of the same participants in each discussion. Events can include many types of actors involved in influencing policy: public officials, civil servants at various levels of government, public servants in a delivery function (e.g. policy officers, healthcare practitioners), voluntary sector staff and advocates, those in the private sector, and researchers within independent research organisations and academia. Events can be designed and led by an academic and/or an academic knowledge broker or can be designed by a policy actor who invites researchers and stakeholders into policymaking spaces.

The study of policy engagement events engages with research focussing on the interaction between evidence and policy. Recent work from Oliver et al. (2020) builds upon Best and Holmes (2010) to understand and categorise engagement events within three different perspectives. *Linear* approaches focus primarily on evidence dissemination and are illustrated by events like seminars that announce new research findings. *Relational* approaches focus on 'how knowledge is shared among diverse stakeholders ... and how to create partnerships underpinned by common interest' (Oliver et al. 2020), and often take the form of discussion-focussed events with stakeholders. Finally, *systems* approaches focus on 'infrastructure and systems that need to be in place to support research use in government' (Oliver et al. 2020). Choosing between these approaches is dependent upon the type of engagement you wish to foster.

Initial work from Oliver et al. (2020) found that most events sit within the first two categories.

Individual researchers benefit from participating in policy engagement events by sharing their research directly with influential policy actors, fostering relationships and making connections with actors inside policymaking spaces for future collaborations. Additionally, these engagements allow researchers to learn more about the type and form of evidence that policy actors are interested in and the research questions being asked inside policy spaces they can contribute to. Policy partners/collaborators benefit by being able to quickly tap into new and emerging evidence in their areas of interest, hear from a diverse range of stakeholders to inform policy development or implementation decisions, and make connections with knowledge producers and experts to help answer questions and fill research gaps.

This chapter will detail some of the common features of targeted policy engagement events from the perspective of an academic knowledge broker in a university and will detail two engagement events – one in person and one virtual – to draw out useful tips for implementing them.

11.2   DESIGNING AN ENGAGEMENT EVENT

Targeted policy engagement events often occur when a policy issue requires new evidence and insights to be considered and/or a variety of research and policy stakeholders should be brought together in discussion to influence policy design, implementation, or evaluation. There are many situations wherein a policy engagement event would be a useful way to bring experts from academia and policy spaces together, and the reasons for designing one may come from either partner. The impetus for engagement can often inform whether an engagement should be 'linear' in its approach, or whether the event tends towards a more 'relational' or dialogue-focussed event.

11.2.1   Identifying Opportunities for Engagement

One of the key horizon-scanning activities for a knowledge broker is identifying the opportunities that are ripe for engagement. These can include:

- Periods of national crisis in a policy area, which requires the marshalling of new evidence and ideas to solve problems (e.g. social recovery from Covid-19)
- Changes of government/elections which may necessitate different approaches to address policy problems
- A new policy agenda or strategy from the current government (e.g. Programme for Government, Autumn/Spring Budgets)

- Large changes in certain policy areas (e.g. devolution of social security, changes to international development budgets)
- Requests from government departments for new research based on documents like the UK's 'Areas of Research Interest'
- New studies or pieces of evidence that have changed the policy debate on an issue.

Once an opportunity is identified by an academic, knowledge broker, or policy partner, an important task is understanding what research evidence and expertise is needed to improve understanding of the policy problem. For knowledge brokers in academic institutions, this means first connecting with the network of academic experts both inside and outside your institution to understand how their knowledge and evidence can be utilised. Academic experts can serve active roles as presenters, panellists, discussants, or facilitators on the day or simply attend.

One of the important ways that academic experts aid in the design and delivery of policy engagement events is by serving as the gatekeeper to the field. They help a knowledge broker identify the aims and outcomes for the event, what issues require discussion, and, importantly, have a keen sense of who needs to be around the table to meet the event's objectives. For most targeted engagement events, identifying an academic lead (or team of academics) to work with you is a vital part of the design process. An academic lead is important to establish early on because knowledge brokers will likely not be able to identify every actor working in a policy area. These academic leads help brokers make a 'way in' to a policy and knowledge network and will work closely with them to ensure the event is timely, appropriate, and useful for all those in attendance.

Top Tip

Approach and meet with an academic lead early on in the event planning to help determine the core aims of the event and identify others in their knowledge network inside and outside academia to be involved.

11.2.2   Getting Buy-In

Targeted policy engagement events work well when they are designed to meet the needs of both parties at a point in time and can include discussions of issues that are 'hot' as well as issues that are perennial, 'wicked' problems. They enable new knowledge and connections to be brought to policy actors quickly and personally. The motivations for policy actors to be involved in a policy engagement event often centre around the desire for more and new evidence and different approaches to be brought to an existing debate. Academics are important actors to provide this type of knowledge as they not only produce cutting edge research, but are important advisors, partners, and critical friends for policymakers (Haynes et al. 2011 and see Chapter 10 in this book). Having an academic lead may also improve buy-in from policy partners to participate in this event. An academic who has done policy-relevant work in the past may be well known to the policy partner you wish to engage with, and the strength of these existing relationships will help to buttress the reputation of the event.

Academic participants often find value in policy engagement events which enable their work or expertise to inform policy action but also find value in opportunities for policy actors to inform their research activities. Academics should try and participate in or design engagement events not just at the end of a research process as a 'dissemination' event but at various stages of research to help form new questions for inquiry, identify potential partners for co-produced research, identify policy implications for their research, and create a network of stakeholders. Participating in targeted policy engagement events is a useful way to make connections for future work, which can be done most notably in dialogue-focussed 'relational' types of engagement.

11.3   IMPLEMENTING TARGETED POLICY ENGAGEMENT EVENTS

This section will detail some key considerations in organising and delivering targeted policy engagement events using two case examples, one delivered in person and one online.

11.3.1   In Person: DWP Areas of Research Interest Workshop Day – October 2019

In October 2019, knowledge brokers from the University of Glasgow and University of Edinburgh worked in collaboration with the Department for Work and Pensions (DWP) Evidence and Insight Unit to deliver a one-day workshop event focussed on the DWP's Areas of Research Interest (ARI).[1] There were roughly 60 participants that included academics from universities across Scotland and civil servants from the DWP and the Scottish Government. The aim of this event was to bring together new evidence and build relationships in Scotland to address the ARIs.

Establishing partnerships for event delivery

The two teams of knowledge brokers from Glasgow and Edinburgh agreed that the universities would formally partner to hold this event early in the planning process. One of the reasons for this formal partnership was the status of the policy partner (a UK government unit with little prior engagement in Scotland), which necessitated that more resources were brought to bear to ensure the event was delivered to a high standard. In a project of this scale it was valuable that the formal knowledge exchange (KE) partners had an open discussion to discuss how to use their resources most effectively; a discussion that is also useful to have with any formal policy partner (like the DWP). One of the universities had more KE staff and would have greater access to facilities to hold the event and organise arrangements on the day, while the other university team had more extensive knowledge and connections to the Scottish academics for participation and subject matter expertise. These resource specialties would inform who would lead on operations and who would lead on participant recruitment and agenda content.

Lead time

Day-long policy engagement events that seek to bring together many civil servants and academics must be planned very far in advance. For this event the first discussions between university partners began eight months before the event was held. In that discussion it was agreed to send a proposal to the DWP contact requesting a follow up meeting to discuss the event scope and a timeline for all subsequent planning stages.

> **Top Tip**
>
> If you want to have a high level of participation from civil servants – particularly for an in-person workshop or conference where travel would be required – more than six months of planning is recommended.

Building the community

All events require an important discussion about the network of participants and presenters to be involved, and a formal project partnership enables the creation of a larger network of academics and policy experts. In most research fields knowledge brokers will probably be able to quickly identify the 'key players' that are likely to present their work, but a wider network can help to broaden out invitations for participants. It is important to be clear on the most appropriate policy community to engage with, which is dependent on the policy issue being discussed. Is the policy focussed at a national, regional, or local level? Do you want academia, public, private, and/or voluntary sectors involved? In this case, UK and Scottish civil servants were the most appropriate given the high-level discussions of DWP policy.

Event design
If you are organising the event with a policy partner from the outset (as here), the initial conversation will discuss the best way to organise the day and you will need to keep in regular contact as the agenda develops and speakers confirm. For a day-long workshop in person the day will likely include presentations from the key policy partner, other government units if applicable, and academics, along with times for smaller group discussions (here, one in the morning and one in the afternoon). You will therefore need to collaborate with project partners to recruit appropriate presenters and discussion facilitators.

If working with civil servants from different nations, councils, or government units be aware of the sensitivities they will bring to the event when organising the day. If you give space for one unit to present their work at the beginning of the event (such as the DWP), it is likely that the other unit will want to speak as well.

Top Tip

If there is a document that is guiding the day's events (such as the DWP Areas of Research Interest), try to have presentations that speak to most, if not all, of the subsections included in the document. These specific subtopics can also be used to organise the small group discussion periods.

Event inclusion
In-person events need to take into account accessibility issues for those with physical disabilities and for those with other inclusion needs (e.g. for those hard of hearing). In your initial communication to participants be sure to include information on disabled access to all facilities and request for participants to get in touch with you if they have additional inclusion needs at the earliest possible convenience.

11.3.2   Online: More Different Futures Network, May–July 2020

Online events can also be single policy engagement events, but are more readily adaptable to a series of events and conversations. One such project was the 'More Different Futures Network', a series of online seminars and discussions with housing policy and delivery experts in three countries – the UK,

Canada, and Australia. By the end of the ten discussions, over 150 participants had been included in this international network. The aim of the discussion series was to bring together evidence, policy, and practice insights and innovations early in the Covid-19 crisis to influence policy decisions in the short, medium, and long term.

Establishing partnerships for delivery

This event was organised and implemented within one KE unit and did not include a formal partnership with another KE broker or with a policy partner. However, it was appropriate to create informal partnerships with other academic colleagues to help design the engagement, especially as the project involved international partners. In this case the academic lead in the UK approached colleagues in Canada and Australia to serve as informal academic leads for their countries to ensure the content was context-specific and the appropriate international experts were included. Events that aim to reach a wide range of actors (especially international participants) should consider informal partnerships for each country or 'sector' partner (e.g. civil servants, third sector, etc.) to help deliver the engagement.

Lead time

Organising online events of this type – short seminars or a series of discussions – tend to require less lead time than in-person events of the same type, as there are no travel arrangements to make and no facilities to book. A good rule of thumb is to allow at least two months of lead time from project inception to delivery. For an event series the announcement of the full series of dates and times should be released at least one month before the first discussion and any materials for participants to read or view in advance of the sessions should be available a week before the session.

Building the community

Ensuring the right people are in the room is critical even if that room is in a virtual space. In a discussion series there will likely be different networks of participants you would like to invite for certain sessions alongside a core group invited to all sessions. In this case, as the discussion series progressed the team added new participants who were experts in homelessness, housebuilding and more as the discussion series focussed on their area of expertise.

Top Tip

Online events will likely also need different staff in the project delivery team, including an online platform administrator and backup hosts and event chairs in case event leads have technical issues.

Event design

Much of the core agenda elements are similar for online events, with time for presentations and discussions with large and small groups. Planning online policy engagement events must additionally consider the delivery format, and consider issues such as screen fatigue, encouraging active participation, and organising successful small group discussions.

While presentations using slides are a standard feature of online events, for events that are relational in nature (discussion focussed) you can consider removing presentations from the agenda. Presenters can instead record videos for participants to view before the session or create a briefing paper so that the session is focussed on discussion from the start. This was done with every session in this project. The sessions began with a panel of respondents who discussed key reflections from the videos, chaired by the event's academic lead. This format enabled the conversation to begin in earnest. This also allowed other participants to get comfortable entering their own comments in the platform's chat function or raising their virtual hands. A skilled chair should listen to the panellists while also keeping a note of issues and questions that come up on the chat platform for larger discussion.

Small group discussions are vital in online events as elsewhere. For discussion-focussed policy engagement events it is often useful to assign participants to rooms to ensure that stakeholders with similar areas of expertise from different sectors are in a group together to collaborate. Online breakout groups also require a skilled facilitator with discussion questions set in advance to ensure the group discussion does not lag.

Top Tip

To avoid screen fatigue, try to limit a single online event to less than two and a half hours; you can also build in five minute 'breaks' if necessary.

Event inclusion

Please include in every invitation for participants to get in touch with you at the earliest possible convenience if they have additional inclusion needs. For larger seminars consider hiring a sign language interpreter, who will be permanently on a split screen alongside presenters. If attendees require captioning it is the responsibility of the organiser to ensure events are captioned. Many online platforms have a live captioning feature, third party captioning services can be integrated, or you can hire a transcriber to caption the event manually to display on screen.

Top Tip

There are some online platforms that government departments do not allow on their networks. If most key policy participants can only use one type of online platform, consider hosting your event using that platform rather than using workarounds for individual participants.

11.4   OUTCOMES AND LOOKING AHEAD

Targeted policy engagement events are one way for policy actors and researchers to engage outside of their offices to receive, consider, and discuss new evidence to make decisions and build relationships around areas of common interest. Three functions of events – engaging with evidence, collaborating in discussion, and building relationships – are all mechanisms by which policy, practice, and evaluation can be influenced and new research can emerge.

It is challenging, if not impossible, to specifically trace a 'policy impact' back to one single policy event or a discussion series. This is because policy is often made, revised, and implemented incrementally based on small decisions using evidence, expertise, emotions, and beliefs (Cairney et al. 2016). Policy engagement events that focus on supporting these three functions among diverse stakeholders can catalyse dialogue and relationships for many years, often with outcomes that the event organiser will never be aware of. However, knowledge brokers or academic leads should try and keep in touch with participants if possible, noting down any new collaborations or outputs that come from it.

Common challenges to delivering high quality and impactful targeted policy engagement events can arise related to academic participation and policy actor participation. For some engagement events academics may simply not see the value in engaging. This may be due to the event not being entirely related to their current academic work, they are overstretched with other commitments (including teaching), or they do not feel like their involvement will make a difference. To address these concerns it may be useful to have a very clear sense of what policy actors will be in the room, the discussion aims, and how their expertise will bring a new viewpoint to the current debate before approaching them. (If you clearly make your case and they do not engage, no need to take it personally!)

Some policy engagement events can also suffer from not being inclusive of all the voices in the policy debate. To help address this knowledge brokers should be aware of and consider constraints on all participants' time. For example, policymakers in government will likely be very busy in the run-up to budget announcements or large annual reports, but may be more available in the period before an election when Parliament is suspended. Voluntary sector participants who have an operational role may find it difficult to attend day-long events due to demands on their time and also may not have the resources to travel long distances to events. Academic participants are more likely to be available in periods without teaching commitments. You can consider shorter but more frequent engagements (such as a discussion series) for groups with schedule demands to accommodate these needs.

In the two cases detailed above, there were some common features that made success possible. First, knowledge brokers formed partnerships (either formal or informal) early in the planning process with academics or policy partners that knew the policy field in detail. These content experts were vital in determining the most appropriate combination of event elements (e.g. presentations versus discussions), the network of stakeholders, and the overall aim of the engagement. Second, the events were tightly organised around a framework document or topic so that new ideas or 'solutions' could emerge from discussion. Try to design policy engagement events that go beyond 'linear' dissemination with discussion that considers gaps in knowledge or new ideas to solve current (and future) problems. Finally, each of these events had a strong 'backstage' team to make this happen. It is useful (if possible) to have a knowledge broker as the event designer who is the academic liaison and network manager, a communications lead who will be responsible for creating or editing any content for the web, and a staff member to run operations on the day (whether in person or virtual) to ensure all technology, facilities, and participants are included in the event.

It is likely that policy engagement units inside higher education will be considering ways to make their engagement more 'hybrid' in the future. This will include hosting some engagements in person, some fully online, or considering ways to have in-person events meaningfully include participants who are unable to be in the room. KE professionals as well as research and teaching staff are also improving the creative tools that can bring people together to work collaboratively in online spaces, and useful learning between these staff members at universities can improve both practices. Openness, innovation, and dialogue will be vital as the university/policy engagement field develops further, and targeted events will likely continue to be an important way for policy actors to collaborate with new and established knowledge producers and brokers to improve their work.

NOTE

1. 'Areas of Research Interest give details about the main research questions facing UK government departments' and aim to improve how government departments: 'align scientific and research evidence from academia with policy development and decision-making, engage with researchers ... [and] access stronger policy evidence bases' (Government Office for Science and Cabinet Office 2017).

REFERENCES

Best, A., Holmes, B., 2010. Systems thinking, knowledge and action: towards better models and methods. *Evidence & Policy* 6: 2, 145–59.

Cairney, P., Oliver, K., Wellstead, A., 2016. To bridge the divide between evidence and policy: reduce ambiguity as much as uncertainty. *Public Administration Review* 76: 3, 399–402.

Government Office for Science and Cabinet Office, 2017. *Areas of Research Interest.* Accessed 12 March 2021 at https://www.gov.uk/government/collections/areas-of -research-interest

Haynes, A.S., Gillespie, J.A., Derrick, G.E., Hall, W.D., Redman, S., Chapman, S., Sturk, H., 2011. Galvanizers, guides, champions, and shields: the many ways that policymakers use public health researchers. *Milbank Quarterly* 89: 4, 564–98.

Oliver, K., Boaz, A., Hopkins, A., 2020. Mapping government-academic engagement initiatives internationally. Transforming Evidence project website. Accessed 10 March 2021 at https://transforming-evidence.org/projects/mapping-government -academic-engagement-initiatives-internationally

12. Collaborative doctoral research

Tim Vorley and Cristian Gherhes

12.1   INTRODUCTION AND CONTEXT

For many early career researchers their doctorate is more than one of the formative steps of their career, it can be career defining. Over the past two decades
there has been a shift in doctoral training beyond the student–supervisor relationship, which has seen more structured forms of doctoral training prevail. In
the social sciences this has taken the form of graduate schools and funded doctoral training partnerships (DTPs). These are often pan university initiatives
providing formal researcher training and development in broadly streamed
subject areas.

Engagement and impact have become an increasingly prominent aspect
of doctoral training, in part reflecting the wider importance of these agendas
within academe. This was in no small part borne from the growing onus on
publicly funded research to justify and demonstrate its relevance and benefit
to economy and society. Early examples privileged knowledge transfer and
commercialisation of research, as embodied by the Co-operative Awards in
Science and Engineering (CASE) studentship programme of the UK Research
Councils which has been operating since the mid 1990s.

While many early CASE studentships had a strong industrial focus in
engineering and the physical sciences, they marked an important shift towards
more collaborative and engaged doctorates. A defining characteristic of CASE
awards was the collaborative training of the PhD student between the university and non-academic partner. The collaborative and engaged basis of CASE
studentships sought to promote the transfer of knowledge between the PhD
student and supervisors (academic and non-academic), as well as improving
opportunities for career mobility.

In the social sciences Demeritt and Lees (2005) highlight how the CASE
awards saw greater collaboration with public sector and voluntary organisations as well as private sector industry – often linked to regional economic
development and local regeneration. The ability to work across academic
and non-academic environments was regarded as crucial to future doctoral
graduates in social sciences, and Kitagawa (2014) notes collaborative doctoral

programmes that enable employer engagement in innovation and skills development remain important.

The remainder of this chapter is structured in three sections. First, we introduce how the Building Economies And Resilient Societies (BEARS) network, see Figure 12.1, was conceived as a cohort of collaborative doctorates established in 2013. Focusing on formation and outcomes of the collaborative interdisciplinary network of PhD projects, the discussion describes the background and basis of the collaboration, as well as setting out some of the key benefits. Second, we broaden the discussion beyond the BEARS project to offer reflections on the opportunities and challenges associated with collaborative doctoral research for all involved, and offer some thoughts about making the most of collaborative doctoral research projects building on the experience of the BEARS network. The chapter finishes with some final thoughts and deflections on the role of collaborative doctoral research in developing stronger links with policymakers.

Figure 12.1   *The BEARS network logo*

12.2   CONCEIVING COLLABORATIVE PHDS

The BEARS network was developed in conjunction with the Policy, Insight & Change Team at Doncaster Metropolitan Borough Council (DMBC) in 2013/14. The BEARS network was comprised of four co-funded PhD projects developed in partnership by the proposed supervisors and partners at DMBC. As a series of four interrelated but independent engaged interdisciplinary projects, the BEARS network attempted to create a 'hybrid institution space' (Lam, 2010) to pursue the production of policy relevant knowledge. A key part of the network of PhD projects was to foster research-led engagement with policymakers, and with it promote more research engaged and evidence-led policymaking.

12.2.1   Becoming BEARS

In many respects, the BEARS network was not in itself pioneering. As noted above, the prevailing policy dialogue in the UK around knowledge exchange as it relates to doctoral collaborations has come to expect genuine non-academic user engagement. The doctoral network was itself based on a previous relationship with DMBC, which had seen several small projects completed and a relationship as a critical friend (see Chapter 10) established between key academics and policy partners. This limited history of academic engagement provided the basis of the institutional partnership, albeit a partnership premised on individual as opposed to organisational relationships.

The initial collaborative relationship with colleagues at DMBC embodied what Lam (2010) describes as strategic entrepreneurialism and institutional 'boundary work' at, in this instance, the academic–policy interface. The managed introduction of new academic partners into the partnership with complementary skills and knowledge further legitimated the partnership and built goodwill over time, although outside of any formal contractual agreement. During this formative phase in the relationship the central challenge was both in building trust and competency through common interests and a shared vision as to the prospective impact of future collaborations.

The prospect of co-funding a series of doctoral studentships was opportunistic, as opposed to a strategic step in the development of the partnership with DMBC. However, the ability to realise the opportunity both consolidated and developed the existing partnership by extending the areas of common interest and shared vision for future impact. This exemplifies what Davenport et al. (1998) refer to in terms of building trust from difference, although it was underpinned by a partnership approach between university researchers and local government officials.

The financial commitment of DMBC was critical to leveraging funding from the University of Sheffield, without which a project of this scale could never have been initiated. The motivations for the collaborative PhDs were different; while the driver for DMBC being the potential insights from the four interrelated but independent projects, the motivation for the University was promoting interdisciplinary PhD research. While not incompatible, the subtle but significant difference related to engagement, and specifically the possibility and intent to benefit local communities.

12.2.2 Being BEARS

Akin to Larner and Mayow (2003), the shared ambition of the BEARS network, albeit implicit, was to improve evidence in political engagement and joined-up policy thinking as well as advancing academic thinking through collaborative project-based research. By their nature the BEARS studentships encouraged the participating doctoral researchers to think about the perspective of local government as a partner from the moment they commenced their research degree. The four doctoral studentships comprising the network were otherwise 'traditional' PhDs, being based within academic departments. The primary difference was the collaborative context of generating new understanding and insights, and the emphasis required to manage and sustain this collaborative context.

The premise of the BEARS Network was to establish four independent but interrelated interdisciplinary projects focused on organisational change, economic development and societal challenges. The projects reflected the research interests of the academics invited to join the network, but were co-produced with colleagues at DMBC. The nature of the research questions being asked were agreed to be substantive enough as the basis for a doctorate over three years, with the projects conceived in a way so as to provide intermediate insights. The focus of the studentships were:

1. Exploring socio-economic spatial polarisation and health and well-being in Doncaster
2. Adaptive capacity and barriers to business growth among small and medium-sized enterprises (SMEs) in Doncaster
3. Perceptions and realities of economy-driven housing market growth in Doncaster
4. Deprivation, educational attainment and resilience in Doncaster.

For the team at DMBC these four projects represented standalone issues, although they also had a degree of crossover at a headline level. In accordance with the 'good practice' of the Economic and Social Research Council (ESRC,

2020), the network and constituent projects sought to contribute to economic competitiveness, the effectiveness of public services and policy, and the quality of life of Doncaster. The premise of the BEARS network was that all of the projects could and should be independent, but that their interdependence would emerge during meetings of the network's students and supervisors. Realising such synergies was a key rationale for the network, especially from the perspective of DMBC.

Given the interdisciplinary basis of the BEARS network, the supervisory arrangements included two academics from different disciplinary backgrounds. Further to the academic supervision, each project was designated a 'professional supervisor', albeit not formally recognised by the university, working in a policy team allied to the project. The premise of the third supervisor was to enrich the learning environment of the doctoral research by aiding their contextual understanding and helping to ensure that potential issues, such as access, were addressed expediently.

Consistent with Borell-Damian (2009), establishing and embedding the professional supervisor within their respective project teams was also key to maximising the prospect of knowledge exchange between academic and policy worlds. The nature of and opportunities for knowledge exchange often related to sharing and applying research ideas and insights with benefit to the policy partner, although this took different forms. Making the most of such ideas and insights was often contingent on the professional supervisor as a key point of contact, who spanned the worlds of research and practice.

As Thune (2010) notes, such supervisory relationships can break down or be lost when key individuals change roles or leave the organisation. To overcome this the BEARS network also had central coordination and connection between the university and DMBC as the policy partner. The connections between the doctoral candidates and their professional supervisors, along with the central coordination, helped to manage and mitigate numerous issues over the duration of the BEARS network. In particular brokering connections and supporting messaging around sensitive issues were two areas where the professional supervisors added potential value beyond their subject expertise.

12.2.3   Benefits of BEARS

The BEARS network was collaborative by design, bringing benefits to the doctoral researchers, academic supervisors and DMBC as the external partner organisation. The vision was to pioneer innovative and impactful interdisciplinary research that could lead to actionable insights for DMBC. All of the four projects set out above included a discreet or comparative focus in their respective areas on Doncaster. For the Policy, Insight & Change Team the BEARS network provided the opportunity to develop an evidence base to better inform policy development and delivery. Fundamentally the network sought to unpack and better understand the policy challenges being addressed, and what factors are likely to inform and impact policy interventions.

Further to the policy relevance of the BEARS network, another driver in convening and forming the network was to promote interdisciplinary social science research. Despite recognising the value of interdisciplinary approaches in studying real-world challenges, academic institutions reduce areas of research to their disciplinary fields (British Academy, 2016). By requiring the co-supervisors to be from different disciplines engineered the interdisciplinarity of the BEARS network, with the aspiration to address and resolve what are complex policy challenges. While the level of interdisciplinarity varied across the projects, all of the four projects were forged 'bottom up' as collaborative interdisciplinary research projects of common interest.

Another benefit of the collaborations was access to data in a way that would have been more challenging if not impossible outside of the collaborative remit of the PhD. For a number of the project teams the access to this data was leveraged by the doctoral researcher and academic supervisors facilitated by the professional supervisor. This provided access to data on the provision of business support and data informing the development of housing and other infrastructure plans. Beyond access to data, the collaborative projects also saw all project partners exposed to wider networks of contacts associated with their respective project and become immersed in broader academic and policy debates.

Through collaboration, the doctoral researcher, academic supervisors and the professional supervisors from local government shared knowledge and gained an appreciation of different perspectives, disciplines and professional experiences at a project level. This was regarded as a key strength and benefit at the project level. At the network level, the Policy, Insight & Change Team at DMBC as central beneficiary and core collaborating partner benefitted from bringing a range of disciplines through the projects to explore policy challenges that could not be addressed from individual disciplinary contexts. That said, and in order to ensure that the doctoral researchers had a disciplinary home, there was at least nominally a lead discipline in which the doctorate was to be examined.

Arguably a key strength of the BEARS projects and the wider network was the hybrid space it created for knowledge production. Kitagawa (2014) highlights the value of collaborative doctorate programmes in the formulation, mediation and translation of new knowledge and knowledge exchange. The notion of the hybrid space created meant that the doctoral research was more applied than may otherwise have been the case, and characterised by higher levels of engagement with, in this case, the DMBC as the local government policy partner. As a format, we concur with Kitagawa (2014) that such collaborative doctoral projects can also enhance the credibility of the research within both academic and policymaking communities.

The contribution of the BEARS network was as much, if not more, about the journey of the doctoral researchers, supervisors and local government officers involved with their individual projects and wider networks as it was the PhDs completed or immediate policy impacts. Through the network's collective learning and shared perspectives forged on prevailing policy priorities and challenges, this enhanced the understanding of the doctoral researchers and supervisors as to the real-world context and policy relevance of their research. For the local government officers involved, the collaborative research provided new insights on what were, in some instances, established issues with findings informing policy thinking.

12.3   DESIGNING AND DOING COLLABORATIVE DOCTORAL RESEARCH

The impact agenda is here to stay, and there is considerable opportunity to inform and impact policy thinking through engaged and/or collaborative doctoral research projects. However, the premise of collaboration with government officers and policymakers should not presuppose an ability to inform or impact policy. Having introduced the BEARS network as an example of a hybrid space, this section reflects on what it takes to make the most of such hybrid spaces. Central to making the most of a collaborative doctoral research project is ensuring that all of those involved are adequately supported and mutually supportive of each other.

First, it is important to recognise that collaborative doctoral research, whether as the basis of the entire PhD or a discrete part thereof, is distinct from more traditional models of doctoral research. As such it should not be expected that either the student or supervisors (academic or professional) embarking on such a mode of study will be familiar or experienced in such ways of working. To this end there is a need to ensure that all parties are adequately supported and expectations are understood and managed to make the most of the collaboration and ultimately inform and impact policy. Indeed, Kieser and Leiner (2012) note that the fruits of collaborative research require the alignment of researchers' and practitioners' interests in the research from the get-go.

From the perspective of the doctoral researcher, there is a need to recognise that developing the skills for collaborative research are typically beyond that of conventional doctoral training. The ability to be reflexive and sensitive to the collaborative context is key, as well as appreciating the 'business as usual' context of government in which the research is taking place. As Reid and McCormick (2010) state, there is also a need to appreciate the working cultures and pressures under which government officers and policymakers operate. To this end, better understanding the needs of end-users and how they use research findings can enable doctoral researchers to pursue more insightful and impactful research.

From the academic supervisors' perspective there is a need to focus on more than the conventional academic grounding and outputs associated with a PhD. For those supervisors not experienced in engaging with policymakers this can represent a paradigm shift, which Kieser and Leiner (2012) explain in terms of different logics. There is a need to move beyond the overly simplistic tendency of academics to privilege abstract knowledge over practical and policy-orientated knowledge described by Peck (1999). To achieve this demands an open-mindedness of the supervisors, and willingness to work with the doctoral researcher and professional supervisor as to the 'rules' of the collaborative PhD as distinct to those of a traditional PhD.

The support for the professional supervisor is particularly important, not least as for many the premise of doctoral research could be an alien concept. There is a need to ensure that the professional supervisor has a substantive role in directing the project, and is not marginalised through the supervision. The knowledge bases of academics and the government officers/policymakers are understandably different, which Kieser and Leiner (2012) contend can culminate in the two groups being experts and laypersons to each other. Managing expectations and forging common frames of reference is crucial, as is establishing milestones and goals as part of the overarching project. This is particularly useful as a part of collaborative projects where expectations around time frames can differ significantly.

Making any kind of collaborative project work depends on effective communication between the parties involved, and this is particularly true of collaborative doctoral projects where there is a need to ensure and maintain effective communication of different groups, i.e. (i) supervisors and supervisee, and (ii) between supervisors. In the case of programmes or networks, such as BEARS, where there are interconnected projects, there is also a need to ensure that there is contact with the programme or network coordinators. In order to make this work Reid and McCormick (2010) suggest making elements of the collaborative arrangement mandatory; these could include supervisions, meetings, network-wide meetings or training sessions.

The ESRC, along with other research councils, have been central to promoting collaboration between postgraduate researchers and non-academic partners, including public, private and third sector partners. The benefits of working collaboratively are widely recognised to improve the research and enhance knowledge exchange, both of which can inform better decision making. Table 12.1 summarises a series of principles and points of good practice, which are intended to inform and support effective collaboration and partnering.

Table 12.1　　*Good practice to support the delivery of collaborative studentships*

Good Practice	Description
Build a work plan	A work plan should be agreed between the student, academic and non-academic supervisors detailing key dates, activities, meetings and milestones and outputs
	Top Tip Agree and specify the format of deliverables so all involved know what to expect
Appropriate training	Further to standard doctoral training, there is a need to ensure that any training appropriate to collaboration is available. This should also include an appropriate induction with the partner organisation
	Top Tip Further to standard Training Needs Analysis, training specific to the collaboration should be considered
Balanced academic and applied foci	Collaborative projects can bring conflicting demands that need to be explicitly considered and agreed
	Top Tip During the formative stages it is critical that a shared focus is developed that meets the needs and expectations of the student and (all) supervisors
Effective reporting	Progress reporting is good practice in any PhD, but in a collaborative project it is particularly important to ensure that the non-academic supervisor is kept in the loop
	Top Tip Circulating a summary of agendas, minutes and actions can help make the most of meetings

Good Practice	Description
Developing relationships	The relationship between the student and supervisors is critical, establishing effective communication and agreed ways of working is important
	Top Tip
	Establish up front preferred communication methods and expectations of level of involvement at each stage, while ensuring regular and consistent communication between the student and (all) supervisors
Managing expectation and delivery	The success of collaborative projects demands managing expectations about what all parties will get out of the project and anticipated timescales
	Top Tip
	Be realistic and transparent about deadlines for proposed deliverables

Source: Adapted from ESRC, 2020.

Further to the preceding discussion, and the principles and points of good practice set out in Table 12.1, as with any collaboration the success is in no small part contingent on the commitment of all parties (Borrell-Damian, 2009; Borrell-Damian et al., 2010). The supervision of collaborative doctoral research can be seen as less hierarchical than traditional doctoral supervision, although this can bring additional complexity which demands additional commitment. Further to the initial institutional co-commitment to the collaboration, there is a need for the academic and non-academic partners to commit to each other, the doctoral researcher and the PhD project (Robertson, 2019). On the part of the doctoral student, there is a commitment to the supervisors and the timely completion of the thesis and key deliverables.

Further to the award of the doctorate as an outcome of collaborative PhD research projects, they can also lay the foundations for enhanced career mobility. For those remaining in academia the collaborative doctorates can provide the skills to bridge with the worlds of industry or policy, while for those pursuing careers outside academe highly skilled doctoral graduates with experience are valued across the public and private sector (Borrell-Damian, 2009). In relation to collaborating with policy partners specifically, whether local, regional or national, working at the research–policy interface has the potential to add considerable value to both the doctoral researcher and their supervisors.

12.4   FINAL THOUGHTS AND REFLECTIONS

The impact agenda has become a fundamental part of academia and policy-making, therefore there is a need to ensure that doctoral researchers are given opportunities to engage in collaborative research. Indeed, understanding the importance of engagement and impact as part of the PhD, in both theory and practice, can enrich the prospects of early career researchers whether they pursue academic or non-academic careers. Reflecting on our experience of the BEARS network and the nature of doctoral collaborations more generally can positively impact research and knowledge exchange outcomes.

There is of course the potential danger that such collaborations may encounter the 'mutually incompatible' described by Peck (1999); here there is a tension between the abstract academic knowledge and more practical policy-orientated knowledge bases. However, where doctoral researchers are given the requisite training and encouraged to dwell in what Bartunek and Rynes (2014) refer to as the 'reflective entanglements' of doctoral collaborations, this can provide the basis to enrich doctoral studies.

To be successful, collaborative doctoral research projects need to be effectively managed from their inception to their delivery. The challenge for the individual and institutional partners is to create a space for the doctoral researcher to undertake their research, and, for some, this can be an alien concept. Where such a hybrid space can be created and the tensions overcome, our experience is that the researchers (doctoral and supervising) came to better understand the research needs of non-academic supervisor and an end-user. This saw research insights created alongside those who can and want to make use of them, as well as providing a strong foundation for future collaborations.

REFERENCES

Bartunek, J.M., and Rynes, S.L. (2014). Academics and practitioners are alike and unlike: the paradoxes of academic–practitioner relationships. *Journal of Management*, 40(5), 1181–201.

Borrell-Damian, L. (2009). *Collaborative Doctoral Education: University-Industry Partnerships for Enhancing Knowledge Exchange*. Report. Brussels: European University Association.

Borrell-Damian, L., Brown, T., Dearing, A., Font, J., Hagen, S., Metcalfe, J., and Smith, J. (2010). Collaborative doctoral education: university-industry partnerships for enhancing knowledge exchange. *Higher Education Policy*, 23, 493–514. https://doi.org/10.1057/hep.2010.20

British Academy (2016). *Crossing Paths: Interdisciplinary Institutions, Careers, Education and Applications*, https://www.thebritishacademy.ac.uk/documents/213/crossing-paths.pdf. Accessed 12 December 2020.

Davenport, S., Davies, J., and Grimes, C. (1998). Collaborative research programmes: building trust from difference. *Technovation*, 19(1), 31–40.

Demeritt, D., and Lees, L. (2005). Research relevance, 'knowledge transfer' and the geographies of CASE studentship collaboration. *Area*, 37(2), 127–37.

ESRC (2020). *Good Practice Guide for Setting up Collaborative Studentship Opportunities*, https://esrc.ukri.org/files/collaboration/good-practice-guide-for-setting-up-collaborative-studentship-opportunities/. Accessed 12 December 2020.

Kieser, A., and Leiner, L. (2012). Collaborate with practitioners: but beware of collaborative research. *Journal of Management Inquiry*, 21(1), 14–28.

Kitagawa, F. (2014). Collaborative doctoral programmes. *Higher Education Quarterly*, 68(3), 328–47. https://doi.org/10.1111/hequ.12049

Lam, A. (2010). From 'ivory tower traditionalists' to 'entrepreneurial scientists'? Academic scientists in fuzzy university–industry boundaries. *Social Studies of Science*, 40(2), 307–40.

Larner, W., and Mayow, T. (2003). Strengthening communities through local partnerships: building a collaborative research project. *Social Policy Journal of New Zealand*, 20 (June), 119–33.

Peck, J. (1999). Editorial: grey geography? *Transactions of the Institute of British Geographers*, 24(2), 131–5.

Reid, L., and McCormick, A. (2010). Knowledge transfer at the research–policy interface: the geography postgraduates' experiences of collaborative studentships. *Journal of Geography in Higher Education*, 34(4), 529–39. https://doi.org/10.1080/03098260903548185

Robertson, M.J. (2019). *Power and Doctoral Supervision Teams: Developing Team Building Skills in Collaborative Doctoral Research*. Abingdon Routledge.

Thune, T. (2010). The training of 'triple helix workers'? Doctoral students in university–industry–government collaborations. *Minerva*, 48(4), 463–83.

13. Doing and making the most of PhD internships

Lauren Tuckerman

13.1 INTRODUCTION

PhD internships are opportunities for PhD researchers to put a hold on their studies (typically 3–6 months) to work with an organisation on a live project. This is usually in their second or third year. They happen across the academic disciplines and are often discussed in academic literature as a means for PhD researchers to build their CV and widen career opportunities (Jones and Warnock, 2015). Many PhD internships are funded (but not all), meaning that those researchers with an existing scholarship still get their stipend over the period of their internship. Internships for PhD students are available from across the research councils as well as sector and industry specific internships being available. Internships can be arranged by intermediary organisations (such as research councils' doctoral training partnerships (DTPs)). There are a few distinct benefits of seeking a PhD internship through an organising body such as the DTPs. Firstly, they have extensive experience of different types of internships and therefore they understand how to create successful internship opportunities. Secondly, they are there to support those involved in the internship should any challenges arise and thirdly they have a good awareness of funders' (such as UK Research and Innovation (UKRI)) require-ments and expectations of internships. In 2012, the Wilson Report (a review of industry and university collaboration undertaken for the UK Government) recommended that 'All full-time PhD students should have an opportunity to experience at least one 8 to 12 week internship during their period of study' (Wilson, 2012, p.8). This suggests that the value of a PhD internship is increasingly acknowledged by governments and, therefore, research funders and universities. Common motivations that PhD researchers might have for undertaking a PhD internship include:

1. To add to their CV
2. To network in policy, industry or government

3. To take a take a step away from their PhD and gain new perspectives
4. To develop and apply new skills.

The benefit of PhD internship programmes extends beyond the individual PhD researcher. The host organisation gains insights from an academic perspective. Those hosting PhD interns have suggested that they provide additional capacity to do research projects that needed focused attention outside of normal workloads. Universities also gain from the PhD internships. PhD researchers return with increased experience and new abilities to conduct research, which benefits not only their PhD but also any teaching they might also do, in that live examples can be used in teaching.

13.2 FINDING, CHOOSING AND APPLYING FOR PHD INTERNSHIPS

There are many routes to finding or establishing a PhD internship. Research councils, DTPs and industry associations often advertise PhD internships; they are also sometimes featured on academic job websites such as jobs.ac.uk. International organisations such as the International Labour Organization (ILO) and the Organisation for Economic Co-operation and Development (OECD) also host PhD interns. To take part in these programmes the PhD intern must be prepared to move to the host's country. This often involves costs associated with moving and sourcing short-term accommodation which can be challenging, although some DTPs (such as the Scottish Graduate School of Social Science) utilise a model which allows for funding relocation and caring responsibilities. However, the rewards of gaining an international perspective and profile could outweigh this. Universities' careers services are a good place to find out about PhD internships and they might be able to help prospective PhD interns find the right internship for them. If a prospective PhD intern is on a visa, they should check the visa regulations to see if they are allowed to undertake the PhD internship alongside or in addition to their studies. University departments and DTPs often organise coordinated internships across the public, private and third sectors. They work with the host organisation to create a project which the intern will work on. Pre-arranged internship programmes such as those organised by DTPs have distinct advantages and disadvantages.

DTPs encourage PhD researchers to undertake internships that do not relate specifically to their PhD topic. Often pre-arranged PhD internships will not relate specifically to the research a PhD researcher is undertaking as part of their PhD or be hosted by an organisation they might want to use in their PhD research. Pre-arranged internships can be advantageous as the projects are well defined and deliverable in the time frame. This does not mean that

PhD researchers cannot arrange their own internship with an organisation that relates to their PhD research, and could contribute data to their PhD data collection, perhaps through an ethnographic approach. This may not always be possible with internships and might require negotiation. For example, internships arranged through the Scottish Graduate School for Social Sciences with the Scottish Government have an agreement contract which states that 'at no time should this Internship be regarded as participant observation or action research' and 'the Intern is also reminded that absence of informed consent precludes any production of case studies, vignettes, narratives or other publications on the work of government' (Scottish Government, n.d.). However, this does not preclude the intern from producing journal articles related to the internship work as long as these are discussed with the Scottish Government and follow their procedures for approval. This is an issue worth being aware of, and a point of negotiation for interns and hosts.

Many PhD internship projects are advertised with a short description of the project and the expectations of the intern. It is worth considering not only the topic of the internships, but how the PhD researcher could address the need expressed in the advert. In some cases, a method or approach might be present in the internship advert. Whether it is or is not, it is important to consider how the internship might build the intern's knowledge not only of the topic of the internship but also how they could build their skills as a researcher. Perhaps they will need to use a method they have not used before, perhaps work with a group they are unfamiliar with and learn how best to communicate with them, these are all valuable skills for an intern to develop.

Applications for internships often rely only on a form and a CV, so speaking to someone in person, ideally over the phone, can really help to form a connection, which is important as the internships can be short and fast paced. Once the PhD researcher has been accepted as an intern, they can again request a call to discuss the details of the project such as prospective start dates, pay, office arrangements, security clearances if applicable and induction.

Top Tip

If the internship advert names a manager or sponsor, the prospective PhD intern could take the initiative by contacting them to express their interest. They could discuss the project, how it has developed and expectations (on both sides) of the internship. This allows them to frame their application in a way to suit the internship as well as making the application stand out; it shows that they are interested in the project, and proactive about seeking the opportunity.

Organisations with prior arranged and advertised PhD internships often have hosted interns before and are aware of what is achievable within the period of the internship. This means that both the intern and the host organisation have a good idea of what the project is, how it will be delivered and what the output of the project will be in advance. The host organisation will also be aware of the level of time and resource needed to support the intern and the project. This is important not only to the PhD intern's experience, but also to the success of the project. This might not be the case in situations where a PhD student seeks to organise their own industry internship, or where projects are expressed in vague terms. In those cases, the PhD student may have to spend additional time considering what can be developed and delivered within the negotiated time frames and communicate this with the industry partner. Jones and Warnock (2015) found similarly that in their pilot of three PhD internships:

> In one case where a more flexible approach was taken, both the student and the stakeholder commented that more could have been achieved during the internship had a more structured approach been adopted at the start. (p.221)

13.3   WHAT CAN BE EXPECTED FROM A PHD INTERNSHIP?

The range of activities that PhD interns can get involved in is broad as there are many different projects from numerous organisations, meaning they could be involved in quantitative work (for example, survey data analysis, mapping, applied sciences), qualitative work (interviews, focus groups, analysis of documents, deep diving into academic literature and reviews) or mixed methods using a combination of techniques. They might be asked to gather primary data, or might be involved in a secondary data analysis. It is important for PhD interns to understand what skills and abilities are needed to do the project and ask for help if they find a gap in their skillset. When considering a PhD internship it is useful for the PhD intern to know that there are parts of the project they are comfortable with to be able to hit the ground running, but they do not have to have experience or understanding of all areas. After all, PhD internships are a learning opportunity. It is worth considering the breadth of learning that can be achieved through a PhD internship; Jones and Warnock (2015) advocate for horizontal development through PhD internships. They describe this type of learning as being achieved through people moving between environments (such as the workplace, lab and policy office). This type of learning includes not only technical skills such as those associated with particular research methods, but also transferable skills where the intern is able to make connections between different environments (Jones and Warnock, 2015).

> **Top Tip**
>
> At the start of the internship, it is useful for PhD interns to try to identify areas they might need extra support with, and parts of the project they are comfortable with. Then they can be clear about what support they need to do the work. Remember that an internship is also a development opportunity and the intern should also get what they want out of it.

Internships usually involve working with people who are experts in their field of practice. This can be intimidating for PhD interns at first, but it is worth remembering that they are people too. PhD interns should remember to show them the respect they have earned, but not be afraid to ask questions. PhD interns are there to learn, as well as deliver a high quality project; they need to ask questions to do both.

> **Top Tip**
>
> PhD internships are also an opportunity to collaborate. PhDs are often quite solitary; this is a chance for the PhD intern to build skills in working collaboratively. An intern might feel like they should get their tasks, do the work and deliver an output, however, often *project impacts are strengthened by sharing thinking, work and raising questions along the way.* This allows the project to be co-produced and means that the intern can get buy-in from the people they are working with, who will take the project forward after the internship finishes.

The outputs and outcomes of a PhD internship should be very clear from the start. It could be a formal report, in which case the intern should be familiar with the templates, form and style of writing expected. It could be a presentation, so the intern needs to understand the audience and create accordingly. It might be a reflective piece on the experience or something less formal altogether. Having this information early on in the internship can make it easier for the PhD intern to work towards a defined goal.

So far the focus of this section has been on delivering a good project outcome during a PhD internship, however, the experience of a PhD internship should be wider than the project. This is an opportunity for PhD researchers to learn about the field and organisation in which they are working temporarily. Interns should ask their manager about other interesting opportunities and express possible areas they are interested in. They should pay close attention to internal communications such as the intranet and email mailouts to see if there are events, meetings or other opportunities they would like to get involved in. They can try to network in other areas; for example, in large organisations such as government bodies, there might be other PhD interns who they can meet, and find out about their internships and PhDs. Interns can have conversations with those around them to find out how others' careers have developed. This is particularly useful if the PhD intern is thinking about a career in industry after their PhD. If you are interested in the experience of a PhD intern, the reflections from an intern highlighted in Box 13.1 provide some useful insights about what to think about and expect to make sure the intern gets the most from the experience.

BOX 13.1 REFLECTIONS FROM THE INTERN

My internship project was entitled 'Improving approaches to consultation in Scottish Government'. It was organised by the Scottish Graduate School for Social Sciences (a DTP) and hosted by the Scottish Government for three months. I felt this project would provide me with an overview of how the perspectives of the public were integrated into the policymaking process. My thesis explored knowledge management in the third sector. Although the internship was not related to this, I found it interesting to observe and understand the role of the third sector in consultation processes. I undertook my internship early in my second year of my PhD and I think this timing worked well. I had not yet started data collection, therefore I did not have to pause building a relationship with my participants.

As a PhD intern I collated and reviewed existing materials and guidance on consultation, and edited, improved and further developed them to create a report with recommendations for Scottish Government policymakers. The outputs from the project aimed to reflect best practice and literature, and meet the legal requirements of Scottish Government consultations. My sponsor at the Scottish Government and I worked together on a research design and plan and sent this to the consultation research group. The research group provided feedback on the research plan, and then provided possible contacts for me to follow up with.

We decided to undertake a review of academic literature as well as a review of internal documents related to how Scottish Government do consultations. Primary data collection included interviews with research analysts, policymakers as well as the digital engagement team. We also conducted a workshop with similar participants. I wrote a report on my findings, presented them at the consultation research group and created a decision tree to be hosted on the intranet.

During my PhD internship, my sponsor highlighted opportunities for me to engage in ongoing work outside of my PhD internship which he felt would be of value to my development and of interest to me. I also met with other PhD interns and people who had previously been interns and had then started working as research analysts at the Scottish Government.

For me as a researcher, this experience opened my eyes to how policymaking worked within the Scottish Government. It broadened my experience of research and I began to think about my own research from the perspective of policymaking, and the scale of considerations in policymaking. The specific nature of the project I was involved in allowed me to engage across policy areas and in this way I developed a broad overview of policymaking processes and consultation processes more specifically.

During this period I gained wider perspective, understanding and experience and added to my ability to communicate my PhD topic and frame findings in a policy relevant way. I believe that having policy experience and impact on my CV helped me when looking for postdoctoral positions. My current role with the Innovation Caucus involves close engagement with policymakers and senior civil servants.

It is important for a prospective PhD intern to get their PhD supervisory team on board with the internship, as in most cases they will have to formally support an application and the break from studies. PhD supervisors should understand that the intern will be working full time on another project for the period of the internship, and therefore will not be working on their PhD. Supervisors may have concerns about the PhD researcher losing momentum with their PhD project, so it is important that the PhD researcher expresses to the supervisors how they think it will benefit them and the overall PhD thesis. Emphasis could be on increased productivity after the internship, an ability to see the bigger picture and possible future collaborations. It is helpful to show that the timing of the PhD internship has been thought through. Creating a project plan for the timings of a PhD project is useful, and showing how the internship fits within that is a convincing way of reassuring supervisors. Taking space out of a PhD might be a concern to the PhD researcher too, however, it is worth remembering that time away from a PhD can allow a return to the PhD with renewed energy and perspective.

13.4   WHAT ARE THE OUTCOMES OF A PHD INTERNSHIP?

While conducting a PhD internship, it is worth keeping in mind what change is the internship there to create? How will the intern's work have some kind of impact? It is also important to remember that the organisations that typically host interns are likely to be complex, and that change might not happen straight away, or at all. That does not mean the intern's work has not been valuable. The intern's time with the organisation is limited. Therefore it is unlikely that they will see impact during their internship period. However, thinking about the change or difference the intern's work might make, it can allow it to be communicated clearly, and be realistic to what can be achieved.

It can also be useful for the PhD intern to reflect on what difference the internship has made to them as a researcher. It can open their eyes to a new field, and broaden their experience of research. It can make them think about how their PhD research is or can be made relevant to practice and policy. Making research impactful is likely to be important to their future career as a researcher, therefore this is a valuable first step for PhD researchers in understanding how that can be achieved. It will also help them understand how to plan and deliver a short-term project, and can provide them with examples to discuss in job applications and interviews. It is useful to remember and understand that the work of a PhD intern has benefits to the organisations that host them, as highlighted in Box 13.2.

BOX 13.2 HOST'S PERSPECTIVE

The Scottish Government decided to create an internship on the project subject at a research group meeting on consultations. The consultation research group is made up of social researchers within the Scottish Government and decided that there was a need for a PhD intern. From the Scottish Government perspective, consulting with stakeholders and the public is a key part of government policymaking. We publish hundreds of documents every year, from highly technical consultations on planning law, to high level consultations on contentious issues such as land reform, fracking or same-sex marriage. Views are incredibly important to policymakers as they develop their policies or legislation but the consultation process is not easy to get right. It is important to the Scottish Government that the consultation process is, and is seen as, appropriate, fair and effective without being burdensome on stakeholders. Prior to the internship project commencing, guidance on consultation did exist in Scottish Government but was outdated and did not match the technical digital advancements nor the spirit of true participation required within the Scottish approach to policymaking, which emphasises co-production and collaborative approaches to policymaking (Cairney et al., 2016; Scottish Government, 2018). The internship was tightly bound to understanding best practices from an academic and practice perspective on how online, survey-based consultation should be conducted. This would then be used to inform an update of the Scottish Government's internal consultation guidelines. This information was made clear from the internship advertisement.

We wanted our consultation guidance to have the same values as the public policies we create, and therefore it was important that we allow those involved in consultation to express what they thought the consultation guidance should include. The idea for the internship project came out of the consultation research group, and therefore it was important that they fed into the development of the research design and plan for the internship. Engagement with the social researchers and policymakers involved in creating consultations allowed the guidance to be more co-produced. It brought together experience from cross-policy areas, which meant that learning from different perspectives were reflected in the report recommendations.

Conducting a PhD internship can make the PhD researcher stand out to future employers. If they are intending on getting a job in industry after their PhD, it provides invaluable real-life experience for them to draw upon. It also shows initiative and supports their claim that they want to work in industry and demonstrates that they understand the demands of industry research. If they intend to work in academia, it is worth thinking about the impact agenda. Since the 1980s, in the UK, there has been a movement towards ensuring outputs from public funding were closely related to the needs of those in industry and policy (Martin, 2011). Therefore researchers in designing projects must consider not only how to contribute to knowledge, but also the societal impact of their contribution (D'Este et al., 2018). Undertaking a PhD internship can show the PhD intern's interest in this area to future academic employers, it can give them insight into how research can impact industry and policy and help them consider impact in future funding applications. PhD researchers can expand their network during their PhD internship and it could be that in the future they can call on those they meet to be collaborators in future research projects, as well as possible participants. Overall, the advantages to the learning, careers and profile of a researcher can be improved by taking part in a PhD internship and it can be the first step in becoming an 'engaged academic'.

ACKNOWLEDGEMENTS

The author gratefully appreciates the feedback she received from those involved in the internship programme, namely Ben Cavanaugh and Liz Hawkins from the Scottish Government and Professor Mhairi Mackenzie from the Scottish Graduate School Social Sciences: Doctoral Training Partnership.

REFERENCES

Cairney, P., Russell, S. and St Denny, E., 2016. The 'Scottish approach' to policy and policymaking: what issues are territorial and what are universal? *Policy & Politics*, 44(3), 333–50, https://doi.org/10.1332/030557315X14353331264538

D'Este, P., Ramos-Vielba, I., Woolley, R. and Amara, N., 2018. How do researchers generate scientific and societal impacts? Toward an analytical and operational framework. *Science and Public Policy*, 45(6), 752–63, https://doi.org/10.1093/scipol/scy023

Jones, H.M., and Warnock, L.J., 2015. When a PhD is not enough: a case study of a UK internship programme to enhance the employability of doctoral researchers. *Higher Education, Skills and Work-Based Learning*, 5(3), 212–27, http://dx.doi.org.sheffield.idm.oclc.org/10.1108/HESWBL-05-2014-0013

Martin, B.R., 2011. The Research Excellence Framework and the 'impact agenda': are we creating a Frankenstein monster? *Research Evaluation*, 20(3), 247–54, https://doi. org/10.3152/095820211X13118583635693

Scottish Government, n.d. Internship Contract. Within the Author's records.

Scottish Government, 2018. PhD Internship Advert. Within the Author's records.

Wilson, T., 2012. A review of business–university collaboration. Accessed 13 July 2020 at https://assets.publishing.service.gov.uk/government/uploads/system/uploads/attachment_data/file/32383/12-610-wilson-review-business-university-collaboration.pdf

14. Enabling collaboration and building capacity through research networks

Phil Wallace, Heidi Hinder, Adam Luqmani and Lisa Hanselmann

14.1 INTRODUCTION

Conducting research that can meaningfully impact on complex policy issues increasingly requires convening and managing a wide network of relationships across diverse disciplines, sectors and geographies. This chapter is about some of the 'nuts and bolts' behind building an impactful network as part of a research grant. Although there are no 'off the shelf' models, given the wide-ranging contexts in which research takes place, there is a growing understanding of the different roles, responsibilities and activities that make up impactful collaborative networks within academic grants. Key players in the core team of a modern collaborative research grant not only include the academic investigators, but also often members of a growing body of specialist professional services colleagues who have the skills to help manage complex networks and span boundaries.

In the spirit of collaboration, the authors have come together from different backgrounds, as funders and project/network managers, to offer reflections based on their experience of working in, and/or supporting, a range of collaborative network initiatives to promote knowledge exchange, collaboration and capacity building. This chapter sets out key thoughts and reflections on what we wish we knew about supporting and delivering research networks when we began working in and with them!

14.2 WHY NETWORKS?

Driven by a range of institutional, cultural and economic factors, research continues to move away from the 'ivory tower' in what Flinders et al. (2016) have called the 'collaborative shift' in academia. Funders such as UK Research and

Innovation (UKRI) can be seen as part of this drive, with collaboration placed at the heart of UKRI's Corporate Plan:

> Our mission is to convene, catalyse and invest in close collaboration with others to build a thriving inclusive research and innovation system that connects discovery to prosperity and public good. (UKRI, 2020, p. 6)

Building and managing networks has become a key component of many research grants, usually with the aim of facilitating greater collaboration between academics, policymakers and practitioners via cross-cutting activities that are typically national or international in reach. For policymakers, interacting with a research network has a number of advantages over interacting with individual academics or, in some cases, individual institutions. These include, but are not limited to:

- Economies of scale. Accessing a breadth of expertise, usually from across multiple institutions and disciplines via one contact point, can be a more efficient use of time (see also Chapter 8 for further practical examples).
- Legitimacy. The wider/deeper expertise of a network (different perspectives/regional and sectoral knowledge) can be more persuasive when it comes to providing evidence for policymaking.
- Professional infrastructure. A network's infrastructure can provide capacity to support effective communication and wider engagement through events, which can be difficult for an individual researcher to manage (more on this later).

For researchers, there are a number of benefits to being part of or interacting with a network, such as:

- Facilitating new connections and wider personal networks, particularly outside of academia.
- Access to dedicated professional support infrastructure. This can offer design support, media contacts, stakeholder relationship management and event support to disseminate research to a much wider audience. Our experience suggests that academics often do not have access to sufficient central communications support to enable the fast turnaround times required in a policy engagement environment.
- Providing a springboard for new ideas and support for promising new collaborations. Often early stage research can be supported, which is unlikely to receive traditional research grant support. Building in small scale early stage research and collaboration support is key when developing new networks and relationships.

- Early career researchers (ECRs) are able to lead projects. Networks can provide infrastructure for small awards enabling ECRs to build their capacity by providing vital experience and career development. Often mentorship is also available from the broader network.
- Co-produced research in a network can carry greater legitimacy and smooth the track towards impact due to policymakers already having a level of involvement in the process.

There are clearly multiple benefits to embedding some form of network within research and knowledge exchange endeavours. However, particularly for larger research grants with multiple deliverables, the prospect of managing the complex and numerous stakeholder interactions entailed in a network can be a daunting one. In the next section, we move from the 'why' of a network to the 'how', providing some practical tips and reflections which will hopefully simplify the process for anyone wishing to build or engage with a network in some way.

14.3   HOW TO PROMOTE COLLABORATION AND BUILD CAPACITY THROUGH A NETWORK

As we move to look at some of the 'nuts and bolts' of convening a network, enabling collaboration and building capacity, we start with a brief look at some of the key roles in a collaborative research network focused policy on impact. Space precludes a comprehensive analysis (Facer and Enright's (2016) typology of roles derived from their work on community–university partnerships is useful here), so we focus on the roles of Director/Co-Director, Network Members/Co-Investigators, Strategic Advisory Board and core 'professional services' roles. In the second half, in keeping with the practical focus of this chapter, we share some of the practicalities of good communications and event management – in our experience some of the greatest ways to facilitate policy impact within a research network.

14.3.1   Direction for the Network

At a meeting of Directors and Coordinators of Networks funded by the Engineering and Physical Sciences Research Council which focused on network good practice, attendees reflected: 'An enthusiastic administrator or coordinator was considered to be a critical success factor as a dynamic and motivational individual would "drive" the network and make things happen. The coordinator may be a Principal Investigator' (EPSRC, 2021). It is suggested that shared leadership, usually through a Co-Director model, can also provide the necessary drive while bringing complementary skills, provided the division of responsibilities is carefully considered at the outset and reviewed as time progresses. An existing network of relationships with relevant stakeholders and a strong expertise in the field will be important catalysts to draw in further collaborators and build capacity. The Director role provides oversight of the network work programme and deliverables, while also acting as an important figurehead externally. However, given network leadership is often only a portion of the Director's time, it is vital to have the support and shared leadership stemming from an inclusive and engaged team.

14.3.2   Convening Academic Network Members

As mentioned in the 'why?' of a network, a key strength is in their ability to assemble a diverse team of multidisciplinary academic talent, a fusion that can create innovative new ways to tackle complex policy problems. This may be in a formal manner as research Co-Investigators, or through more informal ways of associating with the network. As well as different disciplinary perspectives, a diversity of network members can bring different national and regional perspectives, helping to confer greater legitimacy to research outcomes particularly in the context of modern multilayered policymaking. Professor James Wilsdon, Director of the Economic and Social Research Council's first Network Plus investment (the Nexus Network, launched in 2014) remarked that the team's diversity enabled 'a genuine breadth of perspective to the framing and design of the network's activities, and avoid either the appearance or actuality of being captured or overly aligned to particular perspectives' (Wilsdon, 2018, p. 9). Providing some defined responsibilities, either thematic by research expertise, by workstream or through leadership of a defined area, is an important step in providing organisation and milestones to maintain engagement. Although members may lead on one workstream/work package/ module, the beauty of a network approach is that they can still provide advice and insights on other areas of work.

The creation and protection of regular communications processes and channels for network members can easily be neglected amid time pressures, but scheduling monthly virtual meetings for four months in advance, combined with a regular internal members email update, are underrated and important means of maintaining network health (more on this in the communications tips below). A surefire way of building the capacity of future policy-engaged researchers is to build ECR development into the core of your collaborative research work programme. A good place to start is by assigning one of your Co-Investigators or network members leadership responsibility for ECR development. In our experience multidisciplinary and multi-institution networks can be particularly well placed (through scale and breadth) to facilitate the kind of seed funding and sandpit activities that fosters innovative collaborative research and collaborations for a comparatively small investment of time and resource.

14.3.3   Running a Network's Advisory Board

Bringing together a formal group of advisers tasked with maintaining a strategic overview of the project, while providing guidance, expertise and a wide network of contacts, can be incredibly valuable to a research network. Typically an 'Advisory Board' or 'Strategy Group' will consist of 10–20 stakeholders representing the worlds of policy (this could be local, national and/or international if possible, depending on the focus of the network), academia and, depending on the network's focus, could include representatives of other important stakeholder groups such as business or third sector organisations.

The number of members should be large enough to ensure critical mass at meetings in the event of some inevitable diary conflicts. The frequency of the advisory group's meetings will depend on factors such as the length of the collaborative research project, the level of investment and the seniority of the group. In our experience, for a three to four year research network, two meetings a year among senior members of an advisory group can ensure engaging meetings which are a good use of participants' time, when supplemented by additional briefings and communications during the year. For a shorter network-based research grant, quarterly meetings ensured strategic guidance could keep pace with the packed timetable of activity.

Plan well ahead (ideally 8–12 months), starting with the Chair's availability to secure time in busy calendars. Build a range of additional events around each Advisory Board meeting if possible – when bringing members together for a meeting in the morning, why not invite policymakers to participate in a roundtable in the afternoon? In our experience, with plenty of advance planning and some opportunism, an Advisory Board meeting can be combined with a network conference, a policymakers' roundtable and an ECR training event! With their time used constructively and considerately, strategic advisers will be a vital asset for any network.

14.3.4   Network Management

As mentioned previously, running a successful collaborative research network takes shared leadership at multiple levels, and often a key player in this, working closely with the Director/Co-Director, is a Network Manager/Project Manager position. For example, many Network Plus research grants involve administering their own innovative small to medium-sized grant funding competitions, which have a fantastic potential for launching new collaborations, but can also create a significant administrative burden even with the support of central finance and research support functions of host institutions. A Network Manager can bring the organisational skills to realise the full potential of a busy network's work programme, while also helping to span boundaries, both with internal functions and external stakeholders. Often the Network Manager is the key point of contact for the funders for day-to-day activities, helping to maintain a productive working relationship throughout the life of the network. Responsibilities can vary greatly, depending on the network's objectives, and whether the team also includes separate specialist communications/impact/events support. Though demanding and usually entailing a breadth of responsibilities, these Network Management roles can be exciting opportunities for the growing cadre of individuals who want to work at the boundaries of research and policy.

14.3.5   Communications and Impact Management

Alongside a Network Manager or Project Manager, a professional Communications Officer and/or Impact/Knowledge Exchange Officer can be an excellent investment. Modern research engagement is built on multiple communication channels including newsletters, Twitter and LinkedIn. These channels can have high impact, but are also highly time-consuming to get right. While there may be some resources available centrally within institutions, it is unlikely to be able to keep up with the demands of a large and fast-moving collaborative research network. Good design skills can go a long way in helping to catch the attention of stakeholders and build a level of brand recognition to help you stand out. Of equal importance in a diverse team of Co-Investigators, stakeholders and strategic advisers is your internal communication. Management of the schedule of meetings with Co-Investigators, Advisory Board members and funders, including administration around agendas and briefing notes, is a key responsibility that should be clearly assigned within the core team, which might include a Network Manager, Communications Officer and Director. The good news is that mass adoption of virtual meeting technologies since the start of the Covid-19 pandemic makes this much easier, at least for your high frequency shorter meetings with core academic members.

Communications and impact roles in this context, as well as to some extent the Network Manager role, are necessarily multifaceted. They are part communications, part content creation, part knowledge exchange, part events management, part relationship management – and indeed this variety can be part of their appeal – but be careful not to expect excellence in every area all at once and do expect a learning curve as the individual gets to grips with the research that they are communicating (which may be your lifelong work!). A good induction, together with regular meetings, is a worthwhile time investment.

Events are a valuable medium to enable collaboration and build capacity through a network, but can require a lot of preparation to execute successfully. If your network is undertaking a large number of events, perhaps with different academic members leading each, try and create checklists to facilitate continuity and smooth running across the network. The template should provide a checklist of pre-event initial requirements to discuss with the local member/stakeholder leading the event. This is also a helpful way to ensure actions such as collecting relevant impact data (such as pre-/post event evaluations) are completed in line with your various reporting commitments. Once you have managed to secure fantastic speakers, a common error is to then not prepare them adequately. Consider creating a briefing document template which can then be edited with specific guidance for each speaker based on the requirements of the event – ensure to provide a brief background to the network, the audience, the practicalities such as timings, as well as thorough guidance on their role at the event. If holding a network event in person, the budget spent on refreshments is almost always a worthwhile investment! Research outputs may be shared from the presenters' stand, but the vital connections that see knowledge adopted might be made by the coffee table. With the greater adoption of virtual events, all networks will need to reflect on the right blend of in-person and virtual, being mindful of accessibility, cost and what will produce the greatest engagement and impact.

Top Tips for Enabling Collaboration and Building Capacity Through Research Networks

- Build your communications strategy on a strong foundation of internal communications. Efficient management of short monthly meetings between your core members with a basic agenda circulated in advance, supplemented by a fortnightly internal round-up email of the network's activity, will go a long way to building internal capacity, promoting cross-pollination of ideas and avoiding misunderstandings.
- If your institution uses Customer Relationship Management software, which is increasingly available if requested, this can help with impact reporting requirements and also to ensure that key relationships are not lost when staff in your team transition.
- Go the extra mile: personalise your communications with stakeholders wherever possible. For example, if using a newsletter, why not send a personal email to every new sign-up and see if there are any particular research insights that you can point them to or connections that you can make for them? You would be amazed at the conversations and lasting relationships that can flow from this proactive approach.

14.4   CONCLUSION

Collaborative research networks can be a powerful model for co-producing and sharing relevant and impactful research, as many of the chapters in this book are testament to. Though a network's formal lifespan may be tied to the relatively short time frame of a research grant, they can leave a legacy of interconnections and valuable relationships beyond just the tangible research outputs that are initially more measurable. Ensuring that the whole is greater than the sum of its parts, and navigating a complex and shifting policy landscape, requires shared leadership at multiple levels. Given the number of stakeholders involved, networks can feel a little messy at first, but it is hoped that some of the practical guidance provided here can give you a head start to achieving high levels of policy impact. Good luck!

REFERENCES

EPSRC (2021) *Network Grants: Guide to Best Practice*. Accessed 2 September 2021 at https://www.ukri.org/councils/epsrc/guidance-for-applicants/types-of-funding-we -offer/network-grants/guide-to-best-practice/#contents-list

Facer, K., and Enright, B. (2016) Creating living knowledge: The Connected Communities programme, community-university partnerships and the participatory turn in the production of knowledge. Arts and Humanities Research Council. Accessed 15 September 2021 at https://research-information.bris.ac.uk/ ws/portalfiles/portal/75082783/FINAL_FINAL_CC_Creating_Living_Knowledge _Report.pdf

Flinders, M., Wood, M., and Cunningham, M. (2016) The politics of co-production: Risks, limits and pollution. *Evidence and Policy* 12(2): 261–79.

Godsell, J., Kaya, L., Glass, J., Plante, D., Hanselmann, L., and McGilvray, J. (2020) Guide: Creating impact from research. Transforming Construction Network Plus. Accessed 2 September 2021 at https://www.ucl.ac.uk/bartlett/construction/sites/ bartlett/files/guide_-_creating_impact_from_research.pdf

UKRI (2020) *Corporate Plan 2020–2021*. Accessed 2 September 2021 at https://www. ukri.org/wp-content/uploads/2020/10/UKRI-091020-CorporatePlan2020-21.pdf

Wilsdon, J. (2018) ESRC Research Network Plus directors final report, p. 29. Accessed 13 August 2021 at https://www.researchgate.net/publication/330384865_ESRC _Research_Network_Plus_Directors_Final_Report

15. Mission research: experiences from participation in OECD entrepreneurship policy research projects

Helen Lawton Smith

15.1 INTRODUCTION

The mission research discussed in this contribution involves short (but intensive) regional research projects conducted by international policy making organisations on behalf of regional or national governments. It focuses on entrepreneurship policy research undertaken by the Organisation for Economic Co-operation and Development (OECD), often involving academics in the research teams. The process involved in these research missions is that a national or regional government has requested the OECD to prepare a report to assess and advise on current policy in the region. The OECD organises study missions involving an international team of approximately two to five OECD staff members and/or external experts (usually academics). The team interviews local and national stakeholders – policy makers, firms, universities and science parks, etc. Each team member then writes a theoretically and empirically informed chapter on a policy theme, for example on supporting start-ups, scale-ups or clusters in the region. Each chapter includes recommendations and best practice policy models from other countries. The main lines of the discussion and recommendations across the chapters are coordinated by the OECD team manager and a draft report is discussed by stakeholders from the region at a workshop and commented on by regional or national government authorities. The combination of data, insights from interviews and the analysis and recommendations is used to develop more effective policies. Mission research is deemed necessary in order to provide independent advice so that regional policy interventions can better complement national policies. Often this is the focus of mission research.

Missions are always theoretically informed. In recent missions, the entrepreneurial ecosystems framework (Stam, 2015) has been employed and is discussed here. This has been joined by the industry path transition framework proposed by Grillitsch, Asheim and Trippl (2018). As the two approaches target different aspects of regional development, a holistic, context sensitive approach to policy formulation is developed.

15.2   CONTEXT OF OECD MISSIONS

The starting point is the assumption that regions are an appropriate level of delivery for such policies. This helps to avoid bias towards the more prosperous areas and identifies ways in which entrepreneurship and innovation policy can best exploit local clusters.

The missions are led by the OECD secretariat but, where appropriate, academic experts take part, each with a specific area of policy to address. Missions are approximately week-long visits to the region; interviews with key national and regional stakeholders are followed by drafts of reports for comment by the regional or national government.

Each expert includes in the report recommendations and best practice policy models from other countries. It is the combination of use of data, insights from the interviews and the subsequent recommendations that supports the region to develop more effective policies. At the end of the process, there is a validation workshop conducted by the OECD and then the report is finalised. Before the mission there may be fact-finding questionnaires, local diagnostic work and other workshops.

One of the focus areas of a mission is fostering innovative start-ups and scale-ups which drive innovation, productivity and job creation. Therefore a starting point is existing evidence on scale-ups and high growth firms' profiles and performance. Other themes include the role of major firms and higher education institutions (HEIs) in stimulating entrepreneurship and innovation and industrial diversification.

This chapter is written from the personal perspective of an academic expert, who has taken part in a number of missions covering various policy aspects. For example, in Małopolskie in Poland, my theme was Scale-ups and High Growth Firms and how scale-ups in emerging sectors contribute to industrial diversification. The context was the region's approach to the application of the EU's smart specialisation strategy (S3). In Thailand, my focus was on the local entrepreneurial ecosystem in two regions in Northern Thailand. There the policy priority was to build a regional innovation cluster, nested within a national cluster, in the advanced agriculture and biotechnology and food for the future sectors, and develop the capacities of small and medium-sized enterprises (SMEs) and innovative start-ups and scale-ups to integrate research-based knowledge in new products for growing international markets (OECD, 2021).

Some of the general weaknesses in regional policies often identified by missions include:

- Not enough *targeting* of entrepreneurs and SMEs with most economic impact (survivable, ambitious)
- Not enough attention to the impact of *institutional conditions and main-stream policies* as opposed to dedicated programmes
- A need for greater focus on a logic of *market failure and evaluation* evidence
- Policy designed piecewise as individual programmes and not as *holistic packages and ecosystems*
- Insufficient attention to *megatrends* (in particular digitalisation, greening)
- Not securing *equal opportunities* in entrepreneurship
- Not addressing potential to address *spatial disparities*
- *Uneven quality of policy* across regions in terms of strategy and implementation.

Key messages are that the regional 'business environment' – local HEIs, finance, skills, entrepreneurial culture, etc. – has clear impact on the rate of innovative start-ups and scale-ups. Policy interventions in regions can complement national-level policies in supporting innovative start-ups and scale-ups. Priorities include access to equity finance, access to knowledge exchange and entrepreneurial skills and competences. Universities are always a focus of attention, especially the extent of their roles in supplying knowledge and skills to local companies through their teaching and outreach activities.

The purpose of employing the 'entrepreneurial ecosystem' framework is twofold: to identify the main enablers and bottlenecks of the regional entrepreneurial ecosystem, and to consider the types of policy interventions needed to strengthen regional entrepreneurial ecosystems. The concept is defined as, 'A *set* of *interdependent* actors and factors coordinated in such a way that they enable *productive* entrepreneurship within a particular territory' (Stam and van de Ven, 2021, p. 809; emphasis added). The entrepreneurial ecosystems framework comprises ten ecosystem elements, as shown in Figure 15.1, that affect the levels of entrepreneurial activity and see value created through higher levels of productivity, income and employment.

The framework conditions characterise the underlying context in which the ecosystem exists and comprises four elements. They are: (1) *Formal institutions* (i.e. quality government with low levels of corruption, and an entrepreneurship friendly regulatory framework); (2) *Entrepreneurial culture* (i.e. societal attitude and acceptance towards entrepreneurship); (3) *Physical infrastructure* (i.e. road, rail, air and broadband connections giving access to customers, suppliers, collaborators, etc.); and (4) *Demand* (i.e. strong poten-

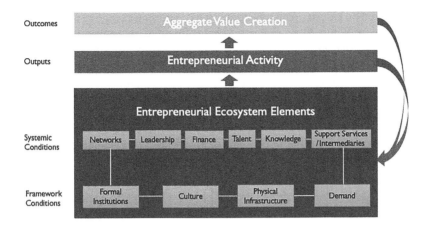

Source: Adapted from Stam (2015).

Figure 15.1   Entrepreneurial ecosystem elements

tial market demand, with good access to customers in domestic and foreign markets). Further to the framework conditions the presence and congruence of the systemic conditions are critical to the success of an entrepreneurial ecosystem.

The six systemic conditions are: (1) *Networks* (i.e. mechanisms of sharing information and knowledge among entrepreneurs, investors, advisors, mentors and supporters and through which they can connect); (2) *Leadership* (i.e. the group are visible, accessible and committed to the entrepreneurial growth of the place/region); (3) *Finance* (i.e. access to investors with entrepreneurial knowledge and experience); (4) *Talent* (i.e. the presence of skilled and diverse labour); (5) *Knowledge* (i.e. access to knowledge from both public and private organisations); and (6) *Intermediaries* (i.e. business support services for entrepreneurs).

The framework is useful in OECD missions in particular as it focuses on start-ups as regional drivers, identifies bottlenecks to be addressed, enables a quantitative approach (through data dashboards) and facilitates discussion among stakeholders. It is a holistic policy approach with packages of actions which can create opportunities for guiding learning from effective policy in similar regions.

In practice on a mission it can be difficult to remain strictly within the expressed policy demand. There may be a need to cover additional issues such as SME innovation, skills development and knowledge exchange, which may become evident as the research progresses. Similarly, the entrepreneurial eco-systems model is essentially static in its approach, so additional analysis might be required on industry path transition – what is driving change and how policy is positioned within those changes. Other difficulties encountered are that the spatial scale of economic interactions may not precisely match the area of the study set out with the government authorities at the outset, requiring open borders for the research, and that the regional ecosystem may differ by sector. The concept lacks explanation of the interdependence of the different pillars. It is therefore difficult to disentangle which parts of the ecosystem drive perfor-mance, and hence to identify and test a key policy lever. In the interviews and report preparation we aim to fill some of these gaps to provide the most useful information possible to the regions.

15.3   EXPERIENCE OF BEING ON A MISSION

Prior to the visit, a local diagnostic report is prepared to provide basic infor-mation and data on framework conditions and policies in the region. This is designed to help each team member with data and information which will inform the questions for their brief. Before the mission, each team member has written a preliminary two-page outline of the proposed content of their chapter. This has to be approved by the project manager. This sets out the key themes to be addressed on the mission. This is often redrafted following feedback. For most missions, the team flies out the day before. We stay in hotels that either offer meeting facilities or are close to meeting venues. We gather at breakfast for travel stories about lost luggage, delayed flights and passport queues.

On the first day, the meetings often start with discussions between the team and the OECD leader and the regional and national government authorities on the context and objectives for the project. At the early meetings the whole team is present. Each expert is keen that their particular angle is addressed. This is where it gets challenging – we compete to make sure that we do not miss out on vital information that will inform thinking and questioning for the rest of the visit. We also support each other by filling in the gaps if someone has misheard something. It is a true collaborative experience. It is an intense experience – like being on *Dancing with the Stars* we make friends for life.

The end of each day is a debriefing with the OECD leader. At this meeting we summarise our preliminary thoughts about the key messages that came out of the meetings and where we need to push harder to get the right kind of insights. We reflect on our own themes and on each other's. This is followed (eventually) by dinner where the conversations continue and team building develops in a social environment.

An example of the type of themes covered is outlined in Box 15.1, which outlines the sessions for day 1 of the Northern Thailand entrepreneurial ecosystems project. This shows the themes explored and the organisations represented at national level, before setting off to the regions. Each session listed below lasted an hour and a half and representatives from organisations ranged from executive level (vice presidents and directors) to policy analysts.

BOX 15.1   DAY 1 PROGRAMME TOPICS AND REPRESENTATIVES, THAILAND

Briefing on BIO-Tech in Thailand and the Industry Technical Assistance Programme (ITAP) – National Science and Technology Development Agency, Food, Agriculture, and Health Industry Innovation Technology Assistance Program (ITAP), Industrial Technology Development Division

Promotion of start-ups in life sciences industry – Thailand Center of Excellence for Life Sciences (TCELS), Department of Industry and Investment Strategy

Macro policies on BIO economy in Thailand and investment promotion policy for BIO-Tech – Office of National Economic and Social Development Council, The Board of Investment of Thailand

National cluster policies/strategies, Thailand 4.0, Programme for Enhancing Regional Integrated SME Promotion (RISMEP)/Macro policies of BIO-Tech of Thailand – Department of Industrial Promotion (DIP), Ministry of Industry, OSMEP, Office of Higher Education Science Research and Innovation Policy Council

Incubation system to support BIO-Tech – National Science and Technology Development Agency

Source: Adapted from Potter (2019).

On subsequent days the team meets a range of local stakeholders. These can be in science parks, government offices and factories. For some meetings, the team stays together if it is someone with interest to all. Often the experts are split into two teams with parallel interviews so that different perspectives can be covered simultaneously. In all cases we meet the most inspirational local actors.

The days are long. Sometimes, as in Thailand, the team moves locations. We moved by air from Bangkok to Chiang Mai on Tuesday and to Chiang Rai – by bus – on Thursday.

It is vital at every meeting to ask for any documentation that is available to help us write the report. These can take the form of official reports, PowerPoint presentations, minutes of meetings, etc. Suitcases are always heavier on the way back than on the way out.

One of the challenges is listening to a translation into English on head-phones. Often the translator goes very fast, making it hard to take notes. One of the best things about the process is that we get to know our translators and local organisers.

There is always a problem of insufficient or missing data and information. This can be simple things such as the number of firms in a sector or the targets for labour market skilling policies. The conceptual framework helps identify potential areas of weakness for entrepreneurship and innovation development in the regions studied. For example, the Stam (2015) framework highlights the role of entrepreneurial leadership in a region, which can be offered by engaged serial entrepreneurs or large anchor firms. These are not always present. In Chiang Mai and Chiang Rai there was only one large domestic firm and that had only just started doing R&D. In Małopolskie the major firms were foreign and did not engage strongly in the local ecosystem.

The framework also highlights the role of networking. This was limited in Małopolskie because of a lack of trust between local firms. In Chiang Mai and Chiang Rai, one of the challenges was to get local networking better organised, for example in biotech and high level agriculture. On completion of the visit, a deadline is set for the first draft report. Challenges in producing the document include finding relevant best practice models and writing recommendations that are specific and actionable. We use local exemplars to make points, for example successful scale-ups or good examples of networking organisations. The hardest part is making appropriate policy recommendations that add value. It is too easy to repeat what has been said numerous times before in other contexts.

An example of the application of the Stam (2015) entrepreneurial ecosystems framework is that of the Małopolskie region of Poland. The framework is used to show the strengths of the regional entrepreneurial ecosystem (Table 15.1).

Best practice policy models follow the same format: description of the approach, what works in this case, what were the challenges and how they were overcome, and relevance to the context. The key is to match the applicability and feasibility to a different context. The report itself undergoes at least two reiterations following feedback on drafts from the OECD and the government authorities.

The drafts require intensive input. In some cases this requires extensive follow-up emails and phone conversations with relevant policy makers and experts. For Małopolskie, I was indebted to a large number of organisations

Table 15.1   The Małopolskie entrepreneurial ecosystem

	Małopolskie
Business	Strong start-up community
	Strong policy support for start-ups (local Entrepreneurship Week, Innovation Voucher initiative, ongoing regulatory burden reduction, etc.)
Innovation	Strong public and private R&D expenditures and outputs
Education	31 HEIs and large numbers of students, 13 university incubators
Governance	Clusters supporting strategically relevant sectors, such as video games, information technology, cyber security and outsourcing

Source: Potter and Lawton Smith (2019).

such as business networks and consultants who provided me with data and insights. For the Chiang Rai and Chiang Mai region, there had to be follow-up to get promised reports and data, as well as searches for evidence to support the policy recommendations.

15.4   REFLECTIONS ON THE PROCESS

From my experience of OECD mission research projects, there are three core reflections that can apply to approaching mission research more generally and six top tips. Firstly, it is important to recognise national and local sensitivities, which can be cultural, political or both. For example, this might be related to local customs when greeting people (as in Thailand) or respecting the systems of governance (as in Poland). It is also important to then do some homework in advance (see Top Tip 1).

Secondly, it is crucial to recognise the organising role of the OECD leaders. They are the lynchpins between regional authorities and the mission teams and therefore set the agenda. They make sure that the team works well together, achieves the goals of the mission research as well as bringing together reports by being integral to drawing up the recommendations, and they lead on presenting to stakeholders. This is just a way in which it is important to work with, and utilise the skills of, your colleagues and collaborators (see Top Tips 2 and 3).

Lastly, for academics there are professional and personal gains from taking part in mission research. From a personal perspective, academics involved in mission research get the opportunity to travel and see places in a unique way. The contacts you make enhance your overall knowledge and understanding of your area of work. Particularly when you can be 'closer to action' during regional visits, which may not happen at country level visits where the tendency is to engage with policy makers and strategists.

Professionally, the OECD is a prestigious organisation and there is kudos for the academic in being acknowledged as a contributor to the final report. Many countries now have some concept of 'impact' in informing judgements about academics which lead to subsequent funding (or not) of research. Involvement here can be a clear indicator of impact, especially if it can be shown that notice and actions were taken as a result of recommendations. Furthermore, because regions have distinct problems and characteristics, there is often something novel or interesting that arises that leads to new connections and ideas for future academic research projects. In some ways, Top Tips 4 and 5 can help you build these relationships.

Top Tips

1. Do your homework in advance – to be on top of the brief put in extra time to research the region. This pays dividends in meetings and interviews.
2. Work with colleagues – they will have noted things that you have missed.
3. Daily debriefings are essential.
4. Engage with local stakeholders so that they remember you when you write follow-up emails for further information.
5. Identify additional people who can provide follow-up information – local people and other academics.
6. Decide whether taking handwritten notes works best for you or typing in the interview (which most of us do).

REFERENCES

Grillitsch, M., Asheim, B. and Trippl, M. (2018). Unrelated knowledge combinations: the unexplored potential for regional industrial path development, *Cambridge Journal of Regions, Economy and Society*, 11(2), 257–74.

OECD. (2021). *Local Entrepreneurial Ecosystems and Emerging Industries: Case Study of Chiang Mai and Chiang Rai, Thailand*. Paris: OECD.

Potter, J. (2019). New role for cities and regions in promoting entrepreneurship and SMEs presentation to European Committee of the Regions, Commission for Economic Policy, External Seminar, Helsinki, 27 November 2019.

Potter, J. and Lawton Smith, H. (2019). Smart specialisation in Eastern Europe: insights from two lagging Polish regions, ch 6 in RSA Expo, M. Barzotto, C. Corradini, F. Fai, S. Labory and P. Tomlinson (eds), *Smart Specialisation and Industry 4.0 in Lagging Regions*, Oxon: Taylor and Francis, pp. 43–54.

Stam, E. (2015). Entrepreneurial ecosystems and regional policy: a sympathetic critique, *European Planning Studies*, 23(9), 1759–69.

Stam, E. and van de Ven, A. (2021). Entrepreneurial ecosystem elements. *Small Business Economics*, 56(2), 809–32.

16. Intersectional Anti-Racist Academic Activism for Policy-making (INTARAAP) through community engagement

Ima Jackson and Judy Wasige

16.1 INTRODUCTION

This chapter highlights an approach to integrating research into policy-making through the application of Intersectional Anti-Racist Academic Activism for Policy-making (INTARAAP). It sets out the key theoretical and practical issues in centring the perspectives of those who experience racism into the production of evidence for policy and practice. INTARAAP fosters a better understanding of the mechanisms of marginalisation through racialisation. Case study evidence from the development of Skills Recognition Scotland (SRS) is used – see Box 16.1. SRS is a Scottish Government funded, policy led, new national process to provide an interface between the skills shortages in the public and private sectors and professional and vocational qualifications acquired from beyond the UK.

Predominant anti-racist practices largely focus on tackling interpersonal racism, an array of behaviours ranging from micro-aggressions to verbal and physical violence that threaten, harm and devalue those who are viewed as 'other'. Yet, it is structural racism, the processes that are embedded in laws, policies and societal and institutional practices that create disadvantages in accessing economic, physical and social resources. Critically, these racialising processes often build from research and policy and influence unequal living conditions, which can encourage interpersonal racism (Nazroo et al., 2020). Racialised inequalities are therefore informed by social structures and systems. The differences in the risks and outcomes of racialisation for different groups can therefore be best understood and tackled if interpreted in the context of lived experiences.

16.2 WHAT IS INTERSECTIONAL ANTI-RACIST ACADEMIC ACTIVISM FOR POLICY-MAKING (INTARAAP)?

INTARAAP emphasises the role of societal structures in constituting the conditions communities are situated in and the inherent vulnerability to inadequate interventions which fail to recognise the structural dimensions of their circumstances (Cho et al., 2013). Intersectional analysis is founded on Black feminist thought and attempts to identify how interlocking systems of power impact those who are most marginalised in society (Crenshaw, 1989; Hill Collins and Bilge, 2020). Analysing the role of the interrelated dimensions of racism can foster a better understanding of marginalisation through racialisation and necessitate that their perspectives and practical concerns become critical in decision-making.

INTARAAP involves academics collaborating with communities and policy-makers to redefine how marginalisation through racialisation is experienced. It aims to explore the changes required to address the challenges described and translate the findings into policy-relevant, scalable solutions. Part of the research and writing process is dedicated to thinking carefully about the implications of the work and taking responsibility for the potential impact on communities. The objective is to facilitate access to power for communities, whilst enabling decision makers to access the knowledge they need from communities to shape anti-racist policy. Thus, activities should provide communities access to academic expertise and policy-making insight, enhance opportunities for centring their perspective in decision-making and understanding policy concepts or service issues under discussion.

Further, INTARAAP gives academics and policy-makers an opportunity to understand and reflect on how and why their thinking is unreflective of the experiences of those at risk of marginalisation through racialisation. INTARAAP nurtures communities', researchers' and policy-makers' appreciation of diverse perspectives and alternative views to increase preparedness for engagement with intersectional perspectives and experiences. It has been recognised and applied in key strategic organisations across sectors in Scotland to support systems change.

16.3 WHY INTARAAP?

The inability of academics and policy-makers to critically engage with the mechanisms of marginalisation through racialisation can maintain ignorance of racism and its implication in people's lives. This increases their risk of becoming agents of racism in the very processes which should address it.

Long-standing demands from communities, current social unease and the drive to disrupt the prevailing circumstances have been intensified by events including Brexit, Scottish Independence, the coronavirus pandemic and the articulation of systemic inequity from the #BlackLivesMatter movement. This has exposed people's vulnerabilities to systemic racism in an unprecedented way (Razai et al., 2021). The need for a groundswell of academic researchers and policy-makers keen to address racialised inequality is urgent. In this section we set out some of the ways in which INTARAAP's focus on redressing racialised inequality is vital.

16.3.1 Access to Centres of Power Enhances Potential to Frame Issues in Policy-relevant Formats

Communities that experience racism are largely underrepresented in the academy and policy decision-making. This often motivates their need to create safe spaces for activism and knowledge production to resist their marginalisation. However, these efforts largely remain on the periphery and may therefore contribute little towards policy and social change. This exclusion can further blind people from realising their expertise is the expertise required for more inclusive policy-making. Concurrently, little encouragement comes forth from dominant knowledge production systems to voice that expertise (Arday and Mirza, 2018). Academic activists engaging in these spaces can inspire hope for the long-anticipated changes.

16.3.2 Centring Lived Experiences Can Disrupt Marginalisation Processes

INTARAAP is underpinned by intersectional analysis which hypothesises that the diverse risks and outcomes of racialisation can only be understood and tackled if interpreted in the context of critically engaging with the lived experiences of structural and interpersonal racisms. Therefore, explanations should be critically analysed using data and reference to the testimony of marginalised groups.

Bringing in perspectives directly aligned to a challenge disrupts usual processes founded on preconceived assumptions about racialised identities. However, there must be a clear distinction between expertise of lived experience, understanding of what systemic racism in action is and the mechanisms that it employs. Although that detailed careful thinking created by 'bringing in' can help support the process, lived experience on its own is not sufficient. Researcher or policy-maker interpretations are often overgeneralisations or misinterpretations of the issues, unless they have deep knowledge of the systemic process and understand how racialisation and racism function.

Essentially, INTARAAP counteracts experiences of racism being interpreted by the same systems that create the racialisations. Additionally, it helps recalibrate the power mechanisms that can develop within communities. For example, opportunity hoarding by some 'leaders' and the uncritical partnerships formed by policy-makers with some third sector organisations that form the basis of exploitation and can be difficult, if not impossible, to counter (Verloo, 2013).

BOX 16.1 CASE STUDY DEVELOPING 'SKILLS RECOGNITION SCOTLAND'

Long-standing evidence indicates those who migrate to Scotland are not enabled to function at their skills, qualifications and expertise levels. The overlapping structural disadvantages, including the lack of a formal process to accredit their qualifications and inadequate interventions, largely maintain and perpetuate racialisation, contribute to their vulnerability to poverty and other disadvantages (Netto et al., 2011). Unemployment and underemployment amongst adults in Scotland with overseas skills and experience brings with it not only a cost for the individual concerned but also incurs wider macroeconomic costs, such as a reduction in productivity and deskilling (The Equal Opportunities Committee, 2016; Trevena, 2016) .

Engagement with migrant communities in Scotland clarified the frustration and perceived hopelessness of their circumstances. The significant issues of unemployment and underemployment and well-documented skills shortage for employers in Scotland heightened the urgency for change.

A witness seminar using an INTARAAP framework in 2016 hosted in Glasgow Caledonian University brought together all the relevant policy and service providers, including the Scottish Government, the Scottish Qualifications Authority, the Scottish Credit and Qualifications Framework (SCQF) and third sector migrant support organisations, such as Bridges Programmes and Radiant and Brighter, laid the foundation for SRS implemented in 2018. The SRS is a national process for mapping skills/qualifications achieved abroad to the SCQF.

16.4   FACTORS TO CONSIDER WHEN UNDERTAKING AN INTARAAP APPROACH

16.4.1   Critical Intersectional Analysis of Racism in Existing Structures Must Inform Project Design and Methods

Those who seek to undertake this work should have a good understanding of the policy landscape under exploration, including the associated services, to enable them identify who holds decision-making power. This helps ensure all the key players are involved, and supports incorporation of social justice and transformation goals in project design.

Current UK anti-discrimination initiatives are implemented under 'equalities' legislation, in line with the Equality Act 2010. However, as progress towards anti-racism has been extremely slow, long-held concern amongst equality experts and activists indicate existing tools are inadequate for combating prevalent deep-rooted inequalities (Bi, 2021). Ahmed (2012) argues that 'equalities' does not have the 'strength' to force organisational change, because it is historically seen as an organisational strategy to not make change – conceptualisation as 'equality' denies focus on the inequalities it purports to address.

To use the INTARAAP approach *it is essential to be mindful of the dynamics of the equalities landscape and seek alternative policy contexts that resonate with the vision and understanding of proposed processes.* For the SRS project the tactic was to consider the positive potential, involve decision makers far beyond 'equalities' and seek welcome and support for the ambition of wider work. The economic benefits of accrediting skills/qualifications acquired overseas aligned with Scottish Government departments concerned with demographic change, including Scotland Is Now, TalentScotland, Scottish Enterprise and Population Growth policy. These areas were all successfully encouraged to engage.

16.4.2   Researchers Embedded in and Trusted by Communities Must Lead the Work

INTARAAP works best when the researchers involved are critically engaged with experiences of racism in the context of research. It is important here to differentiate between community engaged researchers and academic activists and why this kind of work should pay attention to inherent challenges and tensions within both.

Community engaged researchers are often skilled in building networks and centring communities' perspectives in their research, however, their work may not foster social justice because they have not critically engaged with racism. Academic activists may seek to foster social justice, but their work may not always build from the intersecting inequalities at the root of marginalisation (Shaw et al., 2020).

16.4.3 Disrupting Dominant Knowledge Structures is Critical

Evidence of racialised discrimination within existing research and policy structures in spite of purported aims to tackle marginalisation indicates a lack of awareness by researchers and policy-makers of their complicity in these processes. Hence a key aim of INTARAAP is to improve understanding of racialisation and racism: how it functions within organisations, how it shifts and changes within society. *You cannot make research and policy decisions about those marginalised through racialisation if you do not understand your own and your organisation's role in these processes.* Researchers involved must understand that *it is the expertise of those who critically understand the experiences of racism that is crucial in developing new ways of knowing how to support the system address itself* – they must be keen to disrupt dominant knowledge structures.

16.4.4 Thought Leadership is Critical in Shaping Perceptions

Real tension exists in policy development and subsequent service provision regarding dedicated funding for anti-racist work, viewed as an extra demand on the system – whereas *from an anti-racist perspective any funding identified is to support the system which discards racist policy processes and tries to redress the manifestation of systemic inequality.* Public perceptions and policy-makers' understanding about the issue determines how concern and anxiety can embed through a sense of spending on 'them' as opposed to anyone else. Critical thought leadership is needed to change this narrative and identify how and why we have been stuck in 'whiteness' and a marginalising interpretation of how and what should be, to ensure inequity (Buccella, 2020).

16.4.5 Engaging Policy-makers in this Approach is Not Always Instantly Successful

In addition to managing public perceptions about the project, building the confidence and trust of a variety of policy-makers and departments is critical. The fluidity of staff in government policy-making necessitates maintaining trust and integrity of project plans. *The historical understanding of how policy is created around communities who experience racism means that processes of engagement with policy-makers are as important as engagement with the communities themselves.*

16.4.6   Flexibility is Integral to INTARAAP Proposals

Due to the multidimensional, diverse and dynamic nature of the issues addressed, flexibility must be integral in INTARAAP working arrangements. In particular, there has to be some flexibility around funding arrangements. Whilst there can be a clear budget, it is important that funders understand it is often unclear what specific areas will be developed over others.

For example, the cost for advisory support may be more in practice than initially intended or it may be less depending on the prevailing circumstances. Flexibility is therefore critical as it allows the potential dynamic needs of the project to be met. However, anxiety around funding addressing racialisation and racism in systemic processes is worth noting because it challenges the status quo of how and what spending is organised around.

16.4.7   Examples from Other Jurisdictions Can Help Build Confidence – but Watch for Demands to Claim More than You Can when You Start

The availability of data about an issue helps to develop public and policy-makers' confidence regarding demand for infrastructure and to justify the project and the spending. Lack of ethnicity recording in Scotland to identify, monitor and address systemically racialised inequalities is well documented. That it is consistently not addressed is itself viewed as a mechanism of systemic racism (Expert Reference Group on Covid 19, 2021). Intersectional analysis of national structures and processes for recognising overseas skills/qualifications in countries like Germany and Canada was critical in articulating Scottish specific structures, processes, practice and pitfalls (Bontenbal and Lillie, 2019).

The 'act' of agreeing to fund the infrastructure can be viewed as the solution. There is pressure to show off the ambition before there is evidence it could and will work. The infrastructure needs developing to a level that the weight and ambition of the work can carry the publicity and anticipated demand. *The pressure to herald policy decisions which mitigate or address racialised inequality can become intense and should be resisted.*

16.4.8   Involving Local, Government and International Expertise in Quality Assurance

Using a steering group to manage local operational issues can help ensure the project stays on track and remains true to its aim. Involving the government throughout is crucial as it positions the work not as something being done to them but done with and for them to address systemic processes. It allows them to engage with the learning required for fostering intersectional social justice. Contributing steering group members may not need to be high level decision makers. The organisational insight into systems, and assumptions in relation to the ambitions of the SRS project were important. As the work progressed the steering group changed to comprise more senior influencers and decision makers within organisations. An international advisory board with relevant expertise lifts the conversation away from localised issues into a much broader international understanding of systemic function.

16.4.9 Developing Trust and Gaining Buy-in

Initial activities must involve articulating plausible evidence of the current situation and the benefits of the proposed infrastructure or strategy and engagement with targeted service users (employers and migrants) and key decision makers.

Mutual trust needs to be maintained with targeted users of the infrastructure. For migrants this was sustained through relying on and valuing their expertise regarding the systemic processes of marginalisation of their own knowledge, qualifications and skills. Alongside, it was recognised that developing national skills recognition structures without buy-in from employers is pointless. Involving civil servants was helpful in deciding which sectors most required the infrastructure from their own policy intelligence within Scotland.

This approach has supported policy-makers to understand that it is '*their learning*' about the usual processes, and increasing their confidence in disrupting these processes, rather than learning about specifics of project content that is essential. In essence an anti-racist approach to learning about the process of policy-making can demonstrate to them how the system marginalises the experiences of those they wish to support. It can create important opportunities for them to both hear the conversations and to understand their own role within the conversations.

16.5   MECHANISMS AND CHALLENGES

Table 16.1 below outlines what we think works and the challenges of the INTARAAP approach.

Table 16.1   Mechanisms, challenges and ways of overcoming them

Mechanism	Challenges and ways of overcoming them
Recognising that systemic racism as it exists means engaging with systemic racism is itself seen as divisive	Everyone and every organisation are on their own journey – this needs to be managed
Collaboratively exploring with communities, researchers, policy-makers and other 'systems change' stakeholders how to best counteract systemic racism	Not all groups (especially white people) realise they are racialised nor do all organisations accept systemic racism exists
Bringing in the national and international conversations about racism to mitigate the tendency to prove racism exists	Building appropriate national and international linkages to ensure that the focus is not proving racism but the mechanisms which create and sustain it
Acknowledging learning from the inclusion of people with experience of migration and racism works best if that process of 'bringing in' is supported by those who understand the mechanisms of systemic racism	Building critical engagement of racialisation and racism to appreciate lived experiences influencing processes
Acknowledging it is easier for researchers and policy-makers not to challenge existing processes as the system is designed to 'protect' from that level of intimacy	Disrupting a system not designed to enable reflection of its own mechanisms is exhausting and time-consuming
Building momentum to enact and sustain societal change requires the moral and activist input from those with lived experiences of racism	Building capacity to enable reflection on the processes indicates many assumptions and biases the system would probably prefer not to see
Recognising that racialisation is normalised within existing processes. Some stakeholders can be obstructive because the 'system' rewards them	Understanding the organisational risks to those invited to participate can help prevent subversion of their existing professional 'agency' to work against
Understanding the landscape, including who currently benefits and whether they have insight into their own role, power and authority is vital	The power base of beneficiaries of current processes can undermine the work you think you are going to do together
Acknowledging migration forces change – this is important but often resisted and undervalued	Building mechanisms that enable lived experiences to inform the system to reflect on itself
Recognising that pandering to media and political expediency can result in 'Policy Clickbait'	Considerable pressure can be placed on 'successful' initiatives, to publicise achievement before processes can 'hold' societal pressure and scrutiny, including people's hopes, needs careful management
Acknowledging that situating scepticism alongside commitment to accomplish research and policy goals is a difficult tension to manage	Maintaining scepticism as a necessary tool is a professional risk

Mechanism	Challenges and ways of overcoming them
Fostering leadership confidence to encourage the process to include those usually excluded from the decision-making table	This can be a professional risk and requires collective agreement in order to sustain it
Developing potential for humility, hope and understanding of the depth and complexity of the issue to be addressed	The professional and personal can become infused and needs managing. Maintaining honest potentially disruptive conversations in these sorts of spaces can be risky as you are never sure how they will be received and interpreted

16.6   CONCLUSION

Projects and initiatives such as the example in this chapter often exist for political expediency. This means there is always a threat that they will be pulled. Maintaining trust in the process, maintaining long-term buy-in of ministers and their departments, despite their often-transitory roles, is important. Concurrently, maintaining trust and supporting those who are basically the 'guinea pigs' of the process in which you are asking them to rely are significant requirements.

The impact of COVID-19 demonstrated at least for a moment how inequalities are created and sustained by the system ostensibly intended for eradicating or ameliorating those same inequalities (Horton, 2020). This moment appears unprecedented in building awareness of systemic racism and other aspects of intersectional inequality.

However, the ability for the system to right itself and recalibrate around this new knowledge and hence ignore it cannot and should not be underestimated. Academic activists with their deep knowledge of the critical thinking required, the 'bringing in' of those marginalised and the building of public policy processes which incorporate these aspects should see this as a moment – a call to action.

REFERENCES

Ahmed, S. (2012). *On Being Included: Racism and Adversity in Institutional Life.* Durham and London: Duke University Press.

Arday, J., and Mirza, H.S. (eds). (2018). *Dismantling Race in Higher Education: Racism, Whiteness and Decolonising the Academy.* London: Palgrave Macmillan.

Bi, S. (2021). Equality Act 10 years on. Equality Act Review. Retrieved 23 July 2021, from https://www.equalityactreview.co.uk/equality-act-10-years-on-report

Bontenbal, I., and Lillie, N. (2019). WP3 Report: Policy barriers and enablers. University of Jyväskylä. Skills and Integration of Migrants, Refugees and Asylum Applicants in European Labour Market (SIRIUS). Retrieved 14 May 2021, from https://www.sirius-project.eu/publications/wp3-report-policy-barriers-and-enablers

Buccella, A. (2020, 22 October). Uncovering the hallmarks of anti-racist institutions: Thought leaders we are reading, listening to, and following right now. Retrieved 14 May 2021, from https://eab.com/insights/expert-insight/academic-affairs/higher-ed -anti-racist-institutions/

Cho, S., Crenshaw, K.W., and Leslie, M. (2013). Toward a field of intersectionality studies: Theory, applications, and araxis. *Signs*, 38(4), 785–810.

Crenshaw, K. (1989). Demarginalizing the intersection of race and sex: A Black feminist critique of antidiscrimination doctrine, feminist theory and antiracist politics. *University of Chicago Legal Forum*, (1), 139–67.

Expert Reference Group on Covid 19. (2021). *Expert Reference Group on Covid 19: Initial Advice & Recommendations on Systemic Issues.* Edinburgh: The Scottish Government. Retrieved 14 May 2021, from https://www.gov.scot/binaries/content/ documents/govscot/publications/research-and-analysis/2020/09/expert-reference -group-on-covid-19-and-ethnicity-recommendations-to-scottish-government/ documents/systemic-issues-and-risk-initial-advice-and-recommendation

Hill Collins, P., and Bilge, S. (2020). *Intersectionality.* 2nd edn. Cambridge, Medford: Polity Press.

Horton, R. (2020). Offline: COVID-19 is not a pandemic. *Lancet*, 396(10255). doi: https://doi.org/10.1016/S0140-6736(20)32000-6

Nazroo, J.Y., Bhui, K.S., and Rhodes, J. (2020). Where next for understanding race/ ethnic inequalities in severe mental illness? Structural, interpersonal and institutional racism. *Sociology of Health and Illness*, 42(2), 262–76. doi:https://doi.org/10.1111/ 1467-9566.13001

Netto, G., Sosenko, F., and Bramley, G. (2011). Poverty and ethnicity in Scotland: Review of the literature and data sets. York: Joseph Rowntree Foundation. Retrieved 8 April 2022, from https://www.jrf.org.uk/report/review-poverty-and-ethnicity -scotland

Razai, M.S., Kankam, H.K., Majeed, A., Esmail, A., and Williams, D.R. (2021). Mitigating ethnic disparities in covid-19 and beyond. *British Medical Journal*, 372(m4921), 1–5. doi:https://doi.org/10.1136/bmj.m4921

Shaw, J., Howard, J., and Franco, E.L. (2020). Building inclusive community activism and accountable relations through an intersecting inequalities approach. *Community Development Journal*, 55(1), 7–25. doi:https://doi.org/10.1093/cdj/bsz033

The Equal Opportunities Committee. (2016). *Removing Barriers: Race, Ethnicity and Employment.* Edinburgh: The Scottish Parliament. Retrieved 8 May 2021 from https://www.parliament.scot/S4_EqualOpportunitiesCommittee/Reports/ EOS042016R01Rev.pdf

Trevena, P. (2016). *Attracting and Retaining Migrants in Post-Brexit Scotland: Is a Social Integration Strategy the Answer?* Edinburgh: Scottish Parliament Information Centre.

Verloo, M. (2013). Intersectional and cross-movement politics and policies: Reflections on current practices and debates. *Signs*, 38(4), 893–915.

17. Commissioned research

Dan Hodges and Syahirah Abdul Rahman

17.1 INTRODUCTION

The art of commissioning research for policymaking is often misunderstood, largely due to a neglect of discussion on targeted policy–academia collaborations. A quick search on academic commissioned research in policy on any search engine would generate findings that simply discuss the need for collaborations between academia and the government. These findings feed into the commonly misunderstood perception that commissioned research is any form of research that is funded by policymaking bodies.

The first step to unravelling this misunderstanding is to know that there are various channels through which policy makers' funding of academic research can operate. This is the purpose of this book after all, in which commissioned research happens to be one of the last topics in the modes of engagement part of the book for a reason. It is to show that commissioned research is only *one* of the many ways that academics can engage with policy makers. It also shows that, just like other forms of engagement with policy makers, commissioned research has its own sets of unique characteristics, aims, and expectations, which we will discuss in this chapter. As there are many types of topics that could be covered in terms of commissioned research, this chapter will be outlined in a series of questions, through which the authors will use their experiences of having worked in commissioned research *and* having commissioned research with academics to provide guidelines and insights for conducting commissioned research.

17.2 WHAT IS COMMISSIONED RESEARCH?

As described in other parts of the book, there is a growth of evidence-based policymaking in the UK, which results in greater engagement with academic communities to help create a compelling case for policy action (Kenny et al., 2017). Due to this, public bodies have increasingly used the mode of commissioned research with academics. Though evidence-based policymaking does come with its criticisms, especially due to the preference of public bodies to use positivistic and quantitative-based research (Ansell and Geyer, 2017), academics who do not use these types of methodologies need not worry as there is currently a growing demand for qualitative evidences to support more nuanced and multi-dimensional evidences for policy discussions (Stoker and Evans, 2016).

While academic knowledge on commissioned research in policymaking is currently scarce, especially in relation to more qualitative-based research commonly found in humanities and social sciences, more has been written on it by the private and third sectors. Take the works of Race on the Agenda (ROTA), for example, a social policy research organisation focusing on issues impacting on Black, Asian, and Minority Ethnic (BAME) communities. ROTA has consistently published policy briefings that guide its members on frameworks of conducting research, including understanding the subtleties between commissioned, grant-based, and contracted research projects (ROTA, 2009). ROTA explains that when working with public bodies, there is a need for research groups to understand the different expectations that procurers (public bodies) have in terms of aims and processes of funding and commissioning different forms of research projects.

Specific to this chapter, ROTA's description of commissioned research against grant-based and contracted research projects could be useful. ROTA describes commissioned research as a process that public bodies undertake in order to meet a specific policy aim. Firstly, the public body assesses this aim, identifying the research question that needs resolving. Secondly, the public body identifies and plans how much resources they have in order to resolve this question. Thirdly, the public body arranges which party would be most suitable to deliver the project that would be able to resolve the question in the time frame and budget allocated. It is often the case that the monitoring and reviewing plans have already been decided by the public body, although it is common that further negotiations could be made between the procurer and the commissioned researcher(s).

Commissioned research is often time-sensitive, used specifically 'in influencing the debate around an upcoming policy decision' (International Centre for Policy Advocacy [ICPA], 2014). It is in the pre-identification of the 'question' in commissioned research that makes it very different from securing grants or contracts with policy makers. Unlike grants (where the research group is awarded funding based on their planning of how the money will be spent) or contracts (where the funding awarded can be spent freely by the research group as long as the contract specifications are met), commissioned research assumes a much more closely involved researcher–procurer relationship.

From the authors' experiences, there are two main reasons that policy makers would have for turning to commissioned research. First is to gain independent, credible evidence to use in justifying expenditure of public money, and second, to gain independent, credible evidence to help develop impactful programmes. To policy makers, academic researchers come with their own set of values. In policymaking spaces, they are generally considered to come with greater independence compared to private sector researchers, and as such, important in assisting the development of policy positions. In facing the public domain, the value of research independence is integral when policy makers need to deliver specific policy targets and respond to policy-related challenges. As such, the delivery of the commissioned research needs to include 'explanations, evidence, rationale, and arguments to support all aspects of a policy position' identified by the procurers (ICPA, 2014).

In practice, a common approach is actually to commission a consortium of academic and private sector researchers. One such model would be 'academic led', with the academic partners designing the method, analysing the data, and crafting the findings and the private sector partners perhaps conducting the data collection. Another, 'private sector led', model would be to have a private sector organisation such as a consultancy firm designing the method and analysis tool, collecting data, and analysing the results. In such instances, it is common to have an academic advisor or consultant to help with some aspects of the commissioned project, such as method design or analysis, and to review the results of the project.

The key thing that policy makers are looking for is an independent view to support policy discussions so that government bodies, for example, HM Treasury officials, can have confidence that the research outputs are not biased or in favour of our activity. Policy makers are keen to set the research questions, although much more commonly, the research questions could be set in collaboration between the procurer and the researcher only to ensure that the right questions are being asked. A reciprocal relationship between the procurer and the researcher as well as close involvement in the discussion of the commissioned research are valuable in ensuring that the programme and/or topic in question is fully understood by all parties before the project is carried out. That said, procurers often expect live conversations to carry on throughout the lifetime of the commissioned project, not just at the initial stages of the research, to limit the amount of misunderstandings that may occur.

17.3 WHAT IS EXPECTED FROM COMMISSIONED RESEARCH?

UK Research Councils invest around £3 billion each year on cross-council research programmes, through which different government departments can commission research to external actors such as academics. Despite the assumption that policy makers tend to favour positivistic and quantitative research, in reality, qualitative research is also viewed by policy makers as having its own sets of values. For example, they are useful in initial discussions of a policy research area or a problem. Qualitative research findings also provide in-depth nuances that can be used by policy makers to identify a more narrowed and niche area of policy research to develop further. Due to its usefulness, more and more government departments have commissioned research projects that are also in-depth and broad in scope, which are more suitable for qualitative research methodologies.

From a policy maker's perspective, it is key to build expectations upfront that the commissioned research is carried out to feed into the procurer's specific programmes and/or strategies to a deadline. As per the Government Office for Science's (GOS's) guide on engaging with academics outlines, research commissioned to external actors, including academics, can have 'relatively high financial implications', as public funding is being mobilised for the research's purposes (GOS, 2013, p. 4). Academics need to understand upfront the implications of these key characteristics of commissioned research and set their expectations accordingly when pursuing these types of research projects.

The policymaking world has different sets of challenges than that of academia. Policy makers often operate at short timescales, with pressure to deliver, and with goalposts often moving. Public bodies commission research from academics specifically to build a case for policy action, develop options, respond to urgent issues and/or monitor impacts – activities that need timely expert perspectives (GOS, 2013), rather than the pursuit of novel knowledge. Academic researchers need to be responsive to the pressures that policy makers are under without unduly sacrificing the quality of outputs.

Often, policy makers may have preconceived notions that academics might not understand their needs for research to be conducted. They might assume that academics are used to working in novel-thinking types of research, following long-term research plans that can be rigid due to the requirements of research grants and institutional expectations. In reality, this assumption is true to some level. Academics often have teaching and administrative duties, research councils' requirements, university-based accountability and are limited by institutional bureaucracy. These characteristics may not allow them to have much flexibility in adjusting their research procedures, especially with demands of producing academic outputs for their career advancements. Furthermore, there is often a tension in academia, in which academics are often seeking the right balance of *slowing down* in pursuit of fundamental knowledge creation versus doing more applied research that has quicker impacts (Treanor, 2009).

Despite this sentiment, academics are also trained to respond to the needs of a research question and the stakeholders they are working with. With proper engagement and communication, the expectations of a research question and the deliverables required from a research project can be made clear.

Furthermore, many academics value fast-paced, shorter-term research projects too, as they provide opportunities for data collection much needed for continuous productions of academic outputs, if planned well.

Once procurers and academics can have an understanding of what value they can provide to each other, the research commissioning process is relatively straightforward. Research can be commissioned at all key stages of policy development with the purpose of assisting policy makers to deepen their understanding on issues related to the policies they are developing. Commissioned research can help policy makers to explore problems, gain evidence that will help with the formulation of policy response, as well as monitor the impacts of policies implemented. Due to the policy needs of commissioned research, researchers should also be aware that the process of developing policies could be occasionally sensitive. Clear expectations should be made between the two parties at the outset, regarding what (if any) information could be made publicly available for their academic impact work, for example, for producing blog posts, journal articles, or presentation of findings in any public forum. Instances where academics have prematurely released information on a government-commissioned research without consultation could not only be detrimental for the policy itself, but also to the relationship that the researcher has with public bodies and, at a wider angle, to government–academia collaborations (GOS, 2013).

Commissioned research opportunities are usually made publicly available on the webpages of the commissioning government department. Additionally, calls of interest are also commonly published through the official websites of Research Councils or Higher Education Institutions (HEIs). Academics should pay attention to calls of interest from their respective academic departments or proactively seek for these opportunities themselves through a quick web search. Academics seeking commissioned research opportunities might also want to contact their HEIs' research office or knowledge exchange department who may be able to help find local opportunities and provide contacts. It is also possible for some public bodies to use established links with trusted academics, as long as it is within the government department's procurement rules (GOS, 2013). As such, maintaining the networks that you have formed while conducting commissioned research is highly important as it could determine future collaborations with the same procurer(s).

17.4 WHAT ARE THE GOOD PRACTICES OF COMMISSIONED RESEARCH?

Similar to all types of collaborations, good practices can be learned to deliver commissioned research successfully. In this instance, the authors believe that it is fruitful to provide insights into what both parties, procurers and academics, should do for the successful completion and delivery of commissioned research.

Firstly, from the policy makers' standpoint, those who wish to commission research should ensure to have a clear idea from the outset as to why the research is being commissioned and how it is intended to be used. This will help the framing of the research questions and in clearly defining the deliverables, therefore helping the commissioned researcher understand how best to meet your needs.

Typically, policy makers tend to assume that academics work at a much slower pace than policy makers do. Time frames are an important consideration and it is important to agree on the scope and deliverables which are possible within the agreed deadline. Procurers should also be sensitive to the career needs of the researchers they are working with. According to the GOS (2013), both procurers and researchers need to be frank and transparent about the expectations of each party. Academics can often adjust to work with procurers in a more flexible manner and at a pace faster than they are used to as long as expectations are made clear from the onset of the research project. Procurers and researchers should also discuss the payments of research services upfront, preferably after consulting procurement experts on both sides to avoid potential issues on this matter. Academics, who usually have accountability to their universities, may not want to be caught in infinite drafting cycles or not being paid because they are awaiting feedback.

Top Tip

Discussions should be held upfront on the number of revisions to be made and a schedule for report draft deliveries and feedback, allowing for mutual respect on both sides.

From the researchers' standpoint, it is important to note that academics too must listen to the needs of procurers and understand where their own expertise can be augmented by the deeper knowledge of the procurer. A suggested guideline for the initial conversation between the procurer and researcher is as follows:

1. Preparation of project:
   a. How would the research be implemented?
   b. What is the timescale for the project? Is the timescale negotiable or non-negotiable?
   c. How much funding is available and/or required?
   d. What types of data are needed?

    e.   What types of data might be misleading?

    f.   Which methodology is most suitable for the data needed and the time given?

2.   Action:

    a.   How frequently do both parties have to meet for discussions/feedback?

    b.   How many report drafts are needed?

    c.   What types of non-financial support can the procurer provide to the researcher (for example, access to interviewees)?

3.   Closure:

    a.   What types of results are expected?

    b.   What types of outputs are expected?

    c.   How will the findings be disseminated?

Continuous discussions about the commissioned research might sound as if policy makers are monitoring the researcher, and thus putting questions on the value of independence in the research. This is not the case as the need for continuous discussions is mainly to limit any forms of misunderstandings. Continuous discussions help to mitigate unwanted consequences, such as reports needing continuous rewrites or wordsmiths to get things explained on the policy makers' terms. Academics should expect that policy makers often need help in interpreting the findings of the research, especially when the commissioned research involves subjective input of multiple stakeholders. This is when open discussions with the procurer of the commissioned research could really help set the context of the research.

Top Tip

A successful outcome of commissioned research is contingent on finding the right balance: the procurer clearly setting out what they are interested in and their perspectives on it, without seeking to have undue influence on what the results of the research should be.

17.5   CONCLUSION: WHAT ARE THE OUTCOMES OF COMMISSIONED RESEARCH?

With any given piece of collaborative work, the most important factor is its outcome. For commissioned research, its outcome is valued on how the findings of the research help policy makers to build a narrative around the current evidence base. A common output for this purpose are White Papers, which in the UK are government reports that provide information on particular issues, highlight topics for discussions, and/or provide recommendations for policy action. A report by Boa, Johnson and King (2010) on the impact of research on the policy process outlines an important discernment of what researching for policymaking entails. The authors argue that the impact of research on policy is not immediate because, essentially, what underpins policy direction is a *combination* of long-term evidence gathering. Commissioned researchers may not generate immediate policy outcomes but will help in building evidence-based narratives and background data that is integral to policymaking debates that are eventually key to the creation of policies. As the authors' findings have shown, it is rare to attribute a change in the direction of policy to a single piece of evidence or research project. Commissioned research acts as key components of a wider knowledge base in a particular area. It gives policy makers the credibility to show that the positions they make in policy discussions are backed by an established knowledge base, which assists them to answer questions posed by their colleagues within a particular timescale.

Expectations of the outcomes of commissioned research, for example, in terms of the outputs required, should be discussed at the initial commissioning process. Both procurers and researchers need to outline whether peer reviews and proofreading of the outputs are required where appropriate. Common outputs of commissioned research are typically evaluation reports or analyses of the impact of a programme. This would almost always result in a published report, used to improve design or delivery of a programme, or to justify its budget. In these circumstances, procurers of the research require evidence that is rigorous, using quantitative and qualitative methods. The evidence must also align with best practice guidance for conducting evaluations of public programmes, and that the deliverables need to be in either a ready-to-publish format or easily converted to one. Another common form of commissioned research is to help inform the design of a programme, maybe conducting social research amongst target groups, or examining the evidence as to what works. Here, the findings may not be published, but need to be understandable, relevant, and informative. In this instance, both procurers and researchers should be clear on the research questions. They should outline a comprehensive explanation of what the programme is intended to do, and perhaps ask for recommendations for design and delivery.

REFERENCES

Ansell, C. and Geyer, R. (2017) Pragmatic complexity's new foundation for moving beyond 'evidence-based policy making'? *Policy Studies*, *38*(2), 149–67.

Boa, I., Johnson, P. and King, S. (2010) The impact of research on the policy process. Available at: https://assets.publishing.service.gov.uk/government/uploads/system/uploads/attachment_data/file/207544/wp82.pdf (viewed on 1 December 2020).

Government Office for Science [GOS] (2013) *Engaging with Academics: How to Further Strengthen Open Policy Making: A Guide for Policy Makers.* Available at: https://assets.publishing.service. gov.uk/government/uploads/system/uploads/attachment_data/file/283129/13-581-engaging-with-academics-open-policy-making.pdf (viewed on 1 December 2020).

International Centre for Policy Advocacy [ICPA] (2014) *2.3.2 Who Produces and Commissions Policy Research?* Available at: https://advocacyguide .icpolicyadvocacy.org/232-who-produces-and-commissions-policy-research (viewed on 8 December 2020).

Kenny, C., Rose, D.C., Hobbs, A., Tyler, C. and Blackstock, J. (2017) *The Role of Research in the UK Parliament: Volume One.* London, UK: Houses of Parliament.

Race on the Agenda [ROTA] (2009) *All You Need to Know about Commissioning: Grants & Contracts.* Policy Briefing (Issue 24). Available at: https://www.rota. org.uk/sites/default/files/policybriefings/Commisioning%20-%20grants%20and %20contracts-%20Policy%20Briefing%2024.pdf (viewed on 1 December 2020).

Stoker, G. and Evans, M. (eds) (2016) *Evidence-Based Policy Making in the Social Sciences: Methods that Matter.* Bristol: Policy Press.

Treanor, B. (2009) Slow university manifesto. Available at: http://faculty.lmu.edu/briantreanor/slow-university-a-manifesto/ (viewed on 1 December 2020).

PART III

Examples of informing, influencing and impacting policy

18. Engaging with policy makers in emerging markets

Ekkehard Ernst

18.1 BACKGROUND

Applied research in intergovernmental organisations consists of knowledge transfer and comparative studies of policy impact. A key component of this work resides in supporting policy makers in member countries to make use of appropriate tools in identifying policy challenges and providing them with the appropriate instruments to address them. Some membership organisations, such as the Organisation for Economic Co-operation and Development (OECD), make membership dependent on countries committing to building up appropriate state capacity to deliver against a complex policy agenda, including investing in and expanding their capacity to analyse current and emerging challenges. Others, in particular United Nations (UN) organisations with their focus on achieving humanitarian and sustainability goals, leave it to their member countries to decide which level of analytical capacity they are willing to commit to. A key responsibility for UN agencies consists in providing guidelines and support as regards statistical norms, for instance regarding national accounts or labour force surveys. But these guidelines serve as recommendations and countries are by no means required to implement them as part of their membership.

18.1.1 Technical Assistance Provided by International Organisations

To strengthen countries' capacity for policy identification and delivery, many UN agencies provide technical assistance to member countries by transferring knowledge about best practices in different policy domains to policy makers and local experts. This can entail specific training sessions of analysts in using the latest methods – all UN agencies run specialised training centres, often with local presence – or collaborating with ministries in setting up observatories and other institutional structures that support policy delivery in member countries. In many cases it will involve reorganising existing structures and procedures in order to adapt them to changing policy priorities or to streamline them for improved efficacy. For policy researchers this means diving deep into existing institutional structures in order to understand the existing division of labour between ministries and executing agencies. Policy reforms to achieve certain outcomes can easily have unintended consequences when their institutional implications are not fully taken into account.

Traditionally and for the most part, technical assistance programmes are established at the request of the member country. They involve either remote advisory roles or are carried out in collaboration with permanent country missions (see Chapter 15 in this book for more on mission research; Plata-Stenger, 2020). In the case of the International Labour Organization (ILO), the aim of many of these programmes is to build a country's ability to meet international standards in the measurement of the labour market and to address gaps between these standards and the level of expertise in different country contexts. Historically, it was not seen as a tool of economic development, rather a means to support members to reform their labour legislation and to raise awareness of the work that the ILO could deliver (Plata-Stenger, 2020). However, the capacity building that sits at the heart of the ILO's approach to technical assistance has long been associated with international development.

18.1.2   Example: Labour Market Diagnosis and Forecasts

The examples featured in this chapter relate to my experiences of working on technical assistance programmes with the ILO. The ILO is a specialised UN agency, which brings together governments, employers and workers from its 187 member states.[1] Its core aim is to support labour standards, with a focus on promoting social justice through decent work for all.[2] A core means of delivering on this aim is the provision of technical assistance and providing best practice on labour market statistics to ILO members.

This chapter presents recent examples of introducing labour market diagnosis and anticipation tools in an attempt to provide labour market ministries in two emerging economies with the appropriate tools to identify current and upcoming challenges. The objective was to institutionalise experience gained in other countries with labour market observatories to provide up-to-date granular employment information to the relevant minister and the ministerial bureaucracy to enable them to react to labour market challenges, including those that might arise from policy reforms in other areas, such as trade reforms.

This chapter draws on experience gained in two projects carried out between 2012 and 2015 in Colombia and Peru, highlighting the process through which knowledge transfer and capacity building took place. The goal of these two projects had been to strengthen the capacity of the respective labour ministries to undertake detailed labour market analysis and projections to anticipate and support job growth. The experiences gained in Colombia and Peru are contrasted with those obtained in other projects with similar objectives, specifically in Algeria and Ghana. The chapter discusses lessons learnt regarding the role of the country-specific institutional context in designing and implementing such projects across a variety of countries.

18.2 DIMENSIONS OF CAPACITY BUILDING

Labour market interventions hinge importantly on being able to identify precisely the relevant groups that are affected by them. Unemployment benefits should help (only) those who have lost their job, activation measures need to be targeted to those who struggle to return to employment, and skills and training programmes are ideally provided to those with the highest risk of losing out. The more sophisticated the measure, the more costly it is and the better targeted it needs to be, especially in countries with limited fiscal resources. Moreover, it often takes time to build up the administrative capacity to deliver on any particular measure, which makes it important to anticipate potential problems in the labour market well in advance. All of this is particularly relevant in emerging and low-income countries that face tighter fiscal constraints and less state capacity to implement and roll out any such measure.

Part of the work carried out by the ILO, therefore, aims at what is broadly called 'capacity building', an approach to advise governments on best practices in institutional development as identified in other countries. Such experience often has been gained in the context of advanced economies, which means that lessons learnt cannot easily be transferred from one country to another. Three problems, in particular, arise:

1. *The statistical landscape:* The statistical basis on which to build policy advice varies significantly from one country to another, including among more advanced economies. Capacity building, therefore, needs to take into account the statistical landscape, potentially integrating advice on how to improve a state's capacity to identify policy challenges through a larger range of statistical indicators. As a matter of fact, part of the capacity building involves helping countries to provide more granular and reliable data, using the latest techniques and conforming to internationally agreed standards. In particular as regards labour market information, this cannot at all be taken for granted as policy priorities and changing governments often interfere with such efforts. Moreover, data collection in developing countries is often carried out in an ad hoc manner, relying on donor funding and responding to donor objectives. Building up long-term sustainable capacity for the purpose of data collection remains elusive in such an environment.

2. *The use of advanced analytical tools:* Related to a lack of granular and consistent data, the tools and instruments deployed in countries with a more granular statistical basis often require advanced analytical and statistical tools. Whereas labour market policy institutions and ministries in advanced economies, for instance, can rely on detailed micro-econometric analysis of households and firms, analysing several waves of surveys at high frequencies over long periods of time, many low- and middle-income countries only have sporadic surveys that preclude detailed econometric analysis and allows only for a more aggregate view of labour market challenges. As a consequence, detailed analysis of specific labour market challenges, for instance related to occupational transitions, is not available to researchers in countries where such granular data is not available.

3. *Institutional capacity and capabilities:* Finally, the size and depth of state expertise is often not commensurate with the requirements of more advanced technical analysis. Whereas OECD countries, for instance, often rely on a multitude of labour market institutions and ministries at different administrative levels (state, regional, municipal), less well-to-do countries have fewer such institutions, face tighter budget constraints and higher rotation of staff that prevents them from building lasting institutional memory. Part of the capacity building strategy, therefore, also consists in identifying appropriate layers for longer-term deployment of tools that can outlast shifting policy priorities. For instance, where countries dispose of social security institutions, building analytical capacity in such institutions might provide longer-lasting benefits through capacity building than setting up an employment observatory within a labour ministry.

The following sections illustrate these three challenges in the context of capacity building undertaken in Peru and Colombia during the 2010s.[3] This is contrasted with experiences in Algeria and Ghana where similar projects were carried out between 2014 and 2016.

18.3   APPROACH

The ILO has more than 60 regional, subregional and country offices across the world.[4] These local offices maintain close relationships with member country governments in their areas. Member countries can request support from the ILO through their local offices, and if the ILO has capacity, they will offer technical assistance, with Headquarters of the ILO in Geneva acting as a backstop. The Peruvian Government and its Ministry of Labour in particular have a long history of working with the ILO (Dávalos, 2013).

The capacity building projects in Peru and Colombia were instigated by distinct needs identified by the national government of each country. Although both countries required detailed country employment forecasts to improve targeted labour market and social protection measures, they also featured important contextual factors that would shape the delivery of the technical assistance provided by the ILO. In Peru, the challenge was for training providers and public employment services to properly identify the skills needed in the workforce (Dávalos, 2013). The Colombian government, on the other hand, had identified a need to enrich their labour market statistics to inform future policy, and in particular needed information on the informal economy (Arias, 2013).

In contrast to these projects that were meant to enhance the long-term capacity of labour ministries to carry out independent labour market analysis, similar projects in Algeria and Ghana were meant to provide snapshots of current labour market challenges (as of the mid-2010s) to inform longer-term development planning processes. Both countries also dispose of regularly conducted labour force surveys, albeit with less granular information than what was available for Peru and Colombia.

All four countries have middle-income status according to the classification of the World Bank (World Bank, 2021), albeit with large differences in per-capita income levels. All of them are also net commodity exporters, providing them with a larger, non-donor funded but volatile source of fiscal revenues. Nevertheless, general government resources remained more limited in Ghana, restricting their capacity to intervene in the labour market. In contrast, Algeria, Colombia and Peru have developed and implemented a large array of labour market interventions.[5] However, only Peru and Colombia also dispose of regular and detailed labour force surveys, carried out on a quarterly frequency and according to standards set up by the International Conference of Labour Statisticians (ICLS). In contrast, Algeria and Ghana have a more limited capacity to collect granular labour market information, limiting the precision with which they can address labour market imbalances. At the time when the projects were undertaken, none of the four countries disposed of tools for granular labour market analysis and projection within their respective labour ministries.[6] To address this, the Employment Projections Model from the ILO was adapted to the specific country context. To do this, it was important to consider the institutional environment and the ways in which the project could help build institutional capacity.

18.4   OPTIONS FOR AN INSTITUTIONAL SET-UP

A key component of the projects consisted in identifying the most appropriate ministerial or bureaucratic entity at which to locate the capacity building process. Four options were considered in which the ILO could support institutional capacity building: (1) creating a specialised department within the labour ministry of each country, (2) establishing a labour market observatory, which can be independent and function at a national or regional basis (European Training Foundation, 2016), (3) expanding capacity at an existing social security administration, (4) creating a specialised department within a national planning commission department, if it exists.

Three aspects should inform which option to select. First, the decision on which option to pursue depended on the institutional context and the ways in which departments and administrations worked on the ground. Second, the decision needs to be guided by an assessment of the existing capacity. Finally, the decision needs to be informed by the policy objectives that the additional capacity is to support. For instance, if longer-term planning or fiscal sustainability goals are targeted, options 3 and 4 might be the appropriate choice. In contrast, if capacity is being built to inform policy makers about the impact of specific policy interventions, a closer integration with the respective line ministries might be needed.

Top Tip

The first part of any engaged project needs to focus on understanding the institutional context and to find out who the key players are – understanding their perspective and interpretation of the challenge.

Related to the previous point, when looking to provide sustainable knowledge transfer in an emerging economy, it is vital to identify the institution best placed to absorb the knowledge and take the project forward. There are two factors which weigh heavily on the decision of what group of people will take on the task of measuring labour statistics once the ILO project is complete: (1) the ability of the identified recipients to influence ministers to use the information once it is generated, (2) the stability of the position within the institution. Often in middle-income countries, the people who can influence ministers are in institutional contexts which are subject to frequent and sudden change, meaning that building relationships in order to facilitate capacity building and technical assistance is challenging and disrupted without preparing a proper transfer of knowledge.

Top Tip

There is typically a trade-off between institutional continuity and position to leverage policy impact, and this trade-off needs to be considered carefully.

Different options to address these shortcomings exist. In the case of Ghana, for instance, the existence of a National Development Planning Commission provides a strong way to coordinate policy objectives across ministries, but this requires political willpower and support from across government. In the case of strengthening labour market statistics, this can be lacking, especially when such a planning commission does not dispose of centralised resources that it can distribute to support specific ministries. Those most likely to be able to financially support the type of technical assistance the ILO provides are located at the finance ministry or in social security administrations. In Algeria, for instance, the ILO worked to train civil servants in the social security administration who were not directly involved in policymaking but were considered to be more apt at receiving the necessary training. While this allows for more long-term technical capacity building, it also means that the analytical capacity of such institutions is not well aligned with the policy objectives of the relevant ministry. Strengthening labour market analysis of social security administrations, for instance, will mean that shorter-term, occupational breakdowns relevant for the formulation of labour market policies might not be available. A third option, therefore, and one that was initially pursued in the case of Peru and Colombia, is to set up a labour market observation unit responsible for regular briefs and analytical notes to inform the minister and the general public. While such approaches deliver a more integrated policy formulation framework, they often fall prey to limited resources and shifting ministerial prerogatives.

Top Tip

Building ownership is important. This is best achieved when training staff and building capabilities are aligned with policy objectives to be perennial.

18.5 DELIVERY OF TECHNICAL ASSISTANCE

Once the appropriate institutional set-up has been established, the delivery of the technical assistance can begin. Typically for the ILO, a technical assistance programme will last between 6 and 12 months. During this time, bringing on board local expertise and establishing close collaboration with ILO experts is key for the success of such a project. For example, in the case of Peru local consultants were engaged by the government alongside national academics. In this regard, local ownership of the capacity building is essential to guarantee success and long-term adhesion to the project. Only when policy makers consider the task of monitoring labour market trends important to achieve their objectives will they guarantee sufficient resources for staff and data collection on a continuous basis.

Engaging with local expertise also requires adapting the statistical and analytical models to the local context. In both Peru and Colombia, statistical tools originally built in the context of a high-income country (namely the Employment Projection Model developed by the ILO in collaboration with the University of Maryland (Arias, 2013; Dávalos, 2013)) was used to carry out employment projection models. This was a process that had been previously implemented in other middle-income countries, such as Mongolia and the Philippines (Arias, 2013). In order for these models to be fit for purpose and to address questions ministries within government had, it was essential to engage local academics, civil servants and research consultants to identify the appropriate policy questions that these tools were supposed to address. One vital contextual factor which must be considered is the policy cycle within each country's context. The analytical work delivered should be integrated in a regular policy delivery cycle in order to generate regular demand and continuous political commitment to the overall process of gathering, analysing and using the output.

Together with colleagues in the respective countries, the ILO worked with various stakeholders and consultants to help build the Peruvian Employment Projections Model (MPEP) (Dávalos, 2013) and the Model of Employment Trends in Colombia (MPEC) (Arias, 2013). In the case of the MPEP this involved input from the Ministry of Labour and Employment Promotion (MTPE), the National Institute of Statistics and Informatics, and the Ministry of Economy and Finance. In the case of Peru, the MPEP needed to capture the informal market statistics as far as was possible in order to provide a broad picture of labour market activity across the 25 regions in the country. For this, the MPEP used forecasts under different scenarios based on predicted growth patterns to identify regional and occupational mismatches that might emerge from various shocks to growth (Dávalos, 2013). In the case of Colombia, on the other hand, the focus was on intersectoral changes and the dynamics of change in sectors within the economy caused by external shocks and how these impacted on employment (Arias, 2013). Here, the aim of the project was to identify activity and employment across 53 sectors and to integrate them into the MPEC.

Top Tip

Working closely with local experts can help contextualise models and knowledge that has been developed elsewhere and ensures ownership of the project after the intervention has ended.

In Algeria, Colombia and Peru, week-long training courses were delivered on the tailored models which had been developed. Nevertheless, any future updates to the model required further training, in particular regarding the integration of new data and the development of specific scenarios and forecasts developed on behalf of the respective ministry or administration. Providing training increases capacity and capabilities but does not mean that one department can run such a complex model without external support immediately. The purpose remains, however, that over time, national administrations will be able to update and tailor these models independently and to their own policy needs. Out of the four country cases discussed in this chapter, only in Colombia was the model run without external support from inception. In Algeria, Peru and Ghana, given the complex data and analytical tools used, several administrators from different services were involved, creating challenges for the continuous use of these tools.

18.6 OUTCOME

The ILO interventions in Colombia and Peru resulted in some key policy impacts. This included the establishment of a labour market observation group within the Peruvian Labour Ministry, which oversees the use of the MPEP model. Besides the technical challenges of this project, there were also some institutional constraints regarding the mandate of this group. At the time of the inception of the ILO technical assistance project, existing legislation restricted forecasting exercises exclusively to the Central Bank. In order for the MPEP to be adopted, a change to this legislation was, therefore, required and eventually achieved.

In the Colombian project, while there was initial success after the development of the MPEC model through capacity building of a group of five economists within the Colombian Labour Ministry, this group was dissolved within a year of the intervention ending due to shifting policy priorities with the arrival of a new labour minister. The institutional learning which had been carefully created through the ILO's relationship with the Labour Ministry was undermined, as all economists involved in the project left the Labour Ministry after this change.

Top Tip

Working in this type of environment requires an ability to weather change and be resilient.

18.7   CONCLUSIONS AND LESSONS LEARNT

The examples discussed above illustrate some key lessons that are important to consider when looking to engage policy makers in emerging markets. Firstly, there is often a trade-off between policy impact and institutional memory. The changing institutional contexts in middle-income countries means that achieving policy impact can be successful perhaps only for a short while (as in the case of the Colombian project) or can take longer to achieve. As a result of the institutional instability, capacity needs to be built in a modular way, so that the systems in place are robust to withstand disruption and change. Ideally, several different administrations should rely on a broad range of (complementary) tools so that shifting policy objectives in one place do not undermine the technical capacity available in the country more broadly.

Much of the work of the technical assistance projects is reliant on political willpower and capital. It is therefore important to also build up awareness and political interest in the policy areas you are aiming to address. In the ILO case, this means mainstreaming labour and social concerns into broader policy objectives, allowing policy makers to see the bigger picture or the macro-criticality of jobs.

Impacting and influencing policymaking in emerging market contexts brings its own unique challenges. However, there are great opportunities for researchers to have policy impact, with patience, resilience and sensitivity towards each country's context. Involving policy makers, social partners and academia in such an endeavour is key for long-term success and viability of such projects. For a policy-oriented researcher, seeing such projects taking off the ground remains one of the most rewarding experiences.

ACKNOWLEDGEMENT

The author is grateful for the support provided by the editors and in particular Lauren Tuckerman. All remaining errors are mine. The views expressed in this chapter are attributed to the author only and are not necessarily reflective of views at the ILO.

NOTES

1.   See https://www.ilo.org/global/about-the-ilo/how-the-ilo-works/member-states/lang--en/index.htm. Last accessed 13 April 2022.
2.   See https://www.ilo.org/global/about-the-ilo/mission-and-objectives/lang--en/index.htm. Last accessed 13 April 2022.
3.   At the time of the project undertaken in Colombia, the country was not part of the OECD, which it joined in April 2020.

4.   For an overview of the different ILO offices around the world, see https://www .ilo.org/global/about-the-ilo/how-the-ilo-works/departments-and-offices/lang- -en/index.htm. Last accessed 13 April 2022.
5.   ILO (2016); OECD (2016); Mendil (2020).
6.   Only in the case of Colombia did an external (private) provider have some capacity for labour market analysis and projections, which required, however, recurrent – costly – expenses on behalf of the ministry.

REFERENCES

Arias, D. 2013. *Modelo de Proyección de Empleo para Colombia.* Lima: OIT/Oficina de la OIT para los Países Andinos. Available: https://www.ilo.org/wcmsp5/groups/ public/---americas/---ro-lima/---sro-lima/documents/publication/wcms_236123.pdf. Last accessed 27 August 2021.

Dávalos, J. 2013. *Modelo de Proyección de Empleo para el Perú.* Lima: OIT/Oficina de la OIT para los Países Andinos. Available: https://www.ilo.org/lima/publicaciones/ WCMS_236122/lang--es/index.htm. Last accessed 27 August 2021.

European Training Foundation, 2016. *Labour Market and Training Observatories.* Available: http://www.etf.europa.eu/sites/default/files/m/F8E652156F4C 0E9FC12580E60049A5CE_Observatories.pdf. Last accessed 27 August 2021.

ILO, 2016. *What Works: Active Labour Market Policies in Latin America and the Caribbeans.* Geneva: ILO. Available: https://www.ilo.org/wcmsp5/groups/public/ ---dgreports/---dcomm/---publ/documents/publication/wcms_492373.pdf. Last accessed 30 September 2021.

Mendil, D. 2020. Analyse macro-économique des politiques de l'emploi en Algérie dans une perspective d'un développement durable. *Mondes en Développement,* 2(190), 91–110.

OECD, 2016. *Reviews of Labour Market and Social Policies: Colombia.* Paris: OECD.

Plata-Stenger, V. 2020. Technical Assistance 'Experts': ILO Brokers around the World, in *Social Reform, Modernization and Technical Diplomacy: The ILO Contribution to Development (1930–1946).* Berlin, Boston: De Gruyter Oldenbourg, pp. 155–88. https://doi.org/10.1515/9783110616323-010

World Bank, 2021. *Data for Low & Middle Income, Colombia, Peru.* Available: https:// data.worldbank.org/?locations=XO-CO-PE. Last accessed 27 August 2021.

19. The City-Region Economic Development Institute – establishing a successful place-based research institute to support regions in turbulent times and beyond

Rebecca Riley, Simon Collinson, Anne Green and Raquel Ortega-Argilés

19.1 INTRODUCTION

Research institutes are born out of a vision, a few good core ideas, successful funding bids and a dedicated team of researchers. This chapter explores how our vision for geographically based impact (what we also refer to as place-based), which started back in 2015, helped in the development of a research institute called City-Region Economic Development Institute (City-REDI). The chapter will explain key themes that we find are integral to City-REDI's success. We start off by discussing the importance of understanding and choosing the right funding structures. We then go into exploring how our usage of hybrid teams has been important in finding the right skills to match the needs of collaborating with policy makers. We then discuss how important it is to keep engagement with stakeholders a priority from the get-go, in order to have a fruitful and long-lasting relationship between academics and policy makers.

19.2 THE IMPORTANCE OF TYPES OF FUNDING FOR A PLACE-BASED RESEARCH INSTITUTE

The central aim of City-REDI was to develop a better understanding of city-regions as complex, integrated and unique economic, political and social systems. City-regions have different strengths and weaknesses, opportunities and threats and different potential growth paths. Policy interventions, therefore, need to be customised to be effective, and this underlies part of the argument for a certain degree of devolution to enable locally appropriate policies to be developed and applied. Key questions that need to be asked include: How do different combinations of local endowments restrict or facilitate different kinds of growth? *and* What growth impacts can we expect, over what timescales, from different kinds of interventions or investments? These remain intellectually challenging questions but are also highly relevant for policy makers who have responsibility for spending public money efficiently and effectively.

The impetus for establishing City-REDI came in part from local stakeholders looking to improve data and analysis to support policy interventions and provide evidence for necessary investments from the central government. The context of City-REDI's central aim is important, as it had been integral in securing initial funding. In the case of City-REDI, initial funding came from the University of Birmingham's internal 'Discretionary Investment Fund' (DIF), used to catalyse bold new research initiatives. The allocation of DIF funding takes into account the University of Birmingham's identity as a strong civic university with a long history as an anchor institution supporting the city-region. The UK's second city and the three Local Enterprise Partnerships (LEPs) that make up the broader West Midlands Combined Authority area were also ideal candidates for in-depth and focused research on the challenges of local, inclusive economic growth. DIF reflects on these localised factors and allocates its funding with a clear steer that new research centres should be, firstly, self-sustaining over time and, secondly, have a clear set of identified stakeholders who would benefit from the research.

The DIF proposal that secured the initial funding for City-REDI in 2015 focused on the growing importance of city-regions in the UK, as regional comparisons revealed signs of growing spatial, economic and social imbalances across the country. Data and analysis on growth and productivity, regional finances, skills, income and employment opportunities, health and wellbeing and a range of other economic and social metrics pointed to a growing polarisation. Looking back, the timing of this alignment, partly the result of some foresight and luck, was an important factor behind City-REDI's success. But the political agenda, which shapes research funding priorities, changes (often rapidly), so a highly flexible and responsive co-created strategy with stakeholders was needed to ensure longer-term sustainability.

Phase two of City-REDI was enabled in 2019 with the award of a £5 million Research England grant to establish the West Midlands Regional Economic Development Institute (WMREDI). This funding was partly matched by the University of Birmingham and a series of regional partners: the West Midlands Combined Authority, Greater Birmingham Chambers of Commerce, West Midlands Growth Company, Greater Birmingham and Solihull Local Enterprise Partnership, The Black Country Consortium Ltd.,

Aston University, Birmingham City University, and Birmingham City Council on behalf of seven local authorities.

The City-REDI proposal had been developed with, and supported by, a subset of these stakeholders who were united in their aims to: (1) present a coherent and robust strategic economic plan to central government agencies responsible for devolving resources and elements of economic control to the regions, and (2) develop a more sophisticated understanding of the challenges and trade-offs of economic growth in the Greater Birmingham city-region over the longer term. WMREDI represented a step-change in this stakeholder consortium, in terms of breadth and depth, involving co-funding and secondments for the co-production of relevant insights into the city-region. It continued with the original aims of City-REDI but with an additional emphasis on the role of universities as contributors to their regions. This reflected the growing national interest in place-based research and development (R&D) and the impact of universities at the local level as part of the civic universities' 'movement'.

The creation of WMREDI coincided with significant economic and social shocks triggered by Brexit and Covid-19, which impacted regions differently, accelerating underlying inequalities and therefore demands for a new level of responsiveness and adaptation. Understanding different scenarios and impacts to provide real-time insights and intelligence for policy makers at regional and national levels became an even greater priority. It also further highlighted the contribution that could be made by dedicated research institutes, helping to support local and national efforts to respond to these shocks.

19.3   HYBRID STRUCTURES TO COMBINE RIGOUR AND RELEVANCE

Looking back at the evolution of City-REDI we can identify some consistent elements which have underpinned its success. It was established as a hybrid to combine the interests and expertise of academic researchers and those of data analysts and policy specialists. We deliberately set up a hybrid organisation to ensure the institute had the consultancy skill sets which would be needed. The team is built from academic staff who have experience and background in policy-based research and researchers from a policy and consultancy background. This has enabled skills transfer between the different categories of researchers.

The institute had a core aim to advance understanding of place (in robust, objective, evidence-based terms) as well as be relevant to current policy and practice. This is not entirely new: the Institute for Fiscal Studies in the UK and the Economic and Social Research Institute in Ireland are other examples among a wide range of other policy institutes. However, different cultures, incentives, target outcomes and timescales mean that a shared agenda has had to be constantly reaffirmed among stakeholders and, as our focus is on improving intervention development, we have taken an approach to proactively embed our staff in organisations in the regional development landscape.

Relevance to policy and practice was reinforced by co-production structures which differentiated the institute from a linear model of disseminating findings from research initiated solely by academic interests. This is not new but is something that requires active management. Internally, this required consistent effort to steer a balance between short-term outputs, such as blogs, reports, commissioned research and joint events with policy makers and quick-turnaround feedback to senior stakeholders, and longer-term outputs, including academic papers, conferences, methodology workshops and the development of an intellectual contribution to academic national and international networks (such as the Regional Studies Association). Externally, stakeholder partnerships and co-funding activities, a senior-level advisory board with public and private sector representatives, a growing range of secondments, joint posts and projects with the above-listed organisations and others at the national level supported this approach.

The team was consciously developed to be multidisciplinary and interdisciplinary, with expertise including geography, economics, skills and labour markets, firm-level innovation and entrepreneurship, business demographics and local government. It also deliberately aimed to connect different methodological approaches, from input-output economic growth modelling to quantitative and qualitative techniques, surveys and case studies. These combinations of skills and expertise had been important in the development of an evolving toolkit for evaluating the economic impact of different interventions and investments in city-regions, with Birmingham and the West Midlands as the core focus, in comparison with other regions nationally and internationally. This supported an overarching ambition to connect the micro-foundations of growth and change with the aggregate macro-level effects to provide more precise targets for policy interventions and insights into inherent trade-offs between productivity, inclusivity and sustainability.

19.4   PLACE-BASED IMPACT – UNDERSTANDING WHAT POLICY MAKERS WANT

Within this section we look at how we identified stakeholders and established their needs. From the beginning, we took an approach based on identifying, understanding and developing a long-term relationship with partners to support the development of good policy and programme interventions based on sound evidence. We also adopted consultancy-style selling, the tools and techniques of which have been invaluable in ensuring our research findings are used and applied by our stakeholders. This section firstly discusses how we have identified our stakeholders and secondly elaborates on our application of consultancy-based selling in managing the expectations of our stakeholders.

19.4.1   Identifying Key Stakeholders

The first step we took in ensuring that our research had impact was to identify which types of stakeholders our research was more likely to have impact on. We did this by a mapping approach (Mendelow, 1991), which enabled us to look at the power of our stakeholders to utilise our research and ability to act on it, alongside their level of interest in our work. This enabled us to prioritise them and understand where our work could be best utilised as an input into the logic chain of policy and strategy development.

Through understanding the drivers of potential stakeholders and through initial interviews and meetings, we identified stakeholder expectations, power and political priorities. This helped us to identify the most and least important stakeholders according to our core purpose, looking at those who can affect, or be affected by, the work we carry out (Freeman, 1984) to create a 'winning coalition' (Bryson, 2005).

Adapting the framework for our institute, we developed this priority approach to our stakeholders back in 2015 (see Figure 19.1).

Over time, the stakeholders initially identified have not changed, but their position on the matrix has, depending on policy drivers and the research we are producing. This matrix allows us to understand the types of relationships we need to develop at any one time. Stakeholders are prioritised based on their ability to fund, use and act upon our research. This changes over time as policy priorities change and flex.

As a result of this mapping, we created an external advisory board. This board is constituted from those stakeholders with high interest and influence over our work and the greatest ability to utilise it. This included the West Midlands Combined Authority, the Mayor, Local Enterprise Partnerships, Local Authorities and the West Midlands Growth Company. Their role on our board is to help us understand their short- and long-term research needs and challenges while capitalising on a broad set of ongoing projects. This helps us understand key critical issues they may need to address in the future and whether our work can inform it.

Non-governmental organisations have also contributed to the development of the institute, including consultancies and think tanks. These organisations both benefit from using our research to complement their internal work, while bringing their perspectives to enhance ours. We have also built good relationships with several central government departments. This group of original stakeholders have followed us through the process over the last five years. They are the bedrock of our relationship building in the region.

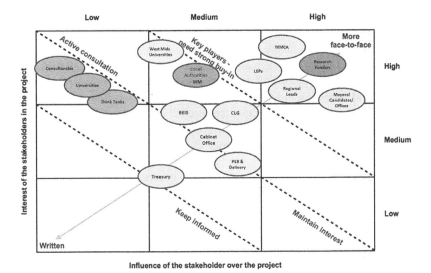

Source: City-REDI internal document; adapted from Mendelow (1981).

Figure 19.1   Stakeholder matrix, City-REDI

Within each organisation we identified economic decision makers. These are the people most likely to make a change based on our work and so generate impact. Thus they were good candidates for our board. We also looked at the technical buyers of our work: the people who understand the research, who can use it day to day and have influence over the decision makers. We built relationships with these actors across the team, based on ongoing topic-based collaborations, including on monitoring indicators for local strategies; understanding the drivers of productivity, skills gaps and shortages; and sector deep dives.

19.4.2   Managing Stakeholder Expectations Using Consultancy-Based Selling

The tools and techniques used in consultancy-style selling can be invaluable to apply in ensuring research findings are used and applied. They allow natural relationships to grow and can create engineered serendipity. The policy environment is a messy, non-linear process, where evidence is one of many inputs to decision making.

We identified that for us to be a successful research institute influencing policy development, we needed to deliver new and innovative research, exploring the underlying structural and long-term issues places face. However, we also needed to ensure our research has an impact on those issues. Therefore, it was key to embed the skills needed to influence policy which already sits in the policy world itself and the consultancy world which supports it. The institute has grown through strategically bringing in skills from these sectors, and by collaborating with people who can develop partner relationships. Key skills in the hybrid model include relationship management, social media, content creation, event management, account and project management. Although these roles sit alongside the academic roles, we are actively building these skills into the development of the early career researchers.

One of the most significant issues facing partners is the lack of capacity to develop evidence. Hence one robust method of generating impact and relationships has been secondments. City-REDI has systematically placed experienced researchers into partner organisations, and funding bids have included this process. This has meant that partners have access to skills and capabilities they need, and they can actively shape research. City-REDI staff also develop their skills and knowledge on impact and understand the challenges of creating policy in a real-world environment.

Contributing to the national policy agenda by taking part in research councils' academic and policy research initiatives, such as the Economic and Social Research Council's (ESRC's) 'The UK in a Changing Europe', has also been instrumental in gaining a national and international academic and evidence-based policy research reputation. Our academic work on Brexit has been presented to audiences including the European Committee of the Regions, the UK government and regional stakeholder meetings around the country. Material from such interactions has enriched academic outputs from these projects. We continue to work with several of these partners, providing academic advice to support their policy agendas.

19.5   DEMONSTRATING IMPACT – DELIVERING CHANGE?

As 'impact' has taken greater weight in the Research Excellence Framework (REF), many academic researchers have had to think explicitly about impact. To define what REF means by impact, the definition from UK Research and Innovation can be used: 'an effect on, change or benefit to the economy, society, culture, public policy or services, health, the environment, or quality of life beyond academia'. However, demonstrating impact and delivering change is broader than the REF and has been a primary concern of some academics/research institutes long before the REF.

Researchers with strong applied research interests rooted in real-world issues tend to display mindsets open to demonstrating impact and delivering change. They tend to gravitate towards, and feel comfortable in, research institutes with a strong applied focus. They learn early on, often implicitly, that there is no single route to achieving and demonstrating impact – in both academia and policy. They also learn that foreseen and unforeseen events can facilitate, obfuscate or stall impact and delivery of change. Some research projects/initiatives are co-created or commissioned to address policy questions and so are set up in a way to inform future policy and/or to evaluate the success of particular policy initiatives. Here the route to demonstrating impact is quite clear cut. In this context, a policy-focused report may come before an academic article. In other instances, research does not have a direct policy focus but yields insights of relevance to policy that may result in commissioning more specific policy-oriented research. Moreover, demonstrating impact and delivering change is often not about a single research project or a series of research projects that are explicitly linked together. In a thriving research institute, constellations of projects may come together to deliver more combined than the sum of individual projects. This requires both formal and informal communication during, as well as at the end of, research projects.

The phrase 'demonstrating impact' suggests a need to systematically collect information on activities and outputs from the outset of a project and thereafter on an ongoing basis. Activities include organising workshops and roundtable events (with policy makers, businesses, investment organisations, other academics, etc.) and taking part in policy-focused and academic conferences. Designing such events with non-academic partners, where applicable, can enhance the reach and impact of such events. It can help achieve a focus on issues and questions of greatest pertinence to current and future policy. Outputs include blogs, policy reports, submissions to parliamentary inquiries, engagements with international organisations, journal articles, etc. These activities and outputs do not represent impact per se but are important ingredients in demonstrating impact. As key components of the impact story, it is important to record these activities and outputs in a systematic way as they are undertaken/produced.

We give an example from City-REDI's and WMREDI's experiences of demonstrating impact and delivering change, in partnership with policy makers in the West Midlands. The example is based on research that was initially commissioned by the West Midlands Combined Authority and draws on previous academic and policy studies that are focused on sectoral and place-based aspects of understanding the business, professional and financial services (BPFS) sector in the region. The research has since spawned a subsequent national government study based on the findings of:

1. The scale and importance of the BPFS sector within the region and Birmingham city centre specifically – which had not been fully appreciated previously and which led to the formation of a Sector Action Plan.
2. The need for a diverse talent pool to achieve innovation and growth – which in turn led to the changes in employers' and skills providers' behaviour to achieve this.
3. The requirement to move place attractiveness up the regional policy agenda due to the demands of employees in the sector and the need for businesses to attract and retain staff – which provided evidence to support changes to place marketing and led to investments in infrastructure.

Specific impacts and changes emanating from the research were felt in innovation, inward investment/destination promotion, infrastructure and skills policy domains and included funding to support specific investments and initiatives.

A second example is work undertaken to monitor the impact of Covid-19 and Brexit to inform planning and interventions of local and regional partners. The project combined various existing and new data, gathering qualitative intelligence from various stakeholders. The findings demonstrated:

1. The requirement for partners to assimilate and examine the evidence to inform policy and practice in a rapidly changing environment.
2. The need to draw together and enhance regional research and evidence resources and capacity to develop better business cases for investment.
3. The need for places to be able to understand and tell their story when competing for scarce resources and influencing national government.

Importantly, capturing and measuring impacts is not solely a mechanistic 'bean counting' exercise. Assessing outcomes and measuring impact is at its heart a relational exercise. Building and maintaining relationships are key to research institutes with an applied policy focus (see Box 19.1). Those relationships, both formal and informal, are key to understanding what research policy makers need and how they might use research evidence, just as maintaining links and keeping abreast of emerging academic agendas is fundamental to good academic research. Moreover, ongoing relationships are crucial given the temporal dimension over which outcomes and impact can occur. Uncertain events such as the effects of Brexit and the Covid-19 pandemic demonstrated to the academic and research community the speed at which economic circumstances and policies can change. As in previous crises, it has also demonstrated how researchers cannot assume that key informants and policy officials will remain in the same roles. But as key informants and policy officials move on, they take their knowledge and contacts with them, underscoring the value of maintaining existing relationships as well as building new ones as circumstances and policies change.

BOX 19.1 TOP TIPS FROM CITY-REDI FOR ACHIEVING IMPACTS

1. Spend time understanding your stakeholders up front. What are their research needs and can you help them? Understanding who has the ability to act on your research means you can engage them from the outset and this improves and strengthens your work. It can give you direct access to new data partners, and enhance access for interviews, focus groups and surveys.
2. Impact is a marathon done in relays and not a sprint. It takes time to build up relationships and handing over your knowledge to the person who can actually make a change requires investment in building trust and knowledge.
3. Recognise policy makers as professional collaborators and co-creators. They are the people who can use and implement your research. They are more than audiences. They often hold access to the information you will need and are experienced researchers in their own right who can add value to academic work.
4. Expect a messy, chaotic journey but enjoy the unexpected. With the examples we highlight in the chapter, we had no idea that the resulting impact would be so far-reaching and still being fed into policy now. Our long-term relationship building means we are still engaged and shaping the impact on an ongoing basis.

REFERENCES

Bryson, J. (2005) 'What to do when stakeholders matter', *Public Management Review*, 6(1), 21–53.

Freeman, R.E. (1984) *Strategic Management: A Stakeholder Approach*, Boston: Pitman.

Mendelow, A.L. (1991) Cited in Johnson, G., Scholes, K. and Whittington, R. (2006) *Exploring Corporate Strategy: Text and Cases* (p. 182), 7th edn, UK: Prentice Hall.

Mendelow, A.L. (1981) 'Environmental scanning: The impact of the stakeholder concept', *ICIS 1981 Proceedings*. 20. Accessed 12 April 2022 at http://aisel.aisnet .org/icis1981/20

UK Research and Innovation (n.d.) Accessed May 2022 at https://www.ukri.org/ about-us/research-england/research-excellence/ref-impact/#:~:text=The%20 Research%20Excellence%20Framework%20(REF,of%20life%2C%20beyond%20 academia

20. Impacting small business policy: the Enterprise Research Centre

Vicki Belt

20.1 INTRODUCTION

The Enterprise Research Centre (ERC) is an academic research centre based jointly at Warwick and Aston University Business Schools and has been funded primarily by the Economic and Social Research Council (ESRC). Since it was first established in 2013, the ERC's mission has been to be the UK's 'go to' centre of research expertise on small and medium-sized enterprises' (SMEs') growth, innovation and productivity. Several other non-academic organisations have also contributed to the funding of the ERC over the years, including the Department for Business, Energy and Industrial Strategy, the British Business Bank, Innovate UK and the Intellectual Property Office. The ERC is a relatively small research centre, with around 20 staff (a mix of post-doctoral research fellows, administrative staff, directors and rotating academic research leads).

The ERC has built up a reputation as a provider of high quality, independent data and insight on SMEs, and for undertaking rigorous research and analysis. Research has focused on SMEs' growth dynamics and drivers of productivity, with a focus on innovation, digital adoption and management and leadership practices. The Centre has sought from the outset to deliver policy-relevant research that focuses on the issues that policy makers and businesses face, giving useful and practical, actionable recommendations, and relevance to a wider audience.

Over the past few years, the ERC has been operating in a fast-moving and somewhat complex policy context. Major concerns around the UK's productivity gap, Brexit uncertainty, and, most recently, COVID-19 have all affected the SME community deeply and have led to an intensification in demand from policy makers for timely and practical research insights and advice. This has happened at the same time as considerable staff 'churn' amongst policy officials.

Despite working in a challenging context, the ERC has had success in shaping several business policy decisions and initiatives through its research and insights, with examples including the UK Industrial Strategy, the Business Basics Programme, the Business Productivity Review, Small Business Leadership Programme and Help to Grow Scheme.[1] It has also influenced government approaches to the allocation of innovation funding for businesses, most recently in response to the COVID-19 crisis.

The experience of the ERC shows that smaller research centres can achieve effective policy influence and impact if they take a strategic approach to research communications, coupled with strong emphasis on soft engagement with key stakeholders. However, achieving this policy impact has taken time, has involved targeted investment, and has depended on a flexible and pragmatic outlook, factors which we will explore more in this chapter.

20.2   APPROACHING POLICY INFLUENCE AND IMPACT THE ERC WAY

20.2.1   A Strategic Approach to Communicating Research

In recent years there has been increasing recognition of the importance of effective and properly planned communication to achieving research impact (Langer et al., 2016). This is reflected in the growing emphasis placed on communications and impact strategies by research funding organisations.[2] It is now widely acknowledged that successfully communicating research to shape policy and practice requires a very different approach to that typically taken by academics when writing for academic publications and audiences (see more in Chapter 4). This has important implications for academic centres and institutes with ambitions to influence and impact policy.

Taking a strategic approach to research communications has been crucial to enabling policy influence and impact at the ERC. Shortly after the Centre was established, the leadership team and advisory board recognised that without successful communications and knowledge exchange activities, the Centre would not be able to achieve its mission and core aims. In response, a decision was taken to invest time in developing a communications and engagement strategy. This strategy has remained a key feature of the ERC's overall strategy over time and has been recognised as an organisational priority.

Properly prioritising research communications means that resources, both human and financial, need to be specifically dedicated to it. At the ERC, a member of staff at the director level has a specific remit to lead on the development and implementation of the communications and engagement strategy, with support from two operational staff members. The strategy is discussed and reviewed regularly at the Centre's management and board meetings. In addition, financial resources have been ring-fenced for research communications. A significant proportion of this budget has been used to buy in long-term support from a specialist communications and public relations (PR) agency, as we recognised early in the life of the ERC the benefits of drawing on professional communications expertise.

Our relationship with the communications agency has been important to our impact and is worth further reflection. It is a relationship that has strengthened over time and there has been considerable learning on both sides. Although at the ERC we have chosen to use an external PR consultancy firm, others may choose to work with the press and communications teams within their institutions. The key point is to ensure that the communications professional that is chosen really understands the target audiences and the specific objectives of your research programme or organisation, and how these translate into communications activities. At the ERC we have worked hard to ensure good dialogues with our lead communications consultant. Over time this has resulted in the development of a deep understanding of the Centre's mission, key research messages and communications needs.

When developing a communications strategy, it can be difficult for those without previous experience in the area to know where to start. In our experience, professional support is particularly beneficial at this stage. At the ERC we found a useful starting point for our strategy was to go 'back to basics', in other words, to clearly articulate the aims and objectives of the Centre, and then align these with a set of specific communications objectives. This was an important task that helped to break down the complexity of communicating the Centre's diverse range of research outputs and insights. It also enabled the development of a set of communications objectives that were clear and simple and relatively easy to measure.

It is also important to spend time identifying target audiences, and we would recommend undertaking a stakeholder mapping exercise to do this. Stakeholder analysis enables audiences and user groups to be prioritised. It can be a very useful tool for researchers seeking policy influence and impact (Slunge et al., 2017). There are a range of mapping techniques available, and it is worth exploring which one would provide the best fit for your needs. At the ERC we chose the 'power-interest' matrix, which enables identification and prioritisation of stakeholders according to their levels of power and interest in a research agenda. The ERC, like many academic research centres, has a potentially wide audience for its research outputs, but we found it helpful to narrow this down into four main target groups to focus our communications.

After identifying target audiences, it is important to spend time thinking carefully about the distinct information needs of each group and the key messages you want to communicate to them. This also raises the associated question of which communication methods would be best to leverage to connect with your target audiences effectively. This involves thinking about the channels most used by each audience, and which ones you are best equipped to make use of. At the ERC we have used a range of channels, including the Centre's website, email newsletters, traditional print/broadcast media and social media channels, as well as stakeholder events to communicate the Centre's research. We would recommend a similar broad-brush approach to others since information is accessed by stakeholders in a variety of ways.

To influence policy maker audiences successfully, however, it is not enough to simply make research easily available to them (although this is of course very important). It is also necessary to make it clear exactly *how* research findings are relevant to them by tailoring outputs accordingly. This requires a considerable amount of work over and above the production of the 'typical' research outputs produced by academic researchers. Over time, the ERC, like many other academic research centres, has realised the importance of creating a variety of types of content designed with different audiences in mind to reflect their specific interests and needs. Consequently, the ERC's outputs now include a range of types of publications, from more traditional academic research papers, to more widely accessible research reports, to shorter, more focused research insight papers, policy briefings, infographic material and blog posts. Academic researchers are often advised by impact experts that when attempting to engage policy makers in research it is important to set out messages in a concise format, and in clear, accessible language. This has arguably become increasingly important in recent times as policy makers face intense pressures and have less time to search and digest complex research outputs. We have frequently found that our shorter papers, briefing notes and blogs focused on topical themes, and infographic materials have been more likely to be noticed and read by policy makers than more substantial technical research reports. It is important that this process of distilling and simplifying should not be regarded as 'dumbing down' research, but rather as a way of making findings more widely understandable and practically applicable.

Most guides to communications strategy development will also emphasise the importance of monitoring and measuring effectiveness by developing key performance indicators (KPIs). Whilst at the ERC we started out with a long list of over 40 performance indicators for our communications strategy, we have learnt over time that it is more useful to have a focused list of 10–12 core KPIs that best reflect the ERC's core communications objectives. These KPIs are reviewed formally on an annual basis, which helps to generate momentum with outputs. However, it is also important to informally monitor communication practices regularly by seeking ongoing feedback from stakeholders about what has worked well and not so well.

In our experience, taking a strategic approach to research communication is a crucial part of the recipe for policy impact. To be successful, communication needs to be regarded as an organisational priority and properly managed. This requires appropriate investment – both financially and in terms of staff resources and time. Using external communications expertise is also beneficial. However, even with the best and most well-resourced communications strategy in place, policy impact is not guaranteed. Our experience at the ERC also shows that nurturing strong relationships with priority stakeholders via 'soft engagement' activity is also vital.

20.2.2 Targeted Soft Engagement

The ERC has always prioritised building strong relationships with its key stakeholders through soft engagement, by which we mean regular, intensive and responsive personal contact. Soft engagement takes place at the ERC in a range of ways. First, we have built structures and mechanisms which enable ERC staff to interact on a regular basis with its main stakeholders. This includes establishing a steering group for the Centre made up of strategically important contacts with an interest in the Centre's research and setting up regular catch-up meetings with policy officials in key stakeholder organisations. Second, when undertaking research projects, we endeavour to follow an 'engaged scholarship' approach. Engaged scholarship has been defined as 'a participative form of research for obtaining the advice and perspectives of key stakeholders (researchers, users, clients, sponsors, and practitioners) to understand a complex social problem' (Van de Ven, 2007). At the ERC, this process begins at the outset of a new project, where discussions take place with relevant stakeholders about key policy questions and knowledge gaps. Then researchers work with stakeholders to sharpen research questions and identify opportunities for achieving impact. During the research, discussions take place about emerging findings, priority messages and the best ways of communicating these. This approach ensures that policy makers and practitioners are engaged in the ERC's research throughout the research cycle, and that outputs are co-created where possible.

Beyond these more 'formal' engagement structures and processes, soft engagement has become more broadly embedded in the ERC's general culture and approach. Over time, our relationships with key stakeholders have evolved into almost daily contact between ERC staff and key stakeholders. A consultation exercise with the ERC's stakeholders in 2017 revealed that policy officials strongly valued the 'openness' of the ERC team. This openness is something we have deliberately aimed for as we have sought to position ourselves as a useful 'critical friend' to our priority stakeholders (see Chapter 10 for more information on the role of critical friends). It has relied on us ensuring the team is as approachable and responsive as possible to stakeholder requests. Building and maintaining these relationships has depended on the development of a strong rapport with policy makers. As well as providing advice, this has also involved time listening to and understanding their needs, being clear and honest about where we can provide advice and where the limitations of our expertise lie.

One useful lesson that we have learnt from this extensive soft engagement is that policy makers are not always interested in the very latest, novel research insights. Instead, they are often looking for reliable summaries of existing research evidence. Reflecting this, we have spent an increasing proportion of our time on 'knowledge curation' activities. As other commentators have observed (e.g. Gavine et al., 2018; Lawrence et al., 2017), in an increasingly time-pressed context, policy makers have less time to conduct systematic, rigorous evidence searches. They often face challenges with 'information overload' (when the amount of possibly relevant evidence becomes overwhelming). There is a role, therefore, for academics in collating and summarising evidence for policy makers providing rapid access to bodies of research evidence.

Recently, for example, the ERC has spent more time delivering evidence reviews, tailored workshops and 'teach-ins' to stakeholders focused on specific themes of interest. The Centre has now published a substantial library of 'State of the Art' reviews covering a variety of topical themes, which has been well received by policy makers. We have also spent more time working directly with policy makers discussing bodies of evidence and their implications to help them frame policy issues more clearly. For example, in the light of the impact of the COVID-19 pandemic, the Centre has convened several 'roundtable' style workshops, frequently at short notice, bringing together evidence that has aided policy makers developing SME support policies. This has included development of the 'Help to Grow' scheme that was launched in June 2021. Through these events the ERC has successfully challenged several policy maker preconceptions about the factors affecting SME performance and innovation. This highly responsive engagement has been especially important in the context of a shifting and highly challenging policy landscape and high staff turnover amongst policy officials, particularly in government departments.

Soft engagement with policy makers has become an intrinsic part of the ERC's work, and we can say with confidence that it has been effective. However, it is also time consuming, and those seeking to follow a similar path need to be aware of this. Stakeholder relationships are never static. There is a constant process of 'keeping up' with key individuals and organisational agendas through a range of channels (e.g. social media networking, conferences, meetings). Relationship-building activities require good soft skills, and there is a considerable amount of background operational and administrative work involved too that is sometimes overlooked in planning and resourcing (e.g. organising meetings and events, keeping stakeholder databases up to date). Sometimes requests for advice and insight come unexpectedly and with short deadlines, and there will also be occasions where a large amount of time will be invested in engagement with no clear impact, and, often, no payment for time used. In short, stakeholder engagement is far from straightforward, neat and easy to manage.

20.3   REFLECTIONS AND OUTCOMES

The ERC has achieved success in research–policy engagement through a combination of strategic research communication and intensive soft engagement. Over time, the Centre has built a reputation of providing trusted expertise to policy makers, which we have achieved by placing the needs of stakeholders centre stage. As Cairney and Kwiatkowski (2017) suggest, we have done this by using insights from psychology to understand the perspectives of stakeholders and the policy processes in which they engage. This has involved taking time to understand stakeholder motives, objectives and pressures. It has also required 'mainstreaming' engagement into the culture of the organisation. In other words, stakeholder engagement is not just something we do at the end of a research project when disseminating findings, but instead we have deliberately and necessarily embedded it into our overall strategy and approach.

For the ERC, as for other organisations, achieving policy influence and impact has had many benefits, including access to increased research funding. But it has not been a simple path. It has involved a considerable amount of time, effort and ongoing learning. Staff at all levels have had to learn new skills and have often had to step outside of their comfort zones. As Cairney and Oliver (2018) note, the 'emotional, practical and cognitive labour' involved in policy maker engagement should not be underestimated. Our experiences at the ERC also confirm their assertion that taking a pragmatic approach is key. Successful engagement involves an acceptance that the world of evidence-based policymaking does not operate in an idealised way. Policy makers frequently use shortcuts, are time-pressed, influenced by political pressures and tend to base judgements on their own beliefs and emotions. Not all engagement is systematic and orderly; rather it is often ad hoc and unexpected (Huzzard, 2021). Academics seeking to achieve policy impact need to acknowledge these realities and work within them.

The realities of the world of policymaking have become more visible in the context of the COVID-19 pandemic, which has placed the role of academic expertise in the spotlight as never before. For the ERC, the pandemic has shown the value of the relationship we have built with policy makers, as the Centre's expertise has been increasingly sought to help with the development of strategies for business support during this highly challenging period. More widely there have been many examples of researchers working to make their research findings available and relevant to policy makers at a much faster rate than ever before. The pandemic has highlighted the importance of academics providing responsive advice and data to inform policy responses in a range of areas. It has also shown that policy makers cannot always afford the luxury of waiting for 'perfect' information before acting, otherwise policy decisions are made too late. Unfortunately, as several authors have noted, much research undertaken in universities, whilst being highly policy-relevant, remains under-utilised by policy makers (Lawrence et al., 2017; Slunge et al., 2017). The unprecedented developments associated with the COVID-19 crisis present new opportunities for academics to work more cooperatively and openly with the policymaking community, and they need to be grasped.

It is hoped that the ERC's experiences add to the available empirical evidence based on research–policy impact and can inform other researchers wishing to create impact through their research. Our approach has been based on prioritising an underpinning communications strategy alongside strong soft engagement practices and a pragmatic outlook. Although there are many challenges to achieving policy impact, for the ERC the rewards have been worthwhile. Not least, as the COVID-19 pandemic has highlighted, giving us the opportunity to contribute to a better understanding of some of the most pressing issues facing businesses and impacting on the policies designed to tackle them.

Top Tips from the ERC for Achieving Research Impact

Reflecting on our experiences over the last few years, we condense our insights into five top tips for achieving research impact:

- *A communications strategy is essential* if you are serious about influencing research through policy. This needs to be carefully aligned with the overall aims and mission of your research programme or organisation. It is helpful to build in some simple evaluation measures to maintain momentum, so that you will know if you have succeeded in meeting your objectives, and where there might be room for improvement. It is well worth buying in specialist help from communications experts to help with strategy formulation, whether this be in the form of external consultants or university-based communications teams.
- *Spend time identifying and understanding your target audiences.* This can be done through processes of stakeholder mapping and ongoing engagement. Properly understand the information needs and the organisational and policy context of your priority stakeholders and produce

a variety of tailored outputs for them. Make your research relevant to them and easily readable. Do not be afraid of simplifying complexity into more simple stories. Make use of a wide range of communications channels to get your research noticed.

- *It is not all about the 'new'.* Knowledge curation is increasingly valued by policy makers. It can often be produced more quickly and can be more persuasive in the sense that it collates, presents and summarises a range of information, thus making a powerful case for action. Getting the right balance between knowledge creation and knowledge curation is key to impact.
- *A long-term view is essential.* Do not underestimate the time that is involved in achieving policy impact. Building relationships with policy makers is time consuming and requires significant time spent listening and building rapport. Expect to spend many hours on engagement activity that may not necessarily lead to any clear impact outcomes. On the other hand, unexpected requests may lead to bigger impacts than you anticipate.
- *Do not be afraid to step out of your comfort zone.* Achieving policy impact requires a range of different skills – technical, creative and social – and staff need to be prepared to try new approaches and to make mistakes. Reflect continuously on whether your engagement is working by seeking feedback from stakeholders and be prepared to be responsive and make changes where they are needed. Learn from your mistakes and from when things go wrong. After all, there is no perfect approach to achieving policy impact.

NOTES

1. More information about all these initiatives can be found on https://www.gov.uk.
2. See for example the ESRC's communications and impact strategy template: available at: https://esrc.ukri.org/research/impact-toolkit/developing-a-communications-and-impact-strategy/ (accessed: 11 April 2022).

REFERENCES

Cairney, P., Kwiatkowski, R. (2017) 'How to communicate effectively with policy makers: combine insights from psychology and policy studies.' *Palgrave Communications* 3(1), 1–8. https://doi.org/10.1057/s41599-017-0046-8

Cairney, P., Oliver, K. (2018) 'How should academics engage in policymaking to achieve impact?' *Political Studies Review*, 18(2), 228–44. doi:10.1177/1478929918807714

Gavine, A., MacGillivray, S., Ross-Davie, M., Campbell, K., White, L., Renfrew, M. (2018) 'Maximising the availability and use of high-quality evidence for policymaking: collaborative, targeted and efficient evidence reviews.' *Palgrave Communications*, 4(1), 1–8. https://doi.org/10.1057/s41599-017-0054-8

Huzzard, T. (2021) 'Achieving impact: exploring the challenge of stakeholder engagement.' *European Journal of Work and Organizational Psychology*, 30(3), 379–89. https://doi.org/10.1080/1359432X.2020.1761875

Langer, L., Tripney, J., Gough, D. (2016) *The Science of Using Science: Researching the Use of Research Evidence in Decision-Making*. London: EPPI-Centre, Social Science Research Unit, UCL Institute of Education, University College London. Available at: https://eppi.ioe.ac.uk/cms/Default.aspx?tabid=3504 (accessed: 23 November 2020).

Lawrence, N.S., Chambers, J.C., Morrison, S.M., Bestmann, S., O'Grady, G., Chambers, C.D., Kythreotis, A.P. (2017) 'The Evidence Information Service as a new platform for supporting evidence-based policy: a consultation of UK parliamentarians.' *Evidence & Policy*, 13(2), 275–316. https://doi.org/10.1332/1744 26416X14643531912169

Slunge, D., Drakenberg, O., Ekbom, A., Göthberg, M., Knaggård, A., Sahlin, U. (2017) 'Stakeholder interaction in research processes: a guide for researchers and research groups.' Available at: https://gupea.ub.gu.se/bitstream/2077/51971/1/gupea_2077 _51971_1.pdf (accessed: 24 January 2021).

Van de Ven, A. (2007) *Engaged Scholarship: A Guide for Organizational and Social Research*. Oxford: Oxford University Press.

21. Impacting policy thinking through partnership: insights from Northern Ireland

Jen Nelles, Tim Vorley and Eoin McFadden

21.1 INTRODUCTION

The productivity puzzle has come to capture the imagination of academics and policymakers since the Great Financial Crisis (McCann and Vorley, 2020; van Ark and Venables, 2020). In 2019, the Northern Ireland Department for the Economy (DfE) was grappling with an important and perennial question: what policies might meaningfully increase productivity outcomes? While low productivity growth had been a concern across the UK, it had been a persistent issue in Northern Ireland, which had consistently been lower than the rest of the UK and had little sign of impact from previous Northern Ireland economic strategies.

The Productivity Insights Network (PIN) was launched in 2018 funded by the Economic and Social Research Council (ESRC) as a multi-disciplinary network of social science researchers engaged with public, private and third sector partners to change the tone of the productivity debate in theory and practice. As part of its mandate, PIN funds research that advances or explores new directions in productivity research in conjunction with key user communities, promoting new research-based partnerships. In this chapter we reflect on the experience of partnering with the DfE, to apply insights from this research using a systems lens to map and explain the complex reality of the productivity puzzle (Nelles et al., 2021a). The research around which this partnership formed argues that approaching productivity policy through familiar silos may be hindering progress in understanding and tackling sluggish post-recession productivity growth (Vorley and Nelles, 2020).

21.2   FROM ESTABLISHING A CONNECTION TO DEVELOPING A PARTNERSHIP

The basis of the partnership with DfE was serendipitous. The research that stimulated the partnership was presented at a PIN workshop with the Department for Business, Energy & Industrial Strategy (BEIS) in the spring of 2019. The presentation was shared on social media (see Box 21.1), which came to the attention of colleagues at DfE. This initial interest from DfE in the presentation resulted in a joint workshop hosted in Belfast, and led to a new project looking to apply a systems thinking lens to the *Economy 2030, the Industrial Strategy for Northern Ireland*. Over the next six months, researchers from PIN and DfE worked together to develop and apply an experimental methodology to policy analysis that resulted in a final report, several public presentations, and academic publications that are under review.

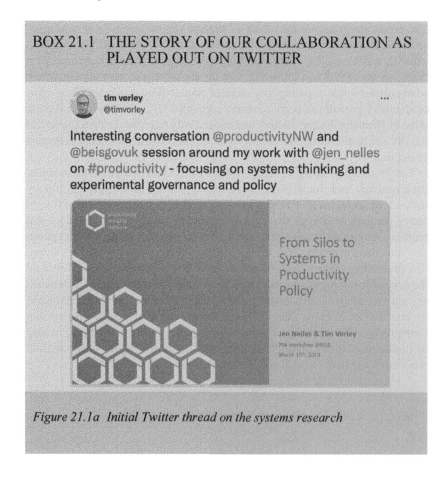

BOX 21.1   THE STORY OF OUR COLLABORATION AS PLAYED OUT ON TWITTER

tim vorley
@timvorley

Interesting conversation @productivityNW and @beisgovuk session around my work with @jen_nelles on #productivity - focusing on systems thinking and experimental governance and policy

From Silos to Systems in Productivity Policy

Jen Nelles & Tim Vorley
PIN Workshop @BEIS
March 15th, 2019

Figure 21.1a Initial Twitter thread on the systems research

Productivity NW+
@productivityNW   ...

Excellent round table with @Economy_NI and the start of an exciting project.

4:05 pm · 9 Sep 2019 · Twitter for Android

Figure 21.1b The follow-up research workshop and presentation in Belfast

The past month has reinforced how important a tool Twitter is for networking, outreach, sourcing views & getting useful insights. #sbri #innovation #policy @instituteforgov @productivityNW @MATRIX_NI 🤓 If only LinkedIn had a decent interface 😬

7:15 pm · 27 Sep 2019 · Twitter for iPhone

Figure 21.1c Reflections from participants

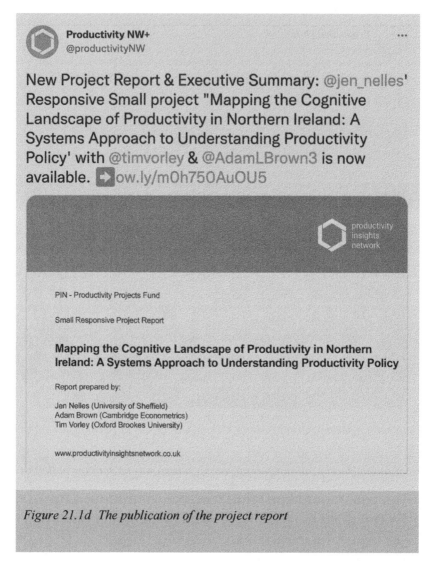

Figure 21.1d The publication of the project report

Further to the workshop and results of the project, a key outcome has been an enduring research and knowledge exchange partnership between DfE and a group of researchers. For DfE, the benefits were principally related to incorporating different ways of thinking and gathering evidence in their policy making process as well as solidifying an enduring partnership with PIN and related organisation partners such as the Productivity Institute and the Innovation Caucus. Issues such as low productivity and innovation performance are complex and addressing them involves engaging with complex eco-systems and multiple interactions and participants. The collaborative approach deepened the researchers' understanding of the policy context and generated impact for stakeholders. DfE regularly works with external stakeholders and research partners as part of the policy development process. Typically, these interactions involve consulting with target communities through represent-atives, such as industry associations. As part of this process, DfE circulates draft policy documents to groups of stakeholders for comments and feedback, although engagement with academics tends to be either as consultees or, more frequently, in commissioning research papers.

As PIN researchers, the work on applying a systems thinking to inform new approaches towards productivity policy was initially conceptual, and the team was looking for opportunities to collaborate on new applied empirical projects. The collaboration with DfE provided an opportunity to get to know policymak-ers better and build longer-term networks, with the opportunity to inform and impact future policy agendas (Evans and Cvitanovic, 2018; Tilley et al., 2017). Listening and responding through dialogue and debate with colleagues at DfE yielded insights about how policy works and offered neutral perspectives on the evidence in relation to policy using work on systems thinking (see Oliver and Cairney, 2019).

PIN has a specific mandate to fund and encourage interdisciplinary projects that engage across a wide variety of stakeholders. Engaging with partners in the government was a natural extension of that agenda and working with DfE presented a fruitful opportunity to develop an empirical project. This partner-ship was also prioritised within PIN as it looked to expand its engagement with devolved regions in relation to the Industrial Strategy, which was a flagship policy. The opportunity to connect with policymakers and other economic actors in Northern Ireland fulfilled an ambition to develop more robust policy connections outside of England and to bring regional stories more centrally into PIN's evolving evidence base.

This confluence of motivations ultimately led to the development of a joint workshop with participants from PIN and various stakeholders in Northern Ireland. The workshop was used to share research experiences on productivity, policy making and impact, and helped in the development of a formal collabo-rative project. While the workshop built some important connections between researchers and stakeholders, the collaborative project created the most unex-pected and enduring outcomes for DfE.

21.3   CO-PRODUCING THE PROJECT

Earlier work produced as a part of the book *Productivity Perspectives* (see Vorley and Nelles, 2020) argued that the UK's productivity puzzle may be partially explained by the persistence of siloed approaches to productivity policy. Briefly, governments have tended to list the factors affecting productivity as separate policy streams. The UK Industrial Strategy, for instance, identifies five 'foundations' of productivity: ideas, infrastructure, people, business environment, and places (HM Government, 2017). The white paper lists policy recommendations separately in each section, a structure that seems to have been mirrored in implementation. The chapter then suggested that one potential avenue might be to rethink productivity as an outcome of a system of interactions, rather than simply the result of five categories of inputs. In other words, it argued that policies may have failed to achieve desired results, in part because interventions across the system created, were caught in, or had ignored feedback loops that diminished their impacts. Understanding the problem space as embedded in a complex adaptive system and applying principles of system dynamics might then open up new realisations about the relationships between policy goals and outcomes across silos and generate new insights for policy design.

While these arguments seemed to resonate across academic and policy making audiences, they were, at that point, only a theoretical contribution to the productivity debate. However, the chapter suggested a roadmap to develop an empirical project. When DfE expressed their interest in applying a systems perspective to evaluating the *Economy 2030, the Industrial Strategy for Northern Ireland,* the research team seized the opportunity to design an experimental project to explore the role of productivity and the factors that affect it in Northern Ireland. The project was intended to generate insights for DfE as they considered a refresh of the (then two-year-old) draft Industrial Strategy document, and to pilot an approach that might be used in other regions or geographical contexts to map systems and highlight policy interactions and interdependencies. As opposed to being an academic project, the focus of the collaborative project was co-developed by DfE and a number of stakeholders, and it offered the opportunity for the government, businesses, and academia to develop a shared understanding of the potential benefits of taking a systems-based approach to understanding productivity. The conceptual direction of the project originated from earlier work done by PIN's researchers, which can be found in their first edited volume,

The project involved two phases. First, a text-based analysis and comparison of the Economy 2030 document and the evidence base of approximately 100 documents that fed into its drafting. This text-based approach applied modified concept mapping techniques to extrapolate a map of how concepts were related in the Industrial Strategy versus in the aggregated evidence base, enabling an analysis of how perceptions of the role of productivity and the system portrayed in policy differed from that derived from the evidence base.

This required DfE cooperation in securing access to the evidence base list and documents, some of which were internal.

The second phase consisted of a series of group or participatory mapping workshops with stakeholders with interests in the Industrial Strategy. These sessions asked participants to discuss the function of the Industrial Strategy and identify interactions between factors that fed into those goals. This created a third system map, which helped to triangulate sources and identify similarities and differences between policy, evidence base, and 'real time' perceptions of the economic system. In this phase, DfE was instrumental in identifying workshop participants. Participants were drawn from academia, firms, government (from within DfE as well as other departments), and from organisations representing private sector interests. DfE was also crucial in inviting participants to the event, ensuring broad-based participation, and hosting the sessions. Each session lasted approximately 90 minutes and consisted of an introduction, collaborative mapping session and final discussion.

A central finding was that while the various cognitive maps differed in interesting ways, they were similar in that productivity was not as central to policy or to economic discourse in practice as policymakers and academics would like to think. This may be because it is poorly defined, poorly understood, difficult to engage with, or seen as less (politically) important than other, more popularly accepted factors. It is clear that productivity is affected by a wide variety of policies regardless of whether stakeholders care to discuss the concept or not, and regardless of whether it is central to policy agendas. Nonetheless, if the lack of clear definition and lack of policy centrality observed in the course of the study has been a long-term feature of economic policy in Northern Ireland (and indeed possibly the UK), then it is no surprise that a variety of uncoordinated policies have been unable to meaningfully move the productivity needle. This suggests that in order to effectively tackle the problem of productivity, policymakers may benefit from a much more coordinated approach, in word as well as deed. Full project findings were published in a final report released in 2020 (Nelles et al., 2020).

The project was a joint effort between the academic team and DfE, but the work was led and conducted primarily by the academics. As outlined above, DfE's contribution to the project was vital in securing access to the evidence base and to catalysing stakeholder participation. It also participated by convening a steering group to observe and steer the research process. This was led by senior personnel within DfE's policy division and attended by a wide range of participants from within the Department and external policy organisations. These sessions were valuable to both the academics and government partners in information clearing, identifying ways that DfE could assist with internal assets, and in collaboratively shaping the narrative of the resulting report.

21.4   OUTCOMES

This project had lasting benefits for both the Department and the academic partners, although, significantly, the results of the research itself, while illuminating, were probably the least of these. This is less an indictment of the quality of the research itself than an observation that other factors ended up creating more lasting impact. Rather, the most enduring benefits of this collaboration related to, for DfE, experiences that might ultimately shift internal practices on engaged policy making and, for the academics, increased visibility and impact of the research. For both, the interaction forged new relationships that broadened networks and deepened knowledge exchange. These experiences allowed us, collectively, to draw some important lessons about the value of collaborative research and about the kind of mindset that is required to unlock benefits beyond research output in these types of partnerships.

The academic partners also gained substantially from the experience. The research was useful for developing the empirical aspect of their research agendas, testing hypotheses and refining theory. The findings were disseminated in two working papers and have informed the further development of their research (Nelles et al., 2020; Nelles et al., 2021b). As such, the experience was valuable from the common metrics of academic output and knowledge generation. However, as with DfE, the process itself, and the involvement of DfE as a participant, had benefits beyond the research product.

It is worth acknowledging that this research would not have been possible without the level of access and assistance that DfE provided throughout the course of the project. Its role in convening workshops and sharing evidence base documents was already covered above, but the steering group meetings were also incredibly valuable in interpreting the results. For instance, the research revealed that the Industrial Strategy and the evidence base were biased towards certain policy pillars over others. Discussions with the steering committee provided crucial context to explain those patterns. Without this insight, the conclusions of the academic work risked being inaccurate or misleading. In subsequent interactions with policy actors, the academic team has learned that consulting relevant departments on results before drawing conclusions almost always improves interpretation and that the opportunity to 'get it right' is also much appreciated from the policy side.

The interaction between PIN researchers and DfE also built a lasting relationship between the organisations as well as between the researchers and principals within the Department. DfE has supported successive bids and assisted with subsequent projects. Involvement with DfE has also raised the profile of the researchers' work in policy circles and resulted in more effective knowledge dissemination. In 2020, this profile resulted in invitations to present in webinar series hosted by the Centre for Exploring Complexity Across the Nexus, a research centre hosted at the University of Surrey, and by the Ministry of Housing, Communities and Local Governments. Both of those experiences further developed the researchers' networks and have resulted in additional research partnerships.

The research was beneficial to DfE in demonstrating that the focus of the Industrial Strategy was not productivity as was assumed, but rather included productivity. The study confirmed that jobs and employment were actually much more central and highlighted some significant gaps in some areas of the strategy relative to the evidence base and participatory maps. These findings will be useful in informing the development of a new Industrial Strategy. However, the process of engaging with stakeholders through the research project yielded important additional insights that are likely to have longer-term benefits.

First, the participatory mapping sessions introduced new ways of doing policy consultations and engagement. DfE participants in the group mapping sessions noted that the kinds of feedback that they got on the substance and purpose of the Industrial Strategy differed significantly from what was standard in other policy consultation forums. These sessions were structured as group problem solving exercises. Nothing was presumed in advance – not even the goal(s) positioned at the centre of the map – and so lively discussions resulted not only on what the Industrial Strategy should do, but how best to accomplish that. Again, the content of the discussions generated some insight, but the process revealed more generally that you can get meaningful participation and richer policy feedback through open-ended engagement. DfE officials observed that discussions were much more open and engaging than the more typical policy consultation previously used. DfE intends to begin incorporating participatory policy consultation sessions, alongside typical requests for comment, into its policy design and evaluation process, having experienced the benefits of this kind of open and iterative format.

Second, this collaborative engagement demonstrated that the social sciences have lots to offer policy. Given its economic focus, the Department is accustomed to consulting economists to develop models and forecasts to inform policy. This experience, which involved working with an economic geographer and a political scientist, showed that social scientists come at problems from different and sometimes unexpected perspectives that yield fresh interpretations of old problems. These can add value particularly in the pre-policy thinking phase of policy design. This is particularly valuable when examining complex issues with multiple potential policy levers and stakeholders.

Finally, the process of engaging with researchers and their broader networks – in this case, PIN and the academics and policy players involved with it – helped to expand DfE's own networks and raised the profile of its initiatives.

Following the joint sessions, DfE reported an increase in engagement with governmental departments in London, such as BEIS and with a much wider academic network across the UK (the UK Productivity Institute is likely to be a cornerstone of this).

From DfE's perspective, the biggest takeaways from the experience were that stakeholders looking to engage with academics should be open to flexibility on outcomes and understand that many of the benefits may be intangible and difficult to measure. Those with fixed ideas and looking for specific products – such as a productivity roadmap – may be disappointed. This project did not produce the clear policy direction that some were hoping might result. But, as described above, the experience did yield other benefits that will likely have a lasting impact and easily justify the effort of engaging in this type of collaborative project. This project has resulted in an increased openness in DfE to new approaches to policy development, including system dynamics modelling and horizon scanning, and an appetite for new methods of stakeholder engagement that will be increasingly important in tackling forthcoming economic challenges.

21.5   REFLECTIONS

A partnership between the PIN and DfE that started simply with a Tweet of a system dynamics mapping of productivity served as the foundation for a collaborative project intended to better understand the alignment of policy objectives and outcomes. The project has not yet impacted policy objectives or outcomes, but through the collaboration is challenging thinking among analysts and policy advisors in rethinking the problem and how it might be addressed. In many respects applying the systems lens to policy is not new, however, through this collaborative project the PIN team were able to support the DfE team in moving beyond the hypothetical and highlight new insights and ways of approaching persistent policy challenges

As with any new collaborative research partnership, the ongoing work between PIN and DfE is continuing to evolve. Through the projects there has been important learning on both sides; the academic partners have greater understanding of the policy landscape in a devolved administration, while the policy colleagues have benefitted from co-producing insights with the academics relevant to their core role. The project-based nature of the work and the need to attract funding to undertake research remains a challenge, but the commitment to collaboration provides an important impetus to move the work forward. It is not the case that the research will be permanent or ongoing, but the collaboration has provided an enduring connection that continues outside of the project and with a commitment to identifying future opportunities.

Overall, and from the humble foundations of a lone Tweet, the project that was subsequently conceived and delivered more than achieved its intended outcomes and went on to deliver benefits beyond what was intended. Perhaps this chapter serves to highlight the value of serendipity as part of the research process, although we would suggest that it was the ability and agility to respond and capitalise on the opportunity that enabled things to happen. For now, however, the academic work on productivity and systems continues, enriched by the empirical side project on Northern Ireland, which served to further both conceptual and applied understanding of the field.

REFERENCES

Evans, M.C., and Cvitanovic, C. (2018). An introduction to achieving policy impact for early career researchers. *Palgrave Commun* 4(1):88. https://doi.org/10.1057/s41599-018-0144-2

HM Government. (2017). *Industrial Strategy White Paper: Building a Britain Fit for the Future*. Accessed 15 May 2020 at https://assets.publishing.service.gov. uk/government/uploads/system/uploads/attachment_data/file/664563/industrial-strateg y-white-paper-web-ready-version.pdf

McCann, P., and Vorley, T. (eds) (2020). *Productivity Perspectives.* Cheltenham, UK and Northampton, MA, USA: Edward Elgar Publishing.

Nelles, J., Brown, A., and Vorley, T. (2020). Mapping the cognitive landscape of productivity in Northern Ireland: a systems approach to understanding productivity policy. Productivity Insights Network Report. Accessed 15 May 2020 at https://productivityinsightsnetwork.co.uk/app/uploads/2020/07/JNTVAB-Report -DRAFT_ReportOnlyFormatted.pdf

Nelles, J., Vorley, T., and Brown, A. (2021a). From systems change to systems changed: assuming a systems-based approach in response to crisis. In P. McCann and T. Vorley (eds), *Productivity and the Pandemic*. Cheltenham, UK and Northampton, MA, USA: Edward Elgar Publishing (pp. 250–62).

Nelles, J., Brown, A., Meehan, C., and Vorley, T. (2021b). Adopting a systems perspective on the productivity puzzle: early insights and methodological lessons. Productivity Insights Network Report. Accessed 27 June 2022 at https://productivityinsightsnetwork.co.uk/app/uploads/2021/07/Nelles_PINReport _SystemsMethods_FinalDraft.pdf

Northern Ireland Department for the Economy. (2017). *Economy 2030: A Consultation on an Industrial Strategy for Northern Ireland*. Accessed at https://www.economy-ni .gov.uk/sites/default/files/consultations/economy/industrial-strategy-ni-consultation -document.pdf

Oliver, K., and Cairney, P. (2019). The dos and don'ts of influencing policy: a systematic review of advice to academics. *Palgrave Commun* 5(1), 1–11. https://doi.org/10 .1057/s41599-019-0232-y

Tilley, H., Shaxson, L., Rea, J., Ball, L., and Young, J. (2017). 10 things to know about how to influence policy with research. Accessed 16 August 2021 at https://www .odi. org/publications/ 10671-10-things-know-about-how-influence-policy-research

van Ark, B., and Venables, A.J. (2020). A concerted effort to tackle the UK productivity puzzle, *International Productivity Monitor*, 39(Fall), 3–15.

Vorley, T., and Nelles, J. (2020). From silos to systems: insights and implications for productivity policy. In P. McCann and T. Vorley (eds), *Productivity Perspectives*. Cheltenham, UK and Northampton, MA, USA: Edward Elgar Publishing (pp. 274–92).

22. Critical engagement in diversity and entrepreneurship: lessons from the Centre for Research in Ethnic Minority Entrepreneurship

Monder Ram[1]

22.1   INTRODUCTION

Race, entrepreneurship and policy – quite a heady brew when you put them together. That is what my colleagues and I have been doing at the Centre for Research in Ethnic Minority Entrepreneurship (CREME) for nearly two decades. The centre was established in 2004 as a joint venture between a Regional Development Agency and a university to disseminate research on ethnic minority entrepreneurship to practitioners. CREME has had an impact in mind since its inception: its *raison d'être* is to work with diverse business communities to promote change whilst conducting critically oriented research. The challenge of navigating academic and practitioner domains is often difficult, but it is amplified when the subject matter, race and entrepreneurship, is politically sensitive, contentious and subject to the ideological whims of policy makers.

Nonetheless, CREME researchers have developed a variety of innovative approaches to engage with, and make a difference to, stakeholders, ranging from the banking sector to newly arrived migrant communities. Such approaches are gaining traction with practitioners looking for progressive economic solutions to the ruptures revealed by COVID-19, Black Lives Matter and Brexit. This chapter offers insights derived from CREME's diverse form of engagement with practitioners, comprising stakeholder consultation, action research and new venture creation. Our core argument is that CREME's foundational commitment to engagement has benefits for researchers and practitioners alike.

For researchers, CREME's experience shows how critical research with an applied edge can be invaluable in politically sensitive contexts. Engagement yields both theoretical knowledge and insights into 'what works'. Critically inclined researchers with a commitment to participative forms of inquiry therefore have a distinctive role to play in the policy arena. Practitioners also gain from working with researchers on the *use* of evidence. The process offers practitioners valuable guidance on how research insights can be used to nego-tiate ambiguous and politically contentious policy arenas. It is important to recognise that CREME's distinctive way of operating can challenge standard higher education institutions' operating models that tend to compartmentalise research, engagement and teaching activities. A supportive higher education institution culture is therefore a prerequisite to the critically engaged scholar-ship outlined here. We set out our approach and identify lessons for researchers in the main body of the chapter. But we start by sketching out the context for undertaking engaged research on ethnic minority entrepreneurship.

22.2   CONTEXT OF THE POLICY PROBLEM

Ethnic minority businesses (EMBs) in the UK are of two kinds: firstly, long-established firms, often with roots in South Asia or the Caribbean, and, secondly, new businesses from a wide range of countries, many in eastern Europe or Africa. These new businesses reflect an array of nationalities, and in many UK cities they represent a significant part of the business landscape. A recent large-scale study found 250,000 EMBs contribute £25 billion Gross Value Added to the UK economy (Roberts et al., 2020). The contribution is amplified by EMBs' social role in providing employment and opportunities for social inclusion for ethnic minority communities excluded from wider labour markets.

Policy discourse at one time treated EMBs as a distinct category defined by ethnic origin. That time has long gone. Business owners rarely identify themselves primarily in ethnic terms. The growing diversity of the population of firms underlines this point: there are far too many national origins for a single 'minority' category to mean anything. This does not imply EMBs are indistinguishable from 'mainstream' businesses. First, because of the limited opportunities open to them, they are concentrated in specific sectors and geographical locations. Evidence shows that new businesses tend to reproduce the experience of older ones, in being located in highly competitive and low value-added sectors. Second, many of them rely on personal and family contacts for financial support and sources of labour. Third, many EMBs are detached from formal business support networks, and thus less likely to receive the support they need to survive and grow.

The context of EMBs highlights important barriers. First, there are enduring constraints that US academic Timothy Bates (2011) refers to as the three Ms: money, markets and management. EMBs often struggle to raise finance, break into value-adding supply chains and lack expertise. Second, despite these challenges, EMBs are less likely to use formal sources of business support than their white-owned counterparts (Roberts et al., 2020). This hinders the growth potential of EMBs and means that business support systems are not as inclusive as they could be. Finally, the academic and policy discourse on 'inclusive' entrepreneurship is impoverished by the absence, or at best, stylised depictions of EMBs. CREME's approach to engagement addresses these challenges.

22.3   OUR APPROACH

CREME actively develops relationships with practitioners to pursue its core aim of promoting an understanding of ethnic minority entrepreneurship to non-academic stakeholders. Its ambition is to be both 'critical' academically whilst still being relevant to practitioners, an approach we think of as 'critical engagement'.

To understand the 'critical engagement' approach, it is worthwhile looking into the way we understand both terms. *Critical* research involves the questioning of assumptions and the use of social science to reveal truths, albeit of a necessarily provisional and contested kind. *Engagement* is the process whereby knowledge moves into action. Combining these two has led to a unique, twin commitment approach. In combination, CREME's twin commitment to the sustained study of ethnic minority entrepreneurship and practitioner engagement has allowed CREME to produce several forms of collaboration with practitioners. Table 22.1 identifies three such forms of critical engagement: sharing knowledge, action research and activism: creating new ventures. We elaborate on each of the mechanisms in the table.

22.3.1   Sharing Knowledge

CREME rarely conducts 'contract' or commissioned research, as described in Chapter 17, with the sole aim of producing a report on a predetermined topic. Rather, practitioners' initial interest in a research issue is often a precursor to a more wide-ranging dialogue, and in many instances, a longer-term relationship that encompasses several forms of knowledge exchange. CREME has several relationships with practitioners that developed in this way. Table 22.1 cites examples with finance providers (Ram et al., 2002; 2003) and business support agencies (Ram et al., 2012).

One of the major issues facing EMBs that CREME has focused on is access to finance, which is often seen as a major issue for EMBs (Ram et al., 2002; 2003). Fraser's (2009) important study on banks and ethnic minority firms found no evidence of direct discrimination for EMBs to have access to finance, but highlighted that the continuing perception of unfair treatment was a major issue for minority entrepreneurs and banks. The studies mentioned

Table 22.1   CREME's approach to critical engagement

Study/Issue	Form of Critical Engagement	Outcome
Sharing Knowledge		
Ram et al. (2002; 2003) *Access to finance*	Banking sector representatives involved in project steering group	– Recommendations to banking sector – Joint CREME/bank workshops for migrant entrepreneurs – Long-term engagement with banks
Ram and Smallbone (2003) *Supplier diversity*	National and local state agencies' involvement in overseeing research	– Recommendations to national and local state agencies – Commissioned good practice guides for professional bodies – Creation of supply chain initiative (Supplier Development East Midlands (SDEM))
Ram et al. (2012) *Business support for migrant businesses*	Practitioner involvement in research design and data analysis	– Recommendations to local state agency – Long-term engagement with agency
Action Research		
Beckinsale and Ram (2006) *ICT and migrant businesses*	Collaboration with local state agencies, business and community groups	– ICT support for 20 migrant firms – Increase in 'mainstream' support by migrant businesses
Ram et al. (2015) *New migrants and business support*	Collaboration with local state agencies, migrant associations, researcher secondments	– 165 new migrant businesses engaged – Increase in new migrants using business support – Change in state agency practices
Activism: Creating New Ventures		
Supply chain intermediary	Creation of supply chain intermediary to promote supplier diversity with corporations	– Opening of corporate supply chains to minority firms – Actual contracts exchanged – Successful 'spin-out'

Study/Issue	Form of Critical Engagement	Outcome
Ram and Trehan (2010) *Peer to peer business support*	Creation of peer mentoring support group with eight African-Caribbean entrepreneurs	– Personal development of owners – Business growth – Support for community
Ram et al. (2015) *Migrants and business support*	Creation of cross-sector partnership to deliver support to migrant businesses	– Engagement and business support with 200+ firms – Novel cross-sector partnership – Increase in 'mainstream' support by migrant businesses

above recommend engagement and knowledge exchange strategies to improve mutual understanding between banks and ethnic minority firms, which forms an academic foundation through which CREME has approached its knowledge exchange activities.

Following this, CREME worked with individual banks and their representative bodies to devise practical ways of tackling the issue of perception that banks are discriminative towards EMBs. For example, CREME has convened several workshops in partnership with the individual banks' representative bodies on access to finance. Such events were a direct way of tackling the perception that banks do not wish to lend to EMBs. CREME also created a cross-sector network to support migrant businesses, comprising corporations, banks, professional associations and academics.

22.3.2 Action Research

CREME frequently moves beyond knowledge sharing by collaborating with practitioners to interpret scientific research to accomplish practical tasks. This takes the form of 'action research', a term used to describe a variety of processes that aim to bring about practical change and develop wider knowledge. The examples in Table 22.1 on implementing information and communication technology (ICT) in ethnic minority firms (Beckinsale and Ram, 2006) and business support for new migrants (Ram et al., 2015) highlight key features of CREME's approach to engagement.

First, the interventions were theoretically informed and, therefore, not solely concerned with practical change or 'empowerment' (as in some approaches to action research). In the ICT project, researchers were concerned with testing an ICT model, as well as increasing the uptake of ICT by ethnic minority firms. The business support project aimed to extend a model on conceptualising ethnic minority entrepreneurship and develop the sponsor organisation's capacity to respond to new migrant entrepreneurs.

Second, the role of the researchers was fluid and mindful of the need to maintain a balance between scholarly and practitioner concerns. They were neither insiders nor outsiders, analysts nor activists, consultants nor detached academics. Rather, they were 'enablers', working with participants to bring critical knowledge to bear on organisational practice. Finally, the approach yielded academic and practitioner outcomes. The insights researchers gained from the context of application enabled them to contribute to scholarly conversation on the ICT and ethnic minority firms (Beckinsale and Ram, 2006), and the role of 'superdiverse' communities in ethnic minority entrepreneurship (Ram et al., 2015). Both projects also produced practical changes to the sponsor organisations' practices and led to increased support for ethnic minority entrepreneurs.

22.3.3   Activism: Creating New Ventures

CREME's closeness to EMB research and myriad practitioner networks is highly conducive to innovative collaborations. Some can result in the creation of new ventures. This form of activism extends beyond action research on a discrete project. It involves researchers joining forces with practitioners with the explicit aim of creating a new entity to support ethnic minority enterprise. The three examples in Table 22.1 – which are still operating at the time of writing – comprise: a peer support network for African-Caribbean entrepreneurs, established in 2004 (Ram and Trehan, 2010); a supplier diversity intermediary created in 2004 (Ram et al., 2007); and, initiated in 2015, a community-based support programme for new migrants (Ram et al., 2015). The development of each venture is attributable to social science work. This includes the identification that supplier diversity initiatives are important in EMB development (Ram and Smallbone, 2003), and that new migrant entrepreneurs are interested in growing their businesses, yet remain detached from mainstream business support networks (Ram et al., 2015).

CREME devised and developed the ventures, a process that included mobilising practitioner partners and securing start-up funding. This proactive stance contrasts with action research approaches in which researchers typically respond to overtures from sponsor organisations. CREME's founding role enabled research principles to be embedded in the ventures. In each case, researchers could witness the application of social science concepts in the relevant context; and they gathered evidence that could be used to assess the wider significance of the initiatives.

CREME's role transitioned from founders to enablers once the programmes were securely established. The African-Caribbean peer support group became self-sustaining after a couple of years, with researchers occasionally observing and facilitating meetings. The group provides mutual support, and mentors aspiring entrepreneurs in the wider African-Caribbean community. The supply chain initiative was 'spun-out' to the private sector in 2006 after a successful two-year pilot phase that saw the formation of a network of corporations committed to inclusive procurement, capacity building of ethnic minority suppliers and the actual exchange of supply chain contracts. The community-based initiative created in 2015 has developed into a long-term programme of business support for new migrants, with partners Citizens UK (an independent membership alliance of civil society institutions acting together for the common good) playing a leading role in delivering the programme. Over 300 business owners – none of whom had previously engaged with mainstream providers – have been supported by the programme.

22.4 LESSONS

We can draw several lessons from CREME's various approaches to engagement.

22.4.1 Research as a First Step …

CREME's experience highlights the importance of regarding research as the first step, rather than the last, in an extended conversation with practitioners on the meaning and significance of research findings. This commitment is integral to CREME's approach of viewing researcher–practitioner relationships as an ongoing process of developing trust rather than a transactional exchange of knowledge. Many of CREME's long-term collaborations with practitioners started off as a commission to conduct a specific piece of research. For example, in 2015, the nationally acclaimed social enterprise Ashley Community Housing (ACH)[2] approached CREME to conduct a study on the entrepreneurial aspirations of new migrants. ACH were interested in adding support for self-employment to the other services it offered to resettle migrants to the UK. This has developed into a long-term relationship of multiplex ties, including collaboration on a national campaign to support refugees, the embedding of a CREME researcher in ACH on a project to build the capacity of the social enterprise, and a senior member of the ACH team enrolling into a programme of advanced study at Aston University (where CREME operates).

CREME's association with Citizens UK has also developed from an initial action research project to a multi-stranded programme of knowledge exchange. CREME was instrumental in Aston University becoming a principal partner of Citizens UK Birmingham in September 2018. Aston University's partnership with Citizens UK has helped to develop an innovative and impactful agenda for civic engagement. Key highlights include: successful grant capture involving academic and professional staff across the University; developing links between University staff and local communities (previously disconnected from the academia); and training students in community organising.

22.4.2   Be Careful How You Frame Your Research Agenda …

The 'framing' of ethnic minority entrepreneurship can exert a strong influence on the portrayal of policy problems and practitioner initiatives. CREME's interdisciplinary approach and critical stance informs its interactions with practitioners. The centre's perspective emphasises the need to view ethnic minority entrepreneurship in its context, attributing equal significance to structural conditions and agential strategies. Accordingly, 'ethnicity' is one of many influences that shape the behaviour of ethnic minority enterprises. This approach helps to counter several tendencies that are stubbornly prevalent in policy circles, including:

- 'Over-ethnicised' approaches to business support. The assumption EMBs require support based solely on their ethnicity is questionable. Ram et al.'s (2015) action research study of new migrant businesses highlighted the importance of understanding the context of owners' business support needs (rather than solely 'ethnicity-related' factors alone). The sponsor organisation – a business support agency – changed its organisational practices by focusing business support in the location where migrant businesses were situated, rather than sub-contracting services to a narrow group of specialist ethnic intermediaries.
- The emphasis on quantity rather than quality. Ethnic minorities have often been the target of 'boosterist' measures that aim to inveigle them into self-employment. Yet even though some ethnic groups have much higher than average levels of self-employment, this should not be seen as an unqualified indicator of 'upward mobility'. Many ethnic minority firms operate in highly competitive and precarious market niches (notably, lower-order retailing); are undercapitalised; work long hours, intensively utilising familial and co-ethnic labour; and are struggling to survive in hostile inner-city environments (Ram and Jones, 2008).
- The 'othering' of ethnic minority enterprise. Academic and policy discourse separates EMBs from 'mainstream' debates. In scholarly circles, there is a tendency to attribute certain business practices of family labour, informal methods of recruitment, capital formation and marketing to ethnicity, when, in truth, they are universal to small businesses. Where there are differences, they appear to be of degree, and not of kind. Policy makers are also inclined to view EMBs as a group with distinct issues. Rarely do EMBs feature in 'mainstream' policy discussions on entrepreneurship, innovation and 'inclusive growth'.

22.4.3 Hold Your Ground ...

CREME's position at the centre of diverse networks with distinct and sometimes competing interests reinforces the importance of researcher independence. This is a key challenge of running a centre that is committed to independent research *and* deeply engaged in myriad practitioner domains. Maintaining this approach can be difficult with private sector firms with reputations to preserve, business support intermediaries striving – not always successfully – to be 'inclusive' and community advocates who claim to represent the views of different ethnic minority groups. There is also an underlying tension between a policy discourse insistent on actionable knowledge and utilisation, and scholarly views on ethnicity that stress fluidity, complexity and power. The inconclusive debate on what constitutes an 'ethnic minority business' exemplifies this tension.

Many of the projects and collaborations documented in Table 22.1 have involved tensions, notably in the contentious area of access to finance. CREME's approach in such circumstances takes the form of 'knowledge-based arbitration' (Porter and Shortall, 2009), in which researchers engage with as wide a range of actors as possible to establish their experiences of the policy or mechanism under scrutiny. Multiple perspectives promote a more complete understanding of the research issue. But not all research subjects' accounts are of equal import, and neither can they be accepted at face value. Rather, they form part of the overall explanatory account that characterises CREME's approach.

22.4.4 Leverage the Convening Powers of the University ...

The idea of the University as a means of independent validation (Grey, 2001) can help to mobilise actors from diverse institutional settings. For example, representative bodies, professional associations and corporations often work with CREME to gain insights on ethnic minority entrepreneurship (notably, access to finance, working practices and business support). The national Federation of Small Businesses recently commissioned CREME to conduct the largest study of EMBs to date (Roberts et al., 2020). The final report separated the independent analysis of the findings from the recommendations, which belonged to the Federation of Small Businesses rather than CREME.

The sense of validation provided by working with a University is also a resource for local communities and marginalised voices overlooked by mainstream institutions. CREME's academic research consistently highlights the social and economic contribution of EMBs and community-based networks. Its engagement activities, which include an annual national conference for practitioners started in 1997, provide a platform for these groups to represent themselves in arenas from which they are often excluded.

CREME's convening role and trust-based relationships with a multiplicity of stakeholders provide insights on how research is used (or not) in different practitioner domains. Rather than the unproblematic translation of 'evidence', the process is more akin to argumentation that emerges from dialogue, interpretation, experience and prevailing power structures (Sanderson, 2006; Schwandt, 2002). This policy learning perspective is at odds with the instrumentalist project of evidence-based policy that is in vogue. It powerfully illuminates the conditions, complexities and character of the context in which initiatives operate. This can be valuable to policy makers interested in establishing how the context and nature of interventions produce outcomes.

22.4.5   Never Lose Sight of Structural Issues ...

CREME's closeness to the research based on ethnic minority entrepreneurship means that it is well placed to reinforce the importance of how systemic conditions influence practical initiatives. Practitioner initiatives are often based on an implicit 'deficit model', that is, they promote measures to remedy the perceived deficiencies of ethnic minority entrepreneurs. This explains the emphasis of 'agency-centric' interventions like language training, mentoring and personal skills. Structural forces that exercise a profound influence on ethnic minority entrepreneurship – severe market competition, punitive regulations and endemic racism – are largely ignored in enterprise policy design (Jones et al., 2014; Rath and Swagerman, 2016). Such skewness risks weakening the potential value of EMB support measures.

22.4.6   It Takes a Team ...

Organising research for scientific and practical relevance requires close consideration to the composition of the team. Attention needs to be given to the blend of skills of the research team in order to ensure that the knowledge generated is both 'actionable' and theoretical. CREME's research team is diverse and comprises academics from a range of disciplinary traditions and practitioners with commercial and public sector experience. CREME's team for its action research project on business support for new migrants reflected this arrangement. It comprised novice researchers with great experience of migrant communities and seasoned academics focusing more on theoretical matters. Nonetheless, the approach to the research, analysis and interactions with practitioners was genuinely collaborative, thus fulfilling a key condition of such research: 'Strong connections with practice settings need to be coupled with strategies aimed at achieving sound and non-manipulative knowledge of organizational transformation processes' (Denis and Lehoux, 2010, p. 374).

22.5 CONCLUSION

CREME's experience shows how researchers working in partnership with practitioners can occupy a distinctive role on the 'crowded platform' of small business support measures that have so often been the preserve of well-funded research institutes, lobby groups and consultancies (Storey, 1994). The key is to be *relational*: relational, in the sense of a theoretical approach that sees EMBs as a product of their context and agential strategies (not solely ethnicity); relational, in being committed to working with diverse practitioners (particularly marginalised voices) as part of an ongoing process of building trust; and relational, in working with practitioners to enact insights from research. This core ingredient is at the heart of CREME's approach and is central to its mission of advancing research and practice on ethnic minority entrepreneurship.

NOTES

1. I would like to thank Professor Richard Roberts, Dr Eva Kasperova and Dr Imelda McCarthy for their comments on an earlier draft of this chapter.
2. For more information, see https://www.ach.org.uk.

REFERENCES

Bates, T. (2011) 'Minority entrepreneurship.' *Foundations and Trends in Entrepreneurship*, 7(1/2), 151–311.

Beckinsale, M. and Ram, M. (2006) 'Delivering ICT to ethnic minority businesses: An action research approach.' *Government and Policy (Environment and Planning 'C')*, 24(6), 847–67.

CREME (2020) *Unlocking Opportunity: The Value of Ethnic Minority Firms to UK Economic Activity and Enterprise*. Report prepared for the Federation of Small Businesses. London, UK: Federation of Small Businesses.

Denis, J. and Lehoux, P. (2010) 'Collaborative research: Renewing action and governing science.' In: D. Buchanan and A. Bryman (eds), *Handbook of Organizational Research Methods*, London: Sage, 363–81.

Fraser, S. (2009) 'Is there ethnic discrimination in the UK market for small business credit?' *International Small Business Journal*, 27(5), 583–607.

Grey, C. (2001) 'Reimagining relevance: A response to Starkey and Madan.' *British Journal of Management*, 12(S1), S27–S32.

Jones, T., Ram, M., Edwards, P., Kiselinchev, A. and Muchenje, L. (2014) 'Mixed embeddedness and new migrant enterprise in the UK.' *Entrepreneurship and Regional Development*, 26(5/6), 500–520.

Porter, S. and Shortall, S. (2009) 'Stakeholders and perspectivism in qualitative policy evaluation: A realist reflection.' *Public Administration*, 87(2), 259–73.

Ram, M. and Jones, T. (2008) 'Ethnic minority business: Review of research and policy.' *Government and Policy (Environment and Planning 'C')*, 26(2), 352–74.

Ram, M. and Smallbone, D. (2003) 'Supplier diversity initiatives and the diversification of ethnic minority businesses in the UK.' *Policy Studies*, 24(4), 187–204.

Ram, M. and Trehan, K. (2010) 'Critical action learning, policy learning and small firms: An inquiry.' *Management Learning*, 41(4), 415–28.

Ram, M., Smallbone, D. and Deakins, D. (2002) *The Finance and Business Support Needs of Ethnic Minority Firms in Britain*. British Bankers Association Research Report. London: British Bankers Association.

Ram, M., Theodorakopoulos, N. and Worthington, I. (2007) 'Policy transfer in practice: Implementing supplier diversity in the UK.' *Public Administration*, 85(3), 779–803.

Ram, M., Smallbone, D., Deakins, D. and Jones, T. (2003) 'Banking on "break-out": Finance and the development of ethnic minority businesses. *Journal of Ethnic and Migration Studies*, 29(4), 663–81.

Ram, M., Edwards, P., Jones, T., Kiselinchev, A. and Muchenje, L. (2015) 'Getting your hands dirty.' *Work, Employment and Society*, 29(3), 462–78.

Ram, M., Trehan, K., Rouse, J., Woldesenbet, K. and Jones, T. (2012) 'Ethnic minority business support in the West Midlands: Challenges and developments.' *Government and Policy (Environment and Planning 'C')*, 30(5), 493–512.

Rath, J. and Swagerman, A. (2016) 'Promoting ethnic entrepreneurship in European cities: Sometimes ambitious, mostly absent, rarely addressing structural features.' *International Migration Review*, 54(1), 152–66.

Roberts, R., Ram, M., Jones, T., Idris, B., Hart, M., Ri, A. and Prashar, N. (2020) *Unlocking Opportunity: The Value of Ethnic Minority Firms in UK Economic Activity and Enterprise*. London, UK: The Federation of Small Businesses.

Sanderson, I. (2006) 'Complexity, "practical rationality" and evidence-based policy-making.' *Policy and Politics*, 34(1), 115–32.

Schwandt, T. (2002) *Evaluation Practice Reconsidered*, New York: Peter Lang.

Storey, D. (1994) *Understanding the Small Business Sector*, Basingstoke: Macmillan.

23. Supporting policy towards sustainability

Alice Owen

23.1 INTRODUCTION

Sustainability is a huge topic, and one that has spawned an enormous body of academic literature since 'sustainable development' became a common policy goal. The UN World Commission on Economic Development, the 'Brundtland' Commission, gave us the hard-to-dispute goal of ensuring development today meets today's needs without reducing options for future generations (Brundtland, 1987). Sustainability can be framed as a policy goal in its own right, but perhaps it is more useful here to think about sustainability as a set of outcomes that every policy area has to address. The UN Sustainable Development Goals (SDGs) would certainly suggest that sustainability happens through action on poverty, the economy, housing, food, water, product design, education and more! This means that an academic who wants to help policy makers achieve more sustainable outcomes from their policies needs to identify the policy topics where their research insights are most helpful, such as energy, agriculture, land use planning, business/economic development, health and so on. You also need to think about the scale where your research could reveal most insights. In the UK, that means being clear about whether you are working with national policy, with one or more of the devolved administrations, with English regions, or city regions across the UK, or local authorities. Each scale has a different set of policy frameworks. Your impact is greatest when you offer insights which closely match the levers available at that scale, and the actions which can be taken at that scale.

At this point you may be asking yourself, 'Am I a sustainability researcher?' That may not be the label you wear in your research institution, but you can almost certainly work with policy makers to make their work more likely to produce sustainable outcomes. However, to misquote the 1999 film *Fight Club*, 'The first rule of influencing policy makers towards sustainability is … do not mention sustainability.' If you want to contribute to a policy achieving a more sustainable outcome, then you need to have a clear way of describing what sustainability is, why it matters and why your expertise is important. But this does not mean that you start every conversation with referencing an academic definition. Instead, think about how your understanding of sustainability matches the interests of your audience, the people you are trying to influence. Rather than suggesting that you should become trapped within a single policy topic silo, when one of the demands of sustainability is that we act on a 'whole systems' basis, this approach suggests that you have a focus where your research could be helpful at a given point in time. Using simple metaphors such as 'stopping sawing through the branch we're sitting on' can be useful, rather than talking about climate change or resource scarcity, biodiversity loss, poverty alleviation or any one of the topics that lie within sustainability.

23.2 EXAMPLES OF SUPPORTING SUSTAINABILITY-RELATED POLICYMAKING

The first tip to bear in mind when seeking to enthuse policy makers – or anyone else – about sustainability goals is *start at the other person's position*. Try to see the world, and the many problems that policy makers are meant to address, through the policy maker's eyes. This might mean thinking about their geography.

Working in Northern Ireland, any approach to sustainability needs to foreground issues of social justice because that is the topic that resonates across communities. Any future vision for Northern Ireland has to acknowledge the history of social division and conflict. Working as part of the UK Sustainable Development Commission (SDC) 2006–11, advising the Northern Ireland Executive and then Assembly, I spent most of my time asking questions and learning about the priorities, experiences and perspectives of politicians and policy officers so that in the small amount of time I had to talk about energy policy, or building retrofit, I was responding to the challenges they faced. There is no point in advocating for new zero carbon houses or transport systems unless you also understand why communities, housing locations and employment opportunities are divided spatially.

When I started working at English 'sub national' level, in one of the 'regional development agencies', we had to find a way to put huge changes to the energy system into the regional targets that would then frame action and investment. A 'Regional Energy Forum' was established to develop policies and targets. I knew something of energy generation, distribution and use, but any technical knowledge I had was subservient to the politically savvy governance experts who took the lead in assembling the individuals and representatives who would make up the Forum. Some groups were keen to participate in the Forum – the managers of major biomass energy investment, the electricity grid operators –

but we needed the people who understood where the region had come from as well as where it was going.

In selecting a chair, appointing a peer who had been a local government politician, rather than one who advocated for renewable energy, meant that the unions representing former coal miners and the operators of fossil fuel power plants came to the Forum table. Did we create a regional energy strategy that delivered a zero carbon economy in 2002? No. Did we even use the term net zero? No – this was 2002! But we did have a greenhouse gas emissions reduction target in a regional economic strategy for the first time in the UK. And for the first time we had the energy intensive workforce involved in discussions about the future of energy and the future of their communities. We started to move on from lamenting the damage that had been done to the social fabric of the region from the 1980s onwards, while still acknowledging that this experience of energy transition had done untold, unsustainable damage. In Yorkshire, and in many other places, energy policy is closely intertwined with social policy, housing policy, industrial strategy and labour issues including training and education.

Once you have thought about and understood specific reasons why the policy maker could be interested in sustainability, the second tip is *to assume that you have a shared goal, you just need to work out what it is*.

I have seen a lot of people who are passionate about sustainability, green economy and – more recently – the climate emergency, alienate the people who they want to bring onside by haranguing them with the dire state of the world and by proclaiming that every one of us has the responsibility to act. Such people campaign with sincerity, and while there is of course a truth in identifying the need for every single one of us to act, the truth is that very few people have the capability to change, certainly not in the radical way that some activists demand. Of course, there is a role for campaigning, for non-governmental organisations (NGOs) to demand higher standards, and more action, but that is not the only way to inform policy. In my experience, being an academic offers a privileged opportunity to bring evidence and solutions to bear on a problem and to work with policy makers in the arenas where they hold influence and agency.

In 2001, all English National Parks were required to develop strategic management plans for the first time. In the UK, National Parks are patchworks of private land, home to tens of thousands of people. National Park Authorities do not own or directly manage National Parks. Instead, the Authorities are planning authorities. They have the skills and processes to draw up detailed spatial plans, designating land use and policies to conserve and enhance the special qualities of the area, framed by a set of statutory duties.

At the time, I was working for the Yorkshire Dales National Park Authority, in my first public sector role, and it was my responsibility to lead the process of writing the first management plan. I had no idea what the content of the plan should be, but I did have an idea about how to structure it. A team from the Authority gave that plan a series of themes – Community, Economy, Ecology, Built Environment and so on. Looking back, it is obvious that these themes together spoke of sustainability, but we did not call it that.

While many other National Parks took their expertise from spatial planning to produce detailed, map-based – and very lengthy – management plans, we aimed to fit everything into 24 pages or less, hoping that a short, structured document might actually be read to inform rather than only being referred to for conflict resolution. We ran a consultation process which started with a picture of the Yorkshire Dales and asked people – residents, old and young, and visitors – what they valued, what they wanted to keep, what could change. Amongst the hundreds of responses, a much greater response rate than anyone had really expected, there was a shared view that the landscape was worth protecting, but that it was a living landscape which had to be able to accommodate changing livelihoods for residents as well as being accessed and enjoyed by visitors. We found a small kernel of something everyone agreed on, in amongst the impossible to resolve specific issues of planning permissions for conservatories or barn conversions, the priority of haymeadow flowers or farm viability. By establishing a set of shared principles, we tried to find a way to move towards greater sustainability, benefiting all those who value the dramatic landscape of the Dales.

A powerful way to develop a shared goal is to imagine what is possible. I learnt this as part of the SDC when we were trying to establish the SDC's position on proposals for a tidal barrage across the Severn Estuary (SDC, 2007). At that time, the proposals offered a huge amount of predictable renewable energy, around 4 per cent of the UK's energy demand, and the employment from developing a major infrastructure project, remaking the economic geography of south Wales and the south west of England. However, the Severn Estuary is a dynamic ecosystem, a critical part of the 'flyway' used by migrating birds, home to rare fish and marine life, with layers of nature conservation designations. It looked as if we were back in the zero sum game which 'triple bottom line' thinking (Elkington, 1999) can lead to; what kind of trade off could be made between competing interests and values? But then we were skilfully facilitated into imagining what a shared set of desired outcomes might be. 'Under what conditions' would tidal power development in the estuary be acceptable?

By starting with the assumption that a barrage could be sustainable, if only we could see how, we unlocked entrenched discussions. What emerged was the seemingly impossible: a barrage that did not fundamentally change the estuary's ecology based on its hydrology would be sustainable. The creative energies then moved into working through how this condition could be met, and the idea of tidal lagoons, rather than an estuarine barrage emerged. While supported by Government in 2016 (Hendry, 2016), plans for tidal lagoons off the south Wales coast have been shelved indefinitely, but working with the assumption that solutions could be found did move the debate away from acceptance or rejection of the barrage proposals and back to the absolute need to increase renewable energy provision. Since moving into research, I now recognise the 'under what conditions ...?' framing as a powerful route to divining research questions, and academics are very well placed to use this kind of hypothetical framing in the search for effective sustainability policy.

The third tip for academics who want their research to be used in shaping more sustainable policy outcomes is to *be determined, as well as flexible and adaptable*.

One strand of my own research focuses on how construction firms, and the individuals in those firms, implement energy efficiency measures when they are working on repair and renovation of buildings, especially homes. This is a sustainability issue because it affects both energy demand, housing quality and occupier health, and the economic viability of businesses together with the jobs they provide. It is also a classic systems sustainability issue where no single group can act to change the situation and there are lots of possible entry points to making improvements.

In brief, if improved energy efficiency in more than 20 million houses is to become routine, then policy and practice needs to change across at least two national government departments (in the UK, industrial strategy and housing sit in different ministries), across complex supply chains, across over a million individual workers' habits and practices, across the vocational training system, local planning advice and enforcement. I have to be willing to share the research-based insights into what construction needs to do, and what it actually does, with each of these groups. Sometimes this is in a one-off presentation; sometimes it is participating in the policymaking structures like a city region advisory panel; sometimes I am a member of an industry task-and-finish group; sometimes I am in informal strategy discussions; sometimes I provide formal input to inquiries. In each case, I have to tailor how I share the same key messages so that they relate directly to what the group I am working with cares about most.

Bringing my experience right up to date, it will not have escaped any readers' notice that 2020 has been a testing year for policymaking of all kinds, in all locations. In March, Bradford Metropolitan District Council (BMDC) approved a new Sustainable Development Partnership for the District. Within a few days, England was in its first COVID-19 'lockdown' and Bradford, like all local councils, was suddenly dealing with public health, communications, support for the vulnerable, schools closure and more. The new partnership's chair and deputy chair, both external to the Council, offered the Council leadership the opportunity to press 'pause', but the leadership was adamant that progress needed to be made. The Council had made a statement of climate emergency in 2019; they wanted to demonstrate that something had happened as a result of that declaration, and they also recognised that late 2020 and beyond would be dominated by economic recovery. For Bradford that meant reaching for a different sort of economy, a sustainable one.

And so we pressed on, developing ideas, drawing in existing work across the district, holding the first board meeting, recruiting staff, contributing to the Bradford Economic Recovery plan until, at the end of 2020, we had 11 areas of action ranging from supporting a green business ecosystem to creating the infrastructure to enable an hydrogen-fuelled light commercial vehicle fleet. Each of those areas ties directly into the city's distinct characteristics; we are starting with the assets the city already has, not least its population. This plan and approach may not have been envisaged when the Council chief executive approached the business leader who could chair the partnership, or when that business leader approached an academic to be deputy chair, but it is an inclusive and vibrant programme to build momentum through 2021.

23.3   CONCLUSION

The experience shared above is not to suggest that the way my career has developed is the only, or best, route to become an academic informing policy, but I would offer some ideas for what an individual academic needs to do so that you become well placed to offer assistance in the field where your expertise applies.

Build your network by being actively helpful. There is much more appetite for helpfulness than there is for campaigning. Develop skills in translating, empathising, communicating, listening, encouraging; ask people what challenges they are dealing with, do not try to open a conversation with what you believe their problems are, unless that is what you have been asked. My experience in sustainability-related policy, and I suspect this applies to other areas with strong ethical or moral bases, is that it helps to be an authentic human being. You will struggle to live a fully sustainable life as much as anyone else, because layers of systems shaped by policy – infrastructure, spatial planning, economic management – will limit the changes you can make. Sustainability cannot be achieved through individual action alone. Being open and honest about the limitations on what it is possible to do can actually lend authority to your advice, because it starts from a place of pragmatism.

Building your network will make it much more likely that you will hear about, and be asked to apply for or take up policy advisory roles! When policy makers turn to academics for advice, they are likely to think about who they have spoken to, or which blogs, podcasts or presentations have been interesting, and much less likely to find you through a search for specific expertise.

Be politically aware, if not political. What is the function of an area of policy? Is it ripe for change or does it need shoring up against attack? Where does your research and knowledge fit into that? Remember the national canvas is not the only canvas that you can paint upon. Can you inform policy locally, or regionally? These are often the scales where change can happen, but where support and expertise is lacking. As an academic, you can really help.

For sustainability policy in particular, be willing to offer views and advice from outside your narrow and deep area of research. If a policy body asks you to be on an advisory board, or someone from the policy world asks for a chat about something, say 'yes' if you possibly can. Even if your research does not speak directly to what they want to explore, then you will build a connection, learn about an issue or problem and, because you are focussed on helping, you will almost certainly be able to bring in other colleagues who might have more specific evidence to share. Do not worry about being eclipsed by others in that specific conversation; your position as the bridge builder, the helpful academic, is secure. So do take opportunities when they come up, and see your policy work as a small part of a much bigger system of knowledge development and societal change.

I have focussed on sustainability but there is much here that would apply to other multi-faceted areas of policy. I have found working as an academic in support of policymaking highly satisfying when considered in the round, if not always easy or comfortable in every incidence. In discussions about sustainability, I have learnt a huge amount about the different pressures that policymaking must respond to and that has shaped my own research, and the evidence I present from that research. At the end of 2020, a non-exhaustive audit of my current policy work includes two formal public appointments with local/regional authorities and various topic groups associated with those, a working group with an industry sector, three active informal roles with local authorities discussing 'green recovery', and both national and local advisory panels for particular projects that have a focus on location-specific approaches to sustainability.

Of course, it still takes some time and effort to get that kind of activity recognised in formal monitoring and reward systems and you still have to undertake research so that your input is the most well informed it can be, but when pressure mounts, I am able to remind myself that, yes, my research does make a difference, because there are paths from the research to decision makers. Some paths are well worn, some are still being cut by machete through thickets of custom and practice, but there are connections along which information can flow and change can happen.

REFERENCES

Brundtland, G. (1987). Report of the World Commission on Environment and Development: Our Common Future. United Nations General Assembly document A/42/427.

Elkington, J. (1999). *Cannibals with Forks: Triple Bottom Line of 21st Century Business*, London, Capstone.

Hendry, C. (2016). The Role of Tidal Lagoons. Report for UK Department for Business, Energy and Industrial Strategy (BEIS).

UK Sustainable Development Commission (2007). *Turning the Tide; Tidal Power in the UK*, accessed at: http://www.sd-commission.org.uk/publications.php@id=607. html

24. How to win friends and influence policy: a guide for new researchers

Katy Jones

24.1 INTRODUCTION

Informing and impacting policy is an important, but difficult, skill for researchers to develop. Early career researchers (ECRs) in particular can struggle to identify how they can engage with policy makers, despite often not possessing the profile and networks held by senior colleagues, or the backing of large-scale funding. Drawing on an example of a small-scale, ECR-led project funded by the Economic and Social Research Council's (ESRC's) Productivity Insights Network, this chapter shows how policy engagement is possible regardless of the scale of a research project, and how continued engagement has the potential to lead to bigger and better things. The chapter gives advice on making research findings accessible to a wide audience, engaging with the policymaking process in a variety of ways, and developing good relationships with policy makers. It also emphasises the importance of supportive colleagues and frameworks for ECR development in policy engagement. The chapter illustrates a journey of research engagement from small-scale 'pump-priming' research funding to the award of a prestigious early career grant for larger-scale research. Seizing different opportunities and learning lessons about policy engagement at each stage was central to this journey.

24.2 CONTEXT: UNIVERSAL CREDIT AND IN-WORK CONDITIONALITY – A PRODUCTIVE TURN?

Universal Credit and In-Work Conditionality – a productive turn? (hereafter the IWC Project) was a small-scale project funded through the ESRC's Productivity Insights Network (see Jones et al., 2019 for a full write-up of the study). The project was designed to explore employers' perspectives of the potential impact of new policy developments in relation to Universal Credit, the UK government's flagship welfare reform policy. Universal Credit has been described as the 'most significant change to the welfare system since the Beveridge reforms in 1947' (DWP, 2010, p. 46). It brings together what were previously separate systems of out-of-work benefits (e.g. Job Seekers Allowance) and in-work financial support (e.g. Working Tax Credits). Reforms have also involved the strengthening of 'conditionality' for unemployed benefit claimants, whereby claimants are expected to engage in intensive job searching and work-related activities in exchange for social security benefits (Dwyer and Wright, 2014). As part of this, alongside stricter requirements for out-of-work claimants, Universal Credit also potentially involves the introduction of 'in-work conditionality' (IWC) to welfare claimants on a low income, placing responsibilities on those claiming Universal Credit whilst in work to increase their earnings, as part of the Department for Work and Pensions (DWP) 'In-work progression' policy.

The exact nature of IWC is yet to be determined. Trialling is underway and the government is adopting a 'test and learn' approach. However, the DWP's (2018) Employer Guide to Universal Credit states that workers on a low income who are in receipt of Universal Credit may be expected to: (a) increase their hours, (b) look for ways to progress in their current workplace, (c) search for additional work with a different employer (i.e. take on multiple jobs), (d) take up alternative work elsewhere (i.e. move jobs). This represents a significant policy shift, as those currently receiving tax credits (which were not underpinned by behavioural conditions) are moved on to Universal Credit and suddenly have to engage with the welfare system in a new way.

Most existing research has focused on claimants' experiences of recent welfare reforms. Little attention has been paid (in policy debates or academic literature) to understanding how recent welfare reforms that impose conditions on employed people in receipt of benefits are likely to impact on the labour market. Furthermore, whilst employers are key to outcomes arising from active labour market policy (van Berkel et al., 2017), they have been largely absent from policy discussions as this new policy is being developed.

The IWC Project began to address this gap, through focusing on employer perspectives on proposals to extend new requirements to working Universal Credit claimants. It gathered insights from 12 employers about the potential impact of (and their likely response to) the extension of conditionality to working Universal Credit claimants. Whilst only a small-scale pilot study, it highlighted a number of important issues which policy makers should consider as their 'in-work offer' is developed. It showed how moves to place rigid expectations on individual workers in receipt of Universal Credit to increase their hours or pay are in conflict with the realities of working life in the UK. It also demonstrated that placing conditions solely on workers neglects to consider long-standing issues of poor work quality and management practices which characterise a large proportion of the UK labour market. Furthermore, the policy direction appears to be at odds with broader policy agendas focused on promoting decent work and productivity.

Whilst the policy relevance of the IWC Project was clear from the outset, this small pilot project attracted an unexpected level of interest from UK policy makers. The remainder of this chapter charts the development of this project and related policy engagement activities both prior to and beyond completion, focusing on lessons learned and advice for ECRs.

24.3   PROCESS: BEST-LAID PLANS … SOMETIMES GO QUITE WELL!

24.3.1   Pre-Project Engagement

The first step of good policy engagement is *pre*-project engagement. Researchers keen to conduct research with the potential to impact on policy should ensure ideas are developed with an understanding of the core agendas of policy makers. All government departments also regularly publish *Areas of Research Interest*, which are a helpful in-road for researchers seeking to engage in policy-related research. However, agendas can shift as new policy challenges and contexts emerge, so staying up to date with relevant policy developments in your field is essential for successful policy engagement. Discussing your ideas at the formulation stage directly with policy makers to ensure that your research is genuinely speaking to their interests is important. This can also help to secure buy-in if the research goes ahead.

The IWC Project centred on a live and evolving policy agenda, and as such, policy engagement should always have been a central component. As a social policy researcher, I try to keep a watchful eye on policy developments, and having been involved in previous research relating to UK welfare reform, I knew that there was policy interest in my proposed research area. However, I also knew that most researchers were not exploring these developments in relation to their broader economic impacts.

Extensive efforts were made to consult with policy makers and other relevant stakeholders in order to inform project development. Discussions with key policy stakeholders helped to inform the development of the funding proposal. These included representatives from the DWP, Department for Business, Energy and Industrial Strategy, the Institute of Directors, the Chartered Institute of Personnel and Development, Greater Manchester Combined Authority and Manchester City Council. I shared with each the rationale behind the research project and proposed approach, and invited their reflections, which ultimately helped me to refine my research proposal. Several also agreed to be involved in a project advisory group, if my grant application was successful. This, I think, was a key factor behind the bid's successful outcome.

24.3.2   Sustaining Engagement

Sustaining engagement throughout the project is also important. All stake-holders engaged at the pre-project phase subsequently became members of an expert advisory group once funding for the IWC Project was secured. The advisory group met twice over the duration of the project: first to recap aims and objectives of the study, and to gather feedback on proposed research instruments (topic guide for semi-structured interviews with employers). Second, to share emerging findings, discuss potential policy implications and next steps for further research. I made the decision to meet twice for two key reasons. First to ensure advisory group members could shape the project from the outset (to ensure we were asking the most relevant questions and invite their advice and assistance with recruitment) and also as key findings began to emerge in order to ensure these were clearly presented and relevant for policy stakeholders. Second, more than two meetings may have risked less engage-ment, particularly given the small scale of the project.

Engagement with the DWP here was critical – as an evolving policy agenda, it was important that messaging to employers was accurate (this policy change was something that *might* happen, and we were interested in their views on it). Support from other advisory group members was also crucial in terms of recruiting employers to take part in the study. Being flexible was also impor-tant here, particularly given the small scale of the project. Not all advisory group members were able to meet at the same time, but were able to meet separately or provide written feedback.

24.3.3   Communicating Research Findings

Once you have research findings to share, communicating these effectively to a policy audience is crucial. Policy makers will not use your research if they do not know about it or cannot read it. Engagement through an advisory group is a good start – if it includes policy makers, they will become immediately aware of your research findings and are likely to share with other policymak-ing colleagues if the research is genuinely of relevance. However, thinking widely about policy engagement will help to maximise your potential for impact. There are multiple ways to do this, and the IWC Project team did the following:

- We held two 'learning events': one in Manchester, one in London. These events involved a presentation of the key findings from the study, and an audience discussion regarding the findings, potential policy implications and future research agenda. Targeted invites to policy makers were sent via the advisory group, and through identifying contacts in relevant All

Party Parliamentary Groups and Select Committees (see Box 24.1 for more advice about identifying key policy stakeholders).
- We produced outputs in varying formats: a summary report, a shorter briefing note and a blog.
- We promoted the report and its findings via social media accounts (institutional and project team members).

Especially for those early in their research careers, it can be difficult to know where to start with identifying and connecting with policy stakeholders. This takes time, and can be difficult to do when under competing pressures, and as policy agendas evolve and contacts move on. Engaging with policy makers is a long-term process (but we all have to start somewhere!). Engaging with other researchers and research communities engaging in the same policy space is important.

BOX 24.1   IDENTIFYING AND CONNECTING WITH KEY POLICY STAKEHOLDERS

- *Think broadly about policy stakeholders:* disseminate your research via relevant All Party Parliamentary Groups, Select Committees and particular MPs who are vocal in relation to your policy agenda (this information is all publicly available). Engaging with the training and resources offered by the Parliamentary Office of Science and Technology can help you to map and identify relevant policy stakeholders.
- *Write blogs:* many academics can see writing blogs as a thankless task. For those new to writing them, they can take a lot of time, and this is time that many do not have when they are in hot pursuit of that 'REF[1]-able' output. However, they can be a great way of sharing research findings (for those who are short of time or are unable to access more 'academic' publications – i.e. policy makers) and can also help to build your profile as an academic interested in a particular policy area (see Abbas and Jones, 2018 for an example of a blog demonstrating earlier interest in IWC).
- *Social media:* love it or hate it, social media is a helpful way of getting your research out there. Yes, it can be a bit of an echo chamber, but it is an echo chamber with policy stakeholders in it. Condense key findings into clear and simple tweets, follow key policy stakeholders, tag them into relevant tweets, and have a link to share whenever the opportunity presents itself. Remember that genuine engagement in policy development is not just about pushing your own research but engaging with and supporting other researchers in this space.

24.4   IMPACT: THE JOYS OF 'SURPRISE!' POLICY ENGAGEMENT

The IWC Project was a small-scale pilot study, centred on 12 interviews with employers. Whilst potential for policy engagement from small-scale studies can be limited, the IWC Project demonstrates how this is not always the case. Following project completion, policy engagement activities continued beyond those initially planned. This included taking up invitations to present the research to the Manchester City Council Welfare Reform board, and to a webinar for members of the Employment Related Services Association. But most significantly in relation to national policymaking were invitations to present findings to senior civil servants in the DWP and to give oral evidence in a House of Lords Committee. Each of these were new experiences for me as a principal investigator and are described below.

24.4.1   Giving Evidence in Parliament

Issues explored in the IWC Project resonated with some of the questions central to a House of Lords Economic Affairs Committee's Inquiry into Universal Credit, which explored the extent to which its design meets the needs of claimants in today's labour market. After noticing the call for evidence on Twitter, I was considering providing a written response to the Inquiry when I received instead a request from the Committee's policy analyst for me to give oral evidence directly to the Committee, after they had seen the IWC Project's findings.

This was an intimidating prospect, not least because the presentation of oral evidence to the Economic Affairs Committee would be televised! I was also conscious of not being an economist, and the need to be prepared for questions to provide evidence on a range of questions that had not been directly answered by the specific research projects I have been involved in. However, the whole point of research is to make an impact, and as such it is important to embrace such opportunities when they arise.

In the run-up to the evidence session, I prepared my response to the questions outlined in the call for written evidence, and then additional questions provided a few days beforehand. The support of my colleagues was crucial here – both in offering suggestions, but also reassurance, helping me to realise that I could have an opinion on matters I had studied, even if I had not personally conducted research on those specific issues.

The evidence session itself was nerve-wracking, but I was happy with how it went. Through drawing on my own research and knowledge of the qualitative evidence base, I was able to complement the quantitative knowledge of the other panel members (specific to my example is a senior economist at the Institute for Fiscal Studies). The Committee and their assistants were welcoming and keen to hear about the evidence we brought to the table. It was also helpful to have a colleague with more experience in policy engagement attend the session; as well as providing moral support, discussing the session together directly afterwards providing another helpful learning opportunity. Alongside oral evidence, I also submitted written evidence (Jones, 2020) – and both were cited in the Committee's report (House of Lords, 2020).

The key things I learned from this aspect of policy engagement experience were threefold. Firstly, if invited to give evidence (try to) keep calm, and remember that you have been invited because of your expertise. Imposter syndrome may hit researchers inexperienced in working with policy makers, but this is something that will be overcome with time and experience. Secondly, researchers should not feel constrained by the confines of the particular pieces of research they personally have conducted – remember that you are an expert on your topic and can draw on your knowledge of the wider evidence base. Thirdly, respond to Inquiries if you think your research is in some way relevant.

24.4.2   Department for Work and Pensions Chatham House Seminar

After attending one of the 'learning events' held at the end of *the IWC Project*, a senior civil servant from the DWP contacted me and asked if I would be willing to share the research findings with their colleagues at an internal DWP seminar. This was a great opportunity to share research findings with those involved in making and implementing policy. Held under the Chatham House Rule (see Box 24.2), this was a great opportunity to have an open discussion about the research and related policy, which often is not possible given the highly sensitive and political nature of welfare reform. I also used this as an opportunity to share my ideas and explore their ideas about further related research, and how this could best be designed to be relevant and impactful.

BOX 24.2   CHATHAM HOUSE RULE

The Chatham House Rule helps create a trusted environment to understand and resolve complex problems. Its guiding spirit is: share the information you receive, but do not reveal the identity of who said it. The Rule reads as follows:

> When a meeting, or part thereof, is held under the Chatham House Rule, participants are free to use the information received, but neither the identity nor the affiliation of the speaker(s), nor that of any other participant, may be revealed.

Any group of individuals in any sector can use the Rule as a pre-agreed guide for running an event, particularly when issues of a sensitive nature are to be discussed.

In a polarized world, used effectively, the Chatham House Rule helps to bring people together, break down barriers, generate ideas and agree solutions.

It allows people to speak as individuals, and to express views that may not be those of their organisations, and therefore it encourages free discussion. People usually feel more relaxed if they don't have to worry about their reputation or the implications if they are publicly quoted.

Source: Chatham House, n.d.

24.5   CONCLUSION: BIGGER AND BETTER THINGS?

Following the IWC Project I continued to engage with policy makers and other policy stakeholders. Most significantly, this involved ongoing consultation with the DWP to shape a much larger-scale funding bid – for the ESRC's New Investigator Grant. As part of this, the DWP agreed to come on board as a project partner. They continue to engage with my research through the project's advisory board and may provide further dissemination opportunities with the Department. According to anonymous peer reviewers, continued policy engagement was a key strength of the proposal, as demonstrated through buy-in from a range of senior policy stakeholders who agreed in advance to be part of my expert advisory group, to advise on key, practical policy and practice implications and support the wider dissemination of project findings as they emerge. The bid was successful, and will provide an amazing opportunity to extend my expertise on the 'demand side' of Active Labour Market Policy and continue to engage with policy makers in this area.

As noted at the start of this chapter, informing and impacting policy is a difficult skill for new researchers to develop. Growing networks, understanding, experience and confidence in this area takes time. However, it is much easier with the support of more experienced colleagues, and there are many supportive people, networks and frameworks you can draw upon. For the lucky researcher, these support networks might be obvious and easily identifiable, others may have to work a bit harder to find them.

I have been fortunate to have had exposure to policymaking environments from the beginning of my research career. Starting out in a non-academic research setting as a think tank researcher was invaluable for the insights it provided into the policymaking process and growing the confidence and ambition to engage with it. Opportunities to undertake internships, or at least spend some time in government departments and other policy-focused organisations, are a great way to develop skills and confidence in policy engagement (see e.g. Chapter 13 on PhD internships).

Since moving into an academic research role I have also been fortunate to be part of research teams led by senior academics who both genuinely welcomed and encouraged the input of ECRs in policy engagement activities (see Scullion et al., 2021 for one example). Through developing the New Investigator Grant application, I have also hugely benefited from the encouragement and moral support and mentorship from a senior academic (in my case, Professor Ashwin Kumar) who has extensive experience in and expertise regarding the policymaking process.

Large investments from UK Research Councils increasingly encourage senior academics to create development opportunities for early career academics alongside a policy and impact focus, so looking out for opportunities to engage with these investments could prove fruitful. Even if you are not directly involved as a researcher in such investments, there is often a networking element that is increasingly open to wider ECR involvement. For example, not only was the IWC Project funded through the ESRC's Productivity Insights Network, the proposal for it was developed through multiple ECR-focused workshops organised by the network. More generally, peer support is also incredibly valuable, both within and across institutions (e.g. connections made through the Money, Security and Social Policy ECR network were helpful to me when thinking through my research ideas) in terms of providing 'safe spaces' for new researchers to ask questions and present early stage ideas and share experiences about policy engagement.

Finally, your Higher Education Institution (HEI) should also have dedicated people and resources relating to the Impact Agenda. These can sometimes be difficult to leverage/find out about, especially for ECRs, but stay alert for opportunities as they arise and keep asking what is available.

NOTE

1.   The Research Excellence Framework (REF) refers to a national, UK-wide assessment of British higher education institution. As part of it each academic is evaluated based on their contribution to research impact.

REFERENCES

Abbas, J. and Jones, K. (2018) 'In-work conditionality is based on weak evidence – but will the policy sink or swim?' LSE British Politics and Policy Blog, 12 September 2018. Accessed 8 April 2022 at https://blogs.lse.ac.uk/politicsandpolicy/in-work -conditionality-public-opinion/

Chatham House, n.d. *Chatham House Rule.* Accessed 9 November 2021 at https:// www. chathamhouse.org/about-us/chatham-house-rule

DWP (2010) *Universal Credit: Welfare that Works.* Cm 7957.

DWP (2018) *Employer Guide to Universal Credit.* Accessed 4 October 2019 at https:// bit.ly/2ALw6rW

Dwyer, P. and Wright, S. (2014) 'Universal Credit, ubiquitous conditionality and its implications for social citizenship,' *Journal of Poverty and Social Justice,* 22 (1) 27–35.

House of Lords (2020) *Universal Credit Isn't Working: Proposals for Reform.* HL Paper 105.

Jones, K. (2020) 'House of Lords Economic Affairs Committee Inquiry: The economics of Universal Credit.' Written response from Dr Katy Jones, Manchester Metropolitan University.

Jones, K., Berry, C., Rouse, J. and Whittle, R. (2019) *Universal Credit and In-Work Conditionality – a Productive Turn?* Report. Productivity Insights Network.

Scullion, L., Jones, K., Dwyer, P., Hynes, C. and Martin, P. (2021) 'Military veterans and welfare reform: Bridging two policy worlds through qualitative longitudinal research,' *Social Policy and Society,* 20 (4), 670–83. doi: https://doi.org/10.1017/ s1474746421000166

Van Berkel, R., Ingold, J., McGurk, P., Boselie, P. and Bredgaard, T. (2017) 'An introduction to employer engagement in the field of HRM: Blending social policy and HRM research in promoting vulnerable groups' labour market participation,' *Human Resource Management Journal,* 27 (4) 503–13.

Index

Printed and bound by CPI Group (UK) Ltd, Croydon, CR0 4YY

16/04/2025

14658488-0003